Elevator Music

Elevator Music

**A
Surreal
History
of
Muzak®,
Easy-Listening,
and
Other
Moodsong®**

Revised and Expanded Edition

Joseph Lanza

University of Michigan Press
Ann Arbor

Copyright © Joseph Lanza 2004
All rights reserved
Published in the United States of America by
The University of Michigan Press
Manufactured in the United States of America
⊗ Printed on acid-free paper

2007   2006   2005   2004   4   3   2   1

A CIP catalog record for this book is available from the British Library.

Library of Congress Cataloging-in-Publication Data applied for
ISBN 0-472-08942-0

This book is a result of research and ruminations about a much-neglected musical category, elevator music. Because Muzak® Corporation has been a leading source of this art form, much of this book concerns that company's technological and philosophical genesis. I culled all of my information about Muzak from the existing literature (from both the mainstream press and Muzak's company archives) as well as telephone and in-person interviews with various Muzak employees, and others connected with the company at one time or another, who were generous enough to help me write this story. However, many of my conclusions about Muzak's ultimate cultural impact are speculative and do not necessarily reflect Muzak Corporation's official, present-day policies.

—Joseph Lanza

Muzak® is a registered trademark of Muzak LLC.

Moodsong® is a U.S. registered trademark.

Every effort has been made to locate the holders of copyrighted material.

Preface to the New Edition

In the summer of 1999, I was fortunate enough to get an invitation to travel to Melbourne, Australia, and present a paper at the Royal Melbourne Institute of Technology's Cinesonic conference. I called my presentation "My Aisles of Golden Dreams: The Beauty of Supermarket Music" and—as a sonic complement to my spoken words—had easy-listening instrumentals (custom-made material from the old Beautiful Music stations) piped through the auditorium's overhead speakers. Many audience members approached me afterward with positive responses, but such glad tidings did not prepare me for a rude awakening that following evening.

The nightmare began when all of the Cinesonic participants commingled for a late night party in a local club. There a young, lone musician (perhaps similar to the one I describe in the beginning of my "Canned Avant Garde" chapter) stood dressed in black, exuding a studied aloofness yet looking a bit lonely as he manned his keyboard. He proceeded to program a loud, droning, ear-splitting, electronic death knell. As the evening's paid soundscaper, he seemed resolved to vaporize any scintilla of human conversation—a feat he for the most part accomplished. The situation got stranger as Philip Brophy, a fine gentleman and subsequent friend who had coordinated Cinesonic, decided to be (I hope) mordantly humorous by shouting in my ear: "This is the elevator music of the future!"

At those words, I heard history being rewritten before my very ears. This was not the elevator music I had hoped to inspire. To appropriate a recent ex-President's notorious line: this was not what is *is*! I thought to myself: if a relatively benign, civilized, and clean city like Melbourne practices this kind of background music hygiene, there is no telling what soundscapers in cities from less privileged areas such as North America and Western Europe were plotting in a possible attempt to sever the musical elevator cables once and for all. Such nightmarish thoughts have informed the tone of this new edition, which focuses less on futuristic speculation than on unabashed Muzak® nostalgia. That said, I am heartened by the "electronica" artists who told me they like my book and were nice enough to react with bemused politeness whenever I asked them to experiment with prettier tunes.

Nearly a decade after the first edition of *Elevator Music* was published, the entire idea of mood music (or music in general) as background "manipulation" has become much more accepted and appropriated. This was not the case in the mid-1980s to early 1990s when I did much of my research. Then I felt compelled to provide background music with an ethical defense.

But in a world where merchandising ploys rule the urban landscape, where people joyously sport brand names on their clothes, where it is increasingly difficult to tell commercials from entertainment, and where music of all kinds blares from megastores to fashionable coffee nooks, the old canard against elevator music being manipulative is a red herring. Most people realize that all music is manipulative, and few really seem to care. With the specter of music as "ambient" arbiter no longer controversial, the elevator music "controversy" has switched entirely from matters of social ecology to aesthetic tastes.

I, like many others, hunger for the elevator music of yore—those unobtrusive instrumental versions of movie themes, show tunes, old standards, and "current" pop hits that employed a thousand strings, a hundred pianos, fifty harps and horns, a dozen xylophones, and a modest but effective volley of soft electric guitars. While some faint whispers of it still surface here and there, elevator music can best be apprehended in the past tense. Now more than ever it survives as a mysterious art form that haunts the pop culture horizon like some undying ancestral memory.

How amazing that I have simultaneously managed to annoy a few past Muzak representatives for associating their product with "easy-listening" and eliciting a hissy fit or two from a very tiny and whiny minority of easy-listening "aficionados" who shudder at the thought of their favorite maestros being lumped in with airs of the Otis-inspired variety. The vast majority of easy-listening/Beautiful Music/ pop orchestral fans I have come to know, however, understand the larger picture and have been very supportive.

My appreciation goes to all of the musicians, sound engineers, scholars, theorists, and friends who assisted me then and do so now, especially easy-listening allies such as Jed Hacker, John Leon, Bob Morgan, the late Jim Schulke, and Phil Stout. Special admiration is reserved for the late, great composer, conductor, and arranger Morton Gould, who graciously agreed to be among my first interviewees, and to the "King of the Keyboards," Roger Williams.

Speaking recently with Stu Phillips, I was thrilled to have touched base with the man who brought orchestral reinterpretations of rock songs—or metarock—to elevated heights on his Hollyridge Strings albums. Metaphysical homage goes out to Ronnie Aldrich, Stanley Black, Frank Chacksfield, Ron Goodwin, Brad Miller, Ray Conniff, Paul Weston, and other mood maestros who have since crossed over to conduct even more *heavenly* orchestras.

I was also fortunate enough to strike up a renewed acquaintance with former Muzak vice president and head of programming Jane Jarvis. She put me in touch with Frank Hunter and Nick Perito— two noted arrangers, composers, and conductors who had also arranged many Muzak sessions in the sixties and seventies. Famed guitarist Tony Mottola, another Muzak player, also shared some fond words. Thanks to collector John Leon (and to my subsequent luck in accumulating more Stimulus Progression LPs), I've had a chance to study even more Muzak tracks from the fifties to the early nineties. My afterword is an encomium on some of the men and women who made what I like to call Muzak® Classic.

Because such a healthy chunk of this book is dedicated to Muzak, I wanted to get at least the company's partial blessing this time around. I wish that Muzak had stuck to its elevator music roots but am glad to have corresponded with its main office (now located in South Carolina) and obtained formal permission to include a wonderful Muzak ad from the 1950s.

Although the Howard Johnson's restaurant in Times Square that once played Muzak's Environmental Channel, and still begins my narrative, is due to face the wrecking ball any day, some of the elevator music spirit is still out there. Muzak has retained an Environmental Channel and even added an Easy Instrumental alternative to its abounding array of "foreground" choices. The option of finding a "Beautiful Music" station on the FM dial is now pretty much nonexistent, but the aforementioned Phil Stout has since gone from the now defunct Digital Cable Radio (as referenced in chapter 11) to programming elevating instrumentals on other digital cable outlets that serve malls and private homes alike.

Many familiar with my first edition will likely take notice of the new edition's mind-altering variances in narrative rhythm and tempo, along with redoubled emphases on key themes and carefully calibrated additions/deletions. These tonal shifts should make *Elevator Music* an altogether more mood-enhancing and surreal experience.

So, until the next decade, when the opportunity to enhance this book might again avail itself, I hope everyone who holds *Elevator Music* finds the reading as easy as the listening. Last, but certainly not least, I would like to express my gratitude to Chris Hebert for believing in this enough to let it live again.

Acknowledgments

Thanks go to the following individuals for their help and emotional and spiritual support as well as for fulfilling their various roles in keeping the elevator music spirit alive.

David Ades
Hank Arakelian
Angelo Badalamenti
J. G. Ballard
Dennis Barrow
Rod Baum
Les Baxter
Gary Blandino
Steve Blush
Bill Boyd
Philip Brophy
Richard Burmer
Sammy Cahn
Wendy Carlos
Steve Carlson
Christopher Case
Ray Charles
Susan Chetwin
Irwin Chusid
Joe Coco
Ray Conniff
Connie Cook
Gautam Dasgupta
Tracy Davenport
Chip Davis
Hayden Detje
Lou Dorren
Dawn Eden
Serge Elhaik
Joe Elum
Tom Evans
Jack Fetterman
Jim Fitzgerald
Alison Fraser

Barry Freedman
Ethel Gabriel
David Garland
Tony Gentry
Ellen Goldblatt
Morton Gould
Evie Greenbaum
Jed Hacker
Bill Halvorsen
Chris Hebert
Robert Heide
Stephen Hill
Robert Hull
Frank Hunter
Thom Iwatsubo
Jane Jarvis
Irv Joel
Richard Johnson
Stella Kane
Dr. James E. Keenan
Barry Korkin
Matthias Kuennecke
Leo Kulka
Jeff Kurtti
Frances Leavitt
John Leon
John Lettis
Erik Lindgren
P. J. Littleton
Robert Lowden
Artie Malvin
Dave Mandl
Bonnie Marranca
Howard Martin

Francisco Mattos
Elfi M. Mehan
Brad Miller
Paul D. Miller (DJ Spooky)
Robert M. Miller
Louise Millmann
Bernadette Moore
Jamie Moore
Bob Morgan
John Mortarotti
Mark Mothersbaugh
Tony Mottola
David Mulkins
Ardis Murphy
Reuben Musiker
Bill Myers
National Public Radio Interviewers
Anton Nikkilä
Jerry Nutter
Ole Georg
Tim Onosko
Terry Pavone
Mark Paytress
Nick Perito
George Petros
Stu Phillips
Michael Pietsch
Marcel Proust
Roy Quady
Simon Reynolds
Chris Ring
Todd Rutt
John Sbarra
Jim Schulke

Debra Sherline
Al Sherman
Cathryn Anita Smith
Scott Springer
Carol Stokes
Phil Stout
Mika Taanila

Marlin Taylor
Yuval Taylor
Manfred Thonicke
Frederick Thornton
Jeff Tumarkin
Gregg Turkington
Wayno

Stephen Witt
Byron Werner
Paul Weston
Roger Williams
Gene Zacharewicz

I wish to thank the following former and present employees of Muzak for their help, time, knowledge, and anecdotes.

Rod Baum
Christopher Case
Hayden Detje
Ellen Goldblatt
Dr. James J. Keenan

Bill Boyd
Susan Chetwin
Tom Evans
Jane Jarvis
Elfi M. Mehan

Steve Carlson
Joseph Coco
Barry L. Freedman
Irv Joel
Kimberly Wolff

Thanks go to the following companies, organizations, and entities:

Dryden Historical Museum
Muzak LLC
New York City Transit Authority
Percy Faith Society
Robert Farnon Society
UNESCO
Wurlitzer Company

Mobile Fidelity Sound Lab
National Elevator Industry
Otis Elevator Company
Ray Conniff Society
Three Rivers Arts Festival
United States Broadcasting Corporation
Record Collector magazine

Contents

1 / Probing the Jell-O®

The Howard Johnson's restaurant centered in New York City's theater district offers a spectacle *extraordinaire:* vinyl upholstery, fake wood laminates, Formica *moderne,* and a turnover of players savoring their french fries, overboiled vegetables, and Jell-O® cubes to the latest Muzak® selections.

Muzak is, in fact, the most essential part of this performance: a computerized chorus that judges, reflects, and determines the actions and thoughts of every character. But if this show is too middlebrow, you need only journey to a café in New York's East Village, L.A.'s West Hollywood, or any enclave where *chic* is *kitsch* spelled backward, to find the digitized drones of artists like Brian

Eno counterpointing cappuccino milk steamers and sundry book chat. The actors, sound, context, and coffee brands may differ from theater to theater, but the stage is essentially the same, as modern life evolves into a megalopolis of air-conditioned and sonically monitored atria.

As restaurants, elevators, malls, supermarkets, office complexes, airports, lobbies, hotels, and theme parks proliferate, the background, mood, or easy-listening music needed to fill these spaces becomes more and more a staple in our social diet. Indeed, background music is almost everywhere: avant-garde "sound installations" permeate malls and automobile showrooms, quaint piano recitals comfort us as we wait in bank lines, telephone techno-tunes keep us complacently on hold, brunch Baroque refines our dining pleasure, and even synthesized "nature" sounds further blur the boundary between our high-tech Platonic caves and "real life."

Along with Muzak and elevator music, there is moodsong to accompany our favorite movie scenes, tickle our subconscious fancies on television and radio commercials, alert us to the next network news station break, and lull us in our home entertainment centers.

But just mention the words *Muzak, easy-listening,* or even *contemporary instrumental,* and many critics will lash out with judgments such as "boring," "dehumanized," "vapid," "cheesy," and (insult of insults) "elevator music." All these reactions appear to be based more on cultural prejudice than honest musical appraisal. In these supposedly "enlightened" times, when people are compelled to think twice before passing blanket judgments on most cultures and their contributions, I find it inconsistent for the press (particularly the music press) to relegate "elevator music" to a categorical pejorative with no questions asked. After decades of rock, rhythm and blues, folk, heavy metal, and rap, a desensitized population seems to assume that if music is not hot, heavy, bubbling with jackhammer rhythms, and steaming with emotion or anger, it is somehow less than good or (worse) less than art.

Not every musician should be obligated to reassure us that we are not zombies. There is also a place for music that is subdued, unpresuming, even remote or alien. This is certainly true in the case of many instrumental recording artists—from Percy Faith to Brian Eno—who have from time to time been successful in the art of producing sonic wallpaper.

Championed by Muzak more than half a century ago, the philosophy and musicology of background music have since radiated into a web of styles and applications more complex and engaging than many people realize. What distinguishes such contoured concertos from other music? An artfully contrived regimen of unobtrusive harmonies and pitches; metronomic repetition; melodic segments that overlap into a tonal wash; a concatenation of hypnotic violins, harps, celestes, and other instruments connoting inherited concepts of how heaven sounds; or diaphanous harmonies that seem to issue from a mysterious, invisible source that is more than the sum of its musicians and (to paraphrase a favorite Muzak saying) "more than music."

For a more clinical definition: mood music shifts music from *figure* to *ground*, to encourage peripheral hearing. Psychoanalysts might say that it displaces our attention from music's manifest content to its more surreal latent content. Hearing it, we are inspired to frame an otherwise disordered or boring existence into movie scenes whose accompanying soundtrack alternately follows and anticipates our thoughts and actions—but then shifts (or rather plays on) with a rhythm and logic indifferent to our own. Moodsong reinforces mounting suspicions that we live inside a dream.

Be it mellifluous Mantovani or Philip Glass parsimony, background music provides an illusion of distended time. It makes us feel more relaxed, contemplative, distracted from problems, and prone to whistle over chores we might find unbearable if forced to suffer them in silence. Yet for other hearers, such music can be a source of annoyance or anxiety. The sounds intended to cater to or quell the emotions can also sound aloof or haunting or intolerably peaceful, depending on the listener's mind, ear, and past experiences.

The vast quantity of uncharitable jokes and condescending anecdotes directed against elevator music in general and Muzak in particular betrays a lack of understanding about music's augmented role in a media-dominated culture. English author and playwright J. B. Priestley once bragged of having "had it turned off in some of the best places." Another Brit, the comic Spike Milligan, allegedly claimed that "Tranquility is something that liberates the soul; Muzak destroys it." Comedian Lily Tomlin once expressed fears that the guy who invented Muzak might be inventing something else.

Sometimes the Muzak metaphors are strained, to say the least. A political commentator wrote in *New York* magazine that Bill Clinton "is the political equivalent of Muzak, appropriating pungent themes like opportunity, responsibility, community, creating vast marshmallows of rhetoric from them but never really taking a tough stand." More curious is a travel article about winding roads that appeared in the *Baltimore Sun:* "I always liken curvilinear streets to Muzak: vaguely pleasant but nothing you can remember."

The American Symphony League insists that host personnel turn the Muzak off at every hotel where it holds its conventions. During the League's Fiftieth annual get-together, at the Washington Hilton, one official petulantly explained to the *St. Petersburg Times*, "We want to be sensitized to music, not desensitized to music."

But journalist Bruce MacLeod, writing for *Popular Music and Society*, is much more even-handed: "Complain as we may about its blandness and ability to manipulate, it is inextricably bound up in the social fabric of our times." Andy Warhol went further by being among the very few celebrities with a public endorsement: "I like anything on Muzak—it's so listenable. They should have it on MTV."

Many commentators habitually label all music that reminds them of elevator music "Muzak." But Muzak is just one company's registered trademark, like Kleenex, Xerox, or Vaseline. With the exception of a few commemorative and novelty promotion albums, Muzak is not something you can buy at retail shelves. It is music made and programmed for business environments to reduce stress, combat fatigue, and enhance sales. Nonetheless, many instrumental songs—some by very famous recording artists such as Lawrence Welk, Lionel Hampton, and Kenny G—have played on Muzak from time to time, either as custom-made cuts or from preexisting records.

According to one-time Muzak designer Christopher Case, "There are literally 90 million people listening to Muzak per day. It's a real challenge to put something together that's going to please everyone. . . . Since we have so many people listening at once, we are forced to amalgamate."

Muzak and mood music are, in many respects, aesthetically superior to all other musical forms: they emit music the way the twentieth century is equipped to receive it. They have so successfully blended genres and redefined music appreciation that they have become the music world's Esperanto.

Consider the words of Professor Gary Gumpert of Queens College when he assessed Muzak's maternal role in a 1990 television documentary on background music for Britain's Channel Four. "Muzak is music that is put in a laundromat. It's been bathed; and all of its passion gotten rid of. It's there; it doesn't make a wave. It's just a kind of amniotic fluid that surrounds us; and it never startles us, it is never too loud, it is never too silent; it's always there. . . ."

Part of our social therapy is to bathe and swim in that "amniotic fluid," not just to the sounds of Muzak but to all of the moodsong soundtracks that embellish our lives and that many ungratefully ignore, deride, or take for granted. This book will have succeeded in its purpose if I can help efface (or at least make all the more confusing) the distinction between one person's elevator music and another's prized recording.

2 / Lullabies from Heaven and Hell

MOOD MUSIC'S ANTIQUITY

And now, its strings
Boldlier swept, that long sequacious notes
Over delicious surges sink and rise,
Such a soft floating witchery of sound
As twilight Elfins make, when they at eve
Voyage on gentle gales from Fairy-Land . . .
—Samuel Taylor Coleridge,
"The Aeolian Harp"

From the most ancient times, background music has soothed us one minute and tormented us the next. Orpheus had to play his lyre to assuage and inspire Jason and his Argonauts on their sea-bound quest for the Golden Fleece. But Orpheus's melodies also blocked out the intoxicating chorus of sirens intent on pulling the minds of listeners into a calamitous unknown.

As if he did not have enough problems throughout Homer's *Odyssey*, Odysseus dared himself to withstand the ebb and flow of the Sirens' song. He instructed his sailors to wear ear-plugs, tie him to his ship's mast, and witness him writhe as they sailed past the Sirens' lair. Of course, the sadistic gods also watched.

Philo Judaeus, in his comments on the book of *Genesis,* asks: "For did not the singing of the Sirens, as Homer says, so violently summon listeners that they forgot their country, their home, their friends and necessary foods? And would not that most perfect and most harmonious and truly heavenly music, when it strikes the organ of hearing, compel them to go mad and to be frenzied?"°

Pythagoras was set on the notion of a superhuman symphony playing beyond the listener's reach or will. His "Music of the Spheres" was based on an inferred mathematical correspondence between harmonic ratios and the motions of planetary bodies. The cosmic geometry followed a "doctrine of correspondences" according to which a plucked string resounds through every living tissue in the universe.

Judging from their literature, the Greeks were rarely without some kind of perpetual musical soundtrack. The mythical Hermes satisfied Zeus's request to charm the 100-eyed Argus with a reed flute lullaby. Once Argus was asleep, Hermes slew him and temporarily freed Io from Hera's jealous gaze. Amphion's music brought down the walls of Thebes. Antigenidas, a flute player, was performing martial melodies at an important banquet when Alexander the Great flew into such a rapture that he jumped from his table, grabbed his weapon, and almost bludgeoned the guests.

One of the first pieces of background music technology to emerge from Greek folklore was a self-generating Aeolian harp (named after Aeolis, the God of Winds) that consisted of a box with strings pulled across its openings to make celestial noises on windy days. Shelley, in "Prometheus Unbound," paid tribute to "The Music of the rolling world, Knowledge within the strings of the waved air, Aeolian modulations." The musical lexicon would later include the term "Aeolian Mood," used to denote an airy, soft, or pacifying chord.

Censorinus, a third-century Roman grammarian, wrote that "music serves to make toil as bearable as may be, as when it is used by the steersman in a moving galley; and the legions, fighting with the

°Philo Judaeus, as cited in Joscelyn Godwin, *Music, Mysticism and Magic* (New York and London: Arkana, 1987), p. 56.

sword, even lose the fear of death when the trumpet is sounded."°

The walls of Rome's Messina were purportedly built to the rhythm of a flute orchestra; and Nero's fiddle (more likely a lyre) score for his inflamed Roman Empire was destined for reenactment in a disaster sequence that director Cecil B. DeMille committed to historical memory centuries later in one of his Biblical epics.

Much of early religious history is sprinkled with anecdotes in which music is used not for its attention-grabbing performance but as a disembodied voice to alter environments and invoke the Divine. David's harp saved King Saul from going mad. Bernadette's song helped her heal the sick. Sublime choirs guided Joan of Arc as she led the French troops. The Christian soldiers of the early Crusades hired battlefield musicians to play the same Arabic martial music that the Saracens used to defeat them in previous battles.

Author Dyer T. Thistleton, in his book *The Ghost World*, dedicated a chapter to "Phantom Music," contending that belief in supernatural fairies strumming harps and other sonic intoxicants is widespread in European folklore. Celtic fables spoke of Dagda, the Irish god who played on a harp to welcome Spring. The Teutons bequeathed the Lorelei legend of musical mermaids enticing wayward listeners to dwell among the sea citizens.

By medieval times, various reports celebrated the private relationship between background music and listener, usually as visitations by angels and holy emissaries. Richard Rolle, a medieval English hermit, was only saying his prayers when a "sweet ghostly song" started spinning in his head. The supernatural voices were so beautiful that he rejected the usual church music as redundant and crude.

Voices of the muses and saints had become man-made territorial soundmarks by the fourteenth century as Christendom's clock ticked to parish church bells and carillons. Gregorian chants most likely tranquilized monks for hundreds of years and have a similar relaxing, yet unobtrusive, effect when played at low volume on today's compact-disc players.

°Censorinus, as cited in Joscelyn Godwin, *Music, Mysticism and Magic* (New York and London: Arkana, 1987), p. 19.

Monk musicians would also play Gregorian plainsong, a kind of medieval Muzak® performed outside the monastery to uplift agricultural workers. Unlike the earthy work songs of migrant or slave laborers, plainsong came not from the workers but from an outside source—the descant of deities trickling from the clouds.

Utopian novels, which usually tried to adapt Christian teachings to encroaching technology, were often repositories of background music philosophy. As the Western world made its queasy transition into print culture, Sir Thomas More concocted *Utopia* to impress King Henry VIII with thoughts of a justly ruled egalitarian society where, among other civic niceties, "No supper goes by without music."

Sir Francis Bacon's unfinished novel *New Atlantis* offers a Christian utopia based on the Bible's "natural law." European sailors drift onto a South Sea island and are treated to the hospitality of Salomon House, a Christian institution dedicated to nature studies. But it is a natural philosophy quite different from that of Rousseau's cuddly "noble savage": the castaways get a grand tour of a magic kingdom where nature is inseparable from intervening technology. Bacon's union of religious idealism and liberal arts prefigures today's theme park, as he describes "perspective-houses" representing "all colorations of light, all delusions and deceits of the sight in figures, magnitudes, motions, colours, all demonstrations of shadows." There are also "houses of deceits of the senses . . . where we represent all manner of feats of juggling, false apparitions, impostures, and illusions" as well as "sound-houses" where every effort is made "to convey sounds in trunks and pipes, in strange lines and distances."

We can also trace mood music to the first church organ recitals that pacified worshippers between sermons. The cathedral became the architectural soundscape that would later inspire the builders of malls, atria, and auto showrooms.

Piped-in music filled the European aristocracy's secular confines by the seventeenth century. Baroque gardens celebrated civilization's dominance over nature with hydraulic organs and artificial singing birds. Much of what today's audiophiles reverently call "the Classics" served as background music for bluebloods. David

Weiss, in his novel *Sacred and Profane*, portrays Mozart commenting on Archbishop Coloredo's musical request: "His Grace is having company for dinner. He expects a serenade, something that will please, but which will not disturb his conversation or his digestion."

In the mid-eighteenth century, German composer Georg Philipp Telemann broke down the once rigid barriers between sacred and secular music by devising a series of background "instrumental" pieces called *Musique de Table* ("Table Music"). Admitting to being no great lover of virtuoso concertos, Telemann ignored rigid schemes and favored an uncomplicated melodic line that could turn stuffy court music into "light music."

Johann Sebastian Bach had his own approach to the light instrumental style. His famous "Goldberg Variations" were commissioned by Count Kaiserling, a former Russian ambassador residing in Dresden. The count sent his protegé, Johann Theophilus Goldberg, to Bach to learn some clavier pieces with enough of "a soft and lively character" and a "constant sameness of the fundamental harmony" to cure his insomnia. A probably fatigued Goldberg played this mixture of canon, fugue, and étude in an adjoining room while the count counted sheep.

When Napoléon restored Christianity as France's official religion, François René Chateaubriand (the religion's prime defender) described heaven as a phantom music wonderland: "Music never ceases in these places: music which one hears everywhere, but which is nowhere; sometimes it is a murmuring like that of an Aeolian harp which the soft breath of Zephyr strokes on a night in springtime; sometimes the ear of a mortal believes it hears the plaint of a divine harmonica, those vibrations which have nothing terrestrial about them and which swim in the middle region of the air."*

The Ancient Egyptians may have explained man's cosmic relationship with the dictum "As above, so below," but it took the

---

*François René Chateaubriand, *Les Natchez*, Book IV, in *Oevres Complètes*, vol. 2, Paris, 1834, pp. 491–3, as cited in Joscelyn Godwin, ed., *Music, Mysticism and Magic*, p. 187.

temerity of nineteenth-century Romantics to ask: "How *far* below?" Romanticism further eroded distinctions between heavenly and satanic serenades. Germany's Robert Schumann was at first content to believe that singing angels were visiting him, but he suddenly had a nervous breakdown after concluding that the choirs were "those of demons and in hideous music." Animal magnetism enthusiast Franz Anton Mesmer was notorious for his Paris séances of dimmed lights set against background melodies so soft and pleasing that mortals received the ghost with no discomfort.

Music that could heal or rend the soul had identical effects on the body. Florence Nightingale claimed, in her *Notes on Nursing*, that "wind instruments capable of continuous sound have generally a beneficial effect on the sick, while the pianoforte with such instruments as have no continuity of sound has just the reverse, the pianoforte playing will damage the sick, while an air like 'Home Sweet Home' . . . on the most ordinary grinding organ will sensibly soothe them. . . . "

Arthur Schopenhauer, in *The World as Will and Idea*, was astute enough to predict movie soundtracks: "This deep relation which music has to the true nature of all things also explains the fact that suitable music played to any scene, action, event, or surrounding seems to disclose to us its most secret meaning, and appears as the most accurate and distinct commentary upon it."

Modern capitalism instigated an ecclesiastical rift. If background music was good enough to orchestrate the houses of God, why not the houses of commerce? The nineteenth-century Italian author Mario Morasso anticipated Muzak futurism by declaring that "the holy temple, as a means of satisfying a spiritual need . . . has become the Department Store or the clerical office. . . . "

As the Industrial Revolution introduced the internal combustion engine's roar and the drone of generators, ventilation systems, riveting pistons, and low-frequency electrical lighting, silence became an unwelcome anomaly when it existed at all. There erupted a whole new genus of criminal activity and factory-related illnesses connected with these noisy incursions, such as "Boilermaker's Disease" produced by metal scraping. Music was not mere entertainment but an "audioanalgesia" to kill the pain of urban din. Karlheinz Stockhausen later suggested using computer-programmed "sound swallowers" to neutralize every unwanted noise in a public place with its opposite vibration.

Background music became a piped-in panacea just in time for what many intellectuals and lapsed theologians called "the disappearance of God." But God did not die so much as become transformed into an electromagnetic choir with a center everywhere and a circumference nowhere. Richard Wagner's "universal currents of Divine Thought" became Nikola Tesla's alternating currents of mass communication.

Thomas Edison perfected his wax cylinder machine by 1888, just before Germany's Emil Berliner introduced a sound disk. Soon a thousand electrical bulbs illuminated the Tower of Light at Chicago's 1893 Columbian Exposition, where Tesla demonstrated his alternating current, Edison presented his "cinetophonograph," and music was piped into the fairgrounds by telephone wire from a Manhattan concert.

Tinny Swiss music boxes enabled turn-of-the-century homes to extract music out of a can, although these devices soon lost out to the Duo-Art player-piano, which, in turn, deferred to the gramophone. Mechanical sound reproduction engendered what an unapproving R. Murray Schafer in *The Tuning of the World* calls "schizophonia," a state in which contemporary life is "ventriloquized" by noises duplicated, transmitted, and divorced from their "natural" sources.

Retailing magnate Bradford Peck took a friendler view in his 1900 novel *The World a Department Store*. This was another Christian utopia dedicated to "suffering toilers in all walks of life." The president of B. Peck & Co. (then New England's biggest department store outside Boston), Peck believed that the principles of Jesus Christ were inherent in "a system of life operated on the department store plan, organized so that every one shall be employed."

The novel's protagonist is Percy Brantford, owner of a small dry-goods business, who overdoses on sleeping powders, falls into a coma, and flashes forward to 1925. It is a future run by the "Cooperative Association of America." Architects and engineers are among the nation's moral arbiters, while the ever-present strains of a "grand orchestra" play continuously in public restaurants and other buildings modeled after such consumption monoliths as Macy's and Wanamaker's.

Edison had initiated several background music "mood tests" in the early 1900s. Aided by a "Dr. Bingham," he compiled charts depicting the mood changes of people as they listened to his phonographs. In 1915, Edison used a programmed selection of phonographic music for factories to determine the extent to which it would mask hazardous drones and boost morale. But the infant loudspeaker and transmission technology were still too weak. There were also cigar factories in the United States and Cuba that hired "readers" to recite the contents of books and newspapers aloud while workers rolled tobacco. Sometimes records or radios were used in their place.

Changing economic and social conditions altered musical perception. The days of the feudal town minstrel were long gone by the time musicians were taken off the streets and confined to cabarets, salons, and café-concerts, with admission prices levied, and a maw of union and licensing complications gaping in the middle distance. The confusion grew more profound when recorded sound forever consigned music to a graven image.

Musical greats of yesteryear were no doubt upset by the electronic colonizer's invisible orchestras. John Philip Sousa disliked the wireless and the phonograph so much that broadcasters had to pay handsomely to overcome his scruples and obtain his radio rendition of "Stars and Stripes Forever." With acrimony in his heart, Sousa allegedly coined the term "canned music."

3 / The "Canned"
Avant-Garde

At first glance, the lonely musician depicted in Luigi Russolo's Futurist painting *Music* (1911) looks dejected. He appears to be slumped over his keyboard, dwarfed by a leering electronic chorus that keeps him in the dark and plays on, regardless of whether he lives or dies. But is the musician sad or in a state of ecstatic somnambulism? Perhaps the faces are an electromagnetic halo while the whiplashing snake creeping up from behind is an umbilical wire plugging him into a superior high-voltage nervous system.

Russolo's subject occupies the ambivalent position of any virtuoso forced to abide the twentieth century's fusion of music and megahertz. No musical artistes ever played the game with more élan than the European avant-garde who, in their efforts to subvert consumer society, ended up buttressing the "canned music" revolution.

Luigi Russolo, an Italian Futurist, lauded the modern era's beautiful machine clangor. A painter, not a musician, Russolo was nonetheless committed to being the Futurist movement's musical activist. His 1913 manifesto "The Art of Noises" rejected inherited preferences for harmony in favor of the dissonant masterpieces that serenade us everyday without our conscious awareness. Conventional pianos, violins, harps, and horns were inferior to "the crashing down of metal shop blinds, slamming doors, the hubbub and shuffling of crowds, the variety of din from stations, railways, iron foundries, spinning mills, printing works, electric power stations, and underground railways."

To realize his dream of a life when "every factory will be transformed into an intoxicating orchestra of noises," Russolo created *Intonarumori* ("Noise Intoners")—gangly speaker boxes that transmitted such chainsaw melodies as an internal combustion engine gurgling in ten whole-tones. He concocted four main noise families: the Exploder, the Crackler, the Buzzer, and the Scraper; the pitch and timbre of each were manipulated by a side lever.

Futurism's resident musician, Francesco Balilla Pratella, was so impressed by Russolo's machines that he wrote the "Technical Manifesto of Futurist Music," another encomium on "the musical soul of crowds, great industrial complexes, transatlantic liners, trains, tanks, automobiles and aeroplanes . . . the domination of the machine and the victorious reign of electricity."

When it came to industrial symphonies, the Mussolini-backed Futurists were probably embarrassed to find many of their efforts matched by those of the enemy Soviet camp. Artists from the pre-Stalin halcyon days of 1920 staged a *Concert for Factory Sirens* that consisted of an orchestrated crescendo of sirens calling comrades to their workstations. Only in this cruder Soviet version did life come to imitate art. We can still hear its influence in factories all over the world orchestrating the peak hours of blue-collar travail.

After some exhibitions in England and private shows for Stravinsky and Stockhausen, Russolo's Noise Intoners became more of a novelty than the promised innovation. Russolo eventually combined several of the Intoners into a rudimentary keyboard called the Russolophone, but that too was doomed to the crackpot file of history.

A less clamorous experiment (with Marxist overtones nonetheless) was Germany's *Gebrauchsmusik*, meaning "utility music" or "music to be used." It encompassed tunes that amateurs could play at home without the intimidations of a concert hall. Kurt Weill's career in the later Weimar period was mostly devoted to this movement's efforts to erase the distinctions between "art music" and "use music." Weill wanted to bring music to the masses by making it "capable of expressing simple human emotions and actions." He took pleasure in provoking the snobs who reviled his rank-and-file allegiances, taunting them by declaring that "the fear of banality has finally been overcome ... with the use of the elements of jazz, easily graspable melodies that superficially bear a strong resemblance to light music."

Weill's words may have sounded revolutionary then, but he was merely advocating the mixture of light music and film music we take for granted today. To get an idea of *Gebrauchsmusik*, imagine mixing a mathematical Philip Glass frost, the string syrup of Percy Faith, a hearty scoop of Boston Pops, an Ennio Morricone marshmallow sauce, and the Ray Conniff Singers for the cherry on top.

Gebrauchsmusik often took on rogue themes. Paul Hindemith, another major figure in the movement, centered his opera *Neues vom Tage* (1929) around the lowbrow subject of tabloid newspapers and homespun compositions called *Spielmusik* ("Music for Playing"). His love of technological gadgetry led to pieces made exclusively for pianola, radio, and for an ether-wave machine perfected by Leon Theremin. Hindemith's irreverent swipes at established aesthetics and authority agitated the Nazi Kulturkammer when his *Kammermusik No. 5* concerto satirized German military marches.

Though created to classify a socially conscious art movement, the term *Gebrauchsmusik* took on the same pejorative mantle as Germany's equally volatile term *kitsch*. The final implications of "utility music"? Music for elevators, offices, stores, and house-cleaning—all to Hindemith's dismay. Perhaps this explains why, once ensconced in an Ivy League music department, he attempted to save face by writing off Muzak® and other background music as a "relentlessly running music faucet."

In place of Futurism's rumpus and *Gebrauchsmusik*'s *noblesse oblige*, Erik Satie offered a musical complement to urban life with pieces that retained melody yet were emotionally neutral. Satie was like the Futurists in developing a blueprint for *sound* environments that originated with the most anti-bourgeois intentions but ended as a middle-class champion. He affirmed his role as Muzak's true progenitor in a 1920 manifesto advocating *musique d'ameublement* ("furniture music").

There are several stories about how Satie coined "Furniture Music" as a term and concept. According to one, Satie had overheard Henri Matisse express a desire for some kind of art form without any nagging subject matter—something he likened to an easy chair. Another more conclusive version has Satie at a luncheon with the painter Fernand Léger. The restaurant's resident orchestra was so loud that the diners had to leave. According to Léger, Satie reacted to the situation with an impassioned discourse:

> *You know, there's a need to create furniture music, that is to say, music that would be a part of the surrounding noises and that would take them into account. I see it as melodious, as masking the clatter of knives and forks without drowning it completely, without imposing itself. It would fill up the awkward silences that occasionally descend on guests. It would spare them the usual banalities. Moreover, it would neutralize the street noises that indiscreetly force themselves into the picture.* [*]

Satie elaborated on this idea in a note to Jean Cocteau: "Furniture music for law offices, banks, etc. . . . No marriage ceremony

---

[*]Alan M. Gillmor, *Erik Satie* (Boston: Twayne, 1988), p. 232.

without furniture music. . . . Don't enter a house which does not have furniture music."

Musique d'ameublement (arranged for a piano, three clarinets and a trombone) had its public debut on March 8, 1920, at the Galerie Barbazanges, performed during intermissions of a play written by his friend Max Jacob. Rollo H. Myers, Satie's biographer, claims "the music, which consisted of fragments of popular refrains from *Mignon* and the *Danse Macabre* and isolated phrases repeated over and over again, like the pattern of wallpaper, was meant strictly to be nothing more than a background and was not intended to attract attention in any way."[*]

The patrons, unaccustomed to regarding art with anything but genuflection, were deaf only to Satie's instructions and proceeded to strain their ears. An annoyed Satie leaped into the crowd and implored everyone to talk, make noise, or concentrate on the picture exhibition in the theater hall. Satie's frustration in trying to change the listening habits of people accustomed to sitting on hard-backed chairs with rapt attention contrasts with a similar situation more than fifty years later when John Cage exposed Satie's *musique d'ameublement* to a public all too accustomed to peripheral listenership. In his address to a New York forum called "The Phonograph and Our Musical Life," Cage attempted to break people out of passive listening by forcing them to wind through a darkened corridor made visible only by the scattered spotlights shining on three chamber ensembles playing the piece.

Appearing on Channel Four's British documentary *"Beautiful Music,"* Professor Roderick Swanston of London's Royal College of Music claims that furniture music was "a reaction against composers taking themselves too seriously." This could also have been Satie's last laugh at all of the tony patrons who ignored him during his dark days as a cabaret pianist.

The Galerie Barbazanges presented the only official "public" furniture music show, but Satie arranged several private installations. When the wife of *Washington Post* owner Eugene Meyer requested the musician's autograph, Satie instead sent the man-

---

[*]Rollo H. Myers, *Erik Satie* (New York: Dover, 1948, 1968), p. 60.

uscript for a musical piece called "Wall Hanging for a Prefectural Office," scored for a small orchestra and intended to be "decorative and sumptuous in appearance." Satie soon created smaller works such as "Forged Iron Tapestry" (to be played in house vestibules for guests as they arrived) and "Phonic Floor Tiles" (designed to complement either luncheons or marriage proposals).

Furniture music, far from being just another smug Dadaist hoax, was Satie's serious attempt to facilitate the simultaneous rise of canned music and silent movie tunes. The cinema impelled musicians to compose viscerally while staying subtle enough not to overscore the screen action, a challenge Satie had met with his score entitled *Cinema* for Rene Clair's *Entr'acte,* in which he cut up, juxtaposed, and repeated musical phrases until they were devoid of any intrinsic meaning.

Long before furniture music, Satie had experienced deep, metaphysical yearnings that prompted him to make unorthodox conclusions not only about music but about how harmony (as opposed to melody) brings us closer to the great beyond.

Born into the middle-class comforts of a then Germanophile France, Satie spent much of his early career fighting off Wagner's tentacles, which gripped so many of his contemporaries. To purge himself, he extolled the monophonic sounds of Gregorian chant and plainsong, transforming this anachronism from the Middle Ages into an antidote against Teutonic excess.

Like plainsong, Satie's music was stripped of dramatic accent and sounded remote enough to make people more cognizant—at times, more suspicious—of their surroundings. Roderick Swanston (speaking again in the British documentary) contrasts Satie's approach with that of two of his contemporaries: "Debussy and Ravel would certainly be composers whom you listened to and expect to listen to. Ironically, a lot of the language they used in their compositions gave the vocabulary for later composers to write their background music." In contrast to Debussy's "parallel chords" (which made a more lush and sentimental sound later echoed by Mantovani and his disciples), Satie's music was minimal and somewhat glacial. The Debussy versus Satie approach to background music is similar to today's sometimes dubious distinctions between easy-listening (which relies on nostalgic melodies) and more emotionally ambiguous forms like Brian Eno's "ambient" music.

Satie performed his Gregorian experiments around the time of his two-year association with the Rosicrucians, during which he fell under the influence of the sexually ambiguous cult leader Joséphin Péladan. Péladan was part of a *fin-de-siècle* sect that rejected materialism and the influence of Darwin in favor of a metaphysical goulash of spiritual observance, hedonism, and a love of "nature."

For Péladan's salon exhibitions, Satie composed "incidental music" (intended as ancillary to the proceedings)—compositions noted for their aimless, hypnotic quality (due partly to Satie's habit of omitting time signatures or bar lines). Satie maintained an enigmatic front by posing more as an interior decorator than a composer, filling his written music with descriptions like "White and motionless" or "Pale and hieratic."

Satie biographer Alan Gillmor states: "Tonality and rhythm as such did not concern him. His aim was to create a vague, floating . . . atmosphere . . . a nongoal-oriented music, a music that is simply *there*, a kind of quasi-religious 'furniture music' before the fact."

More than a decade before furniture music, Satie's three "Gymnopédies" demonstrated how his "minimalist" work harbored repressed feelings that could leave him wide open to maudlin interpretations. The "Gymnopédies" crop up today in some of the gushiest contexts—particularly Louis Malle's elegiac use of them in *The Fire Within* and during the misty-eyed conclusion of *My Dinner with André*.

Various social and economic forces during Satie's time imply that he did not arrive at furniture music out of an aesthetic bubble. Mid-nineteenth-century Paris was among the first European cities to shift from a market economy to a consumer culture. The Parisian department store, for instance, replaced the quaint, small shop. The Bon Marché appeared by 1870 to transform shoppers into ambulatory voyeurs propelled by a fixed-price system, rendering haggling obsolete and gawking all the more enticing. Émile Zola, in *Au Bonheur des Dames*, saw the Bon Marché as a place where female shoppers became intoxicated by a carefully contrived retail dramaturgy.

Celebrating the French Revolution's centenary, the Universal Exposition of 1898 foreshadowed Busch Gardens with its "exotic" samplings of foreign lands garnished with price tags. Satie stood at the foot of the Exposition's freshly erected Eiffel Tower, so intoxicated by the theme park atmosphere that he composed his "Gnossiennes," among his most elegant and spectral works.

Furniture music represented a transition between Satie's departure from Péladan and his embrace of Dada. By the 1920s, his religious convictions were eclipsed by post–World War I cynicism. Dada, a loosely based movement that started in 1916 and disbanded eight years later, took every opportunity to disrupt Europe's old order with a nihilism so pure that it self-destructed. No surprise then that furniture music ended up thwarting the expectations of both classicists *and* the avant-garde. Just two years after it appeared, an army technocrat named George Owen Squier reinterpreted Satie's dream by devising a system for transmitting canned music via electronic wire into the concert halls of restaurants and typing pools. The year was 1922: Dada was in its death throes as Muzak kicked into life.

4 / Umbilical Chords

THE BIRTH OF MUZAK®

In 1887, Edward Bellamy wrote a fantastic book called *Looking Backward*. In it, he attempted to visualize what would be going on in 2000 A.D.

In one part he wrote: *"Please look at today's music,"* she said, handing me a program, *"and tell me what you prefer."* It was dated September 12th, 2000, and contained a long list of music. I noticed that selections were grouped under headings 6:00 p.m., 7:00 p.m., etc. Then I observed this program was an all-day affair divided into sections corresponding to the hours of the day.

"How is it done?" I asked. *"There are a number of studios,"* she answered, *"adapted to play all kinds of music. They are connected by telephone with hotels, restaurants, and homes throughout the City."*

Fifty years ago Mr. Bellamy came very close to prophesying exactly what "Music by Muzak" is today.

—From a 1937 Muzak® promotional booklet

Before Aldous Huxley and George Orwell confronted us with dystopias of social regimentation and advanced technology gone amok, Edward Bellamy gave us a future where high-tech was a maternalistic marvel. His novel *Looking Backward (2000–1887)* described an orderly society where piped-in music was one of many perquisites in a state-controlled consumer paradise run by a benevolent "Industrial Army."

Homes with "acoustically prepared chambers, connected by wire with subscribers' houses" used a "musical telephone" that soothed people in the evening but also got more lively so that "the halls during the waking hours of morning were always of an inspiring type." The musical programs were "so coordinated that the pieces at any one time simultaneously proceeding in the different halls usually offer a choice, not only between instrumental and vocal, and between different sorts of instruments, but also between different motives from grave to gay, so that all tastes and moods can be suited."

No man was better equipped to realize Bellamy's "musical telephone" and its infinite utility than his contemporary Brigadier General George Owen Squier—the inventor of Muzak and the unsung hero of the electronic age.

Squier shared Bellamy's optimistic view of tomorrow, yet had some notable differences. He was congenial neither to *Looking Backward*'s complete government centralization without private enterprise nor to its voting system, which enfranchised only citizens over forty-five years old.

Bellamy, like all utopians, worked best when his vision was reinterpreted if not distorted. Squier was adept at doing both. While many Americans were forming societies of Bellamy literalists, Squier caught on quickly to the author's tacit suggestion that technology could forge a postindustrial link between the apparatuses of entertainment and of social engineering.

Squier led a life that could have easily paralleled that of Julian West, *Looking Backward*'s upper-middle-class protagonist, who emerges from suspended animation to a tomorrow in keeping with the Victorian ideals of yesterday. Without the advantage of time-travel, however, Squier helped usher in the "global village" by concocting a hook-up system capable of compressing vast areas of time and space previously isolated by geography. This same technology is responsible for today's fiber-optic phone lines and cable television's 500-plus channels.

Squier's life and career illustrate how much Muzak is interlinked with the military, the telephone, and the radio. Born near Dryden, Michigan, on March 21, 1865, Squier was destined for precociousness and pulled his first "believe-it-or-not" stunt by gaining admission to West Point Military Academy just after completing the eighth grade. He graduated seventh in his class and, for six years, was a second lieutenant of Army artillery. He soon experimented with physics, mathematics, and chemistry at Johns Hopkins University, getting a doctorate in electrical science and becoming possibly the first U.S. Army engineer with a Ph.D.

"Georgie" (his school nickname) generated occasional friction with his peers when his rendezvous with the laboratory eclipsed sundry soldierly duties. Still, this did not deter him from fathering his first invention: the high-speed telegraph. Not for a moment did Squier shy away from applying this in the most flamboyant fashion—ringing bells, activating machinery, firing canons, and detonating mines by remote radio control.

The 1893 Columbian Exposition in Chicago may very well have been the place where Squier got the idea of using music as one more implement in his electromagnetic arsenal. Attending as an Army representative, he could not help but notice the electronically transmitted philharmonic infiltrating the festivities.

While still in the Army, Squier convinced his lab crony, Albert C. Crehore of Dartmouth University, to join him in a small business partnership. The Crehore-Squier Intelligence Transmission Company dissolved within a year, but Squier soon received accolades for lending the Army an electromagnetic hand. By 1900, he was among few military men engaged in the Spanish-American War who could fathom the science of underwater communications cables. When one of the Army's two cable ships got stuck in the Philippine Islands, Squier (as Telegraph Line Superintendent) laid out a cable system for the second ship.

Squier helped the military achieve the goal of sending and receiving radio signals without revealing the location of either conversant. As assistant commandant, he showed that previously impenetrable wilderness could be converted into a natural transmitter/receiver, since a tree "provides all the essential elements of a radio antenna." This "tree telephone" or "florograph" could receive messages from as far away as Germany.

In 1906, Squier got a visit from Orville Wright, who wanted to fill the general in on his plans for a biplane. Though at first skeptical about the project (the plane had no gas bag), Squier agreed to join him on a test flight. This made Squier one of the world's first airplane passengers. Thereafter, Congressmen were obliged to adjourn and see the plane for themselves before assigning Squier and Wright to design the military's first wings.

By the time he set up a Signal School at Fort Leavenworth, Squier had convinced Congress to dole out the then-astronomical sum of $30,000 for research and development on wireless telegraphy and telephony. As assistant to the chief Signal Corps officer, Squier met the fruit of his research: the "Wire-Wireless." It offered the military an even better intelligence system, with improved accuracy over the wireless and better safeguards against espionage.

Until Squier's invention, existing telephone lines could transmit only one conversation per pair of wires. But on September 18, 1910, Squier unveiled "multiplexing"—a system allowing multiple conversations. (Later, FM radio engineers would devise a similar layout for sending messages through a single carrier wave.)

American Telephone and Telegraph's Bell Laboratories saw Squier's wires as the best method for saving time, money, and materials while meeting a mounting demand for phone service. AT&T obtained Squier's patents and soon inaugurated the electronic revolution that Marshall McLuhan would later describe in *The Gutenberg Galaxy* as "a single constricted space resonant with tribal drums."

But Squier, the eternal public servant, got edgy about his ideas being gobbled up for a private company's vested interests. He sued AT&T, claiming that an allotment of his patent profits should go to the people. The courts did not see it his way, especially since Squier no longer had any legal patent ownership. Congress later changed its position so that some royalties could be funneled into the National Academy of Sciences.

As Squier was proving the benefits of a wired world, his nemesis, the wireless, had also gained popularity. As early as 1896, Guglielmo Marconi had acquired a British patent for his wireless telegraph. Radio's textbook inventor Lee De Forest referred to his "radio telephone" as the "Invisible Empire of the Air, intangible, yet solid as granite." But by the time Woodrow Wilson recited his Fourteen Points across the Atlantic, the wireless and cable were being used simultaneously.

By February of 1917, Squier had become the Army's Chief Signal Officer and was serving on the Joint Army-Navy Board on Aeronautics. This tenure gave him liberty to organize radio and cable communications between military stations in America and the American Expeditionary Forces overseas. He also gained clout with such honors as the Distinguished Service Medal (USA), Knight Commander of the Order of St. Michael and St. George (Great Britain), Commander of the Order of the Crown (Italy), Commander of the Legion of Honor (France), and the Elliott Cresson Gold Medal for his multiplex innovations.

When the Army bought its first airplane, Squier was on hand to draw up the proper specifications. He supervised the assembly of the first Air Corps during World War I after working as a London military attaché. He disagreed with Woodrow Wilson's anti-war proclivities, surmising from the start that America's involvement in the Great War was inevitable. The Wilson Administration grew hawkish two years later and called Squier back to the United States to serve in the Army Air Service as Brigadier General.

But just as he was not a favorite among his classmates, Squier also antagonized the top brass. He was present when Lieutenant Thomas Selfridge became the military's first air-crash casualty. Squier was permitted to name the Macomb County Air Base after Selfridge, but he soon became the focal point of public and media outrage when the Air Corps encountered further technical problems. This led to his forced resignation as Chief Signal Officer.

Squier was near retirement in 1922 when he decided to apply his signal innovations to a music service. The connection between music, mass communication, and military might had been established long before. In the 1820s, a French engineer named François Sudré had submitted the proposal for a musical code to the Académie des Beaux Arts. It was intended as a universal language by which the scale's seven notes could transmit battlefront orders and dispatches. By 1916, future RCA executive David Sarnoff, then working for Marconi, was proposing the "Radio Music Box" for homes.

Scientific applications to civilian life were nurtured years earlier; many people regarded them as incursions. Inventions like Jeremy Bentham's "Panopticon" (designed to observe several prison chambers simultaneously) made mass technology synonymous with repression. As Jerri Husch writes in *Music of the Workspace: A Study of Muzak Culture*, "that both industry and politics gradually came to be influenced by an engineering perspective is dramatically illustrated by the observation that during the 1920s both President Hoover and the five chief executives of the largest and most growth-oriented corporations at the time, General Motors, Singer Sewing Machine Company, Dupont, General Electric and Goodyear, were all past classmates at M.I.T."

While Squier investigated the connection between wired music and crowd control, Frederick Winslow Taylor had already outlined an unprecedented human behavior blueprint with his 1911 book *Principles of Scientific Management.* His "Taylor System" employed time and motion studies to determine optimum clerical performance. A 1912 German study called *Psychology and Industrial Efficiency* led to specialized testing procedures for typists and stenographers. Westinghouse (which would one day own the Muzak corporation for several years) was one of the first companies to finance industrial management. If Taylorism could monitor the time-lag between clerks reaching for pencils and their marking papers, sound engineers could likewise manufacture their version of the optimum work womb.

Squier's ambitions were less overbearing. When presenting his patents to the New York offices of the North American Company, a Cleveland utilities combine, he had in mind servicing homes and retail shops. It was the dream of any corporation to plug electronic lines into homes and businesses, transmitting not only music but advertising and public service announcements. In October of 1922, North American started a new subsidiary called Wired Radio, Inc., to compete with the burgeoning wireless.

North American spent several years conducting preliminary experiments in Ampere, New Jersey, and on Staten Island. By 1930, the Cleveland Electric Illuminating Company of Cleveland, Ohio, attempted to pipe music from an electronic substation into households in the city's Lakeland area. Homes were given a choice of three channels that featured news items and dance music for only $1.50 per month. Engineer Walter H. Thomas (whose parents were among the recipients) recalls the stations being a less sophisticated version of today's FM band. But abundant interference made it a short-lived venture until improvements followed in 1933. Aware that the wireless monopolized private residences, Wired Radio started servicing small businesses—mostly restaurants and hotel dining rooms. It also abandoned the inferior electric wires and started leasing AT&T's phone lines.

Notwithstanding the lure of jazz clubs, Rudolph Valentino, and flappers, the 1920s were the wired music wonder years. Before Muzak transmitted its first note, the subject of background music was seeping into more and more pages of modern folklore. In 1929, playwright Elmer Rice contributed a novel to the *New Yorker* called *Voyage to Purilia* about a distant planet where "melody is as much a condition of life as are light and air." People woke, slept, and caroused to this "swooning sound," an "omnipresent harmony; now pathetic, now gay, now ominous, now martial, now tender, but always awakening familiar memories, always swellingly mellifluous, and always surcharged with a slight but unmistakable tremolo."

Public address serenades also evoked unease. "The air was continuously alive with gay synthetic melodies," wrote a facetious Aldous Huxley in *Brave New World,* describing a future society where "Synthetic Music" piped out "hyper-violin, super-cello and oboe-surrogate" to boost the spirit of techno-tribalism. For him "whenever the masses seized political power, then it was happiness rather than truth and beauty that mattered."

Huxley, like Edward Bellamy, was prescient in understanding how music would ultimately become a disembodied muse in an electronically, magnetically, and (ultimately) digitally reproduced world of absentee players. But where Bellamy envisaged a humanitarian purpose for an everyday background chorus, Huxley could only lament the passing of individual rights, the specter of human engineers, and the triumph of a zombie symphony that filled the empty spaces "with its agreeable languor."

Yevgeny Zamyatin, a precursor to both Huxley and Orwell, wrote a dystopian novel in 1920 called *We*. A former supporter of the Russian Revolution and friend to Maxim Gorky, Zamyatin fashioned his story as a bitterly satirical reaction to the unmistakably totalitarian route the revolution had taken. The book was so disturbing to the Russian Association of Proletarian Writers that its publication was banned, and it did not appear in the Soviet Union until 1957. Zamyatin's hypothetical future is dedicated to the preservation of unanimity, where life is regimented, reason is supreme, and the "soul" is looked upon more as a malignant tumor. To keep citizens in step with the "March of the One State," a "Music Plant" grinds out sonatas composed by a "musicometer" at three sonatas per hour. Describing the music, Zamyatin alludes to at least one leading turn-of-the-century social engineer: "The crystalline chromatic measures of converging and diverging infinite series and the synthesizing chords of Taylor and McLauren formulas; the full-toned, square, heavy tempos of 'Pythagoras' Trousers'; the sad melodies of attenuating vibrations; vivid beats alternating with Frauenhofer lines of pauses. . . . What grandeur! What imperishable logic!"

Without the alarming lyricism of dystopian fiction, however, Professor Jacques Attali, in his book *Noise: The Political Economy of Music*, summarizes Muzak's imminent role in twentieth-century musicology. He points out how music is "one of the first artistic endeavors truly to become a stockpileable consumer product." Standardized music, like standardized labor, was part of the machine process challenging the outmoded worship of originals. Squier's Muzak would eventually establish what Satie hinted at in his many disquisitions and disgruntled letters: that it was no longer the musical instrument that mattered so much as the conduits transmitting the tones.

Squier spent his retirement in Dryden where he reportedly made an apt but premature prediction. Looking around one day at the elaborate movie theaters sprouting along Detroit's thoroughfare, he expressed dismay at how the builders were wasting their time and money since electronic and cable technology would soon bring movies right into living rooms. He died of pneumonia on March 24, 1934, in Washington, D.C. His body lay in Arlington National Cemetery, decorated with full military honors, and the Squier Memorial Park subsequently was listed as a National Historic Site. But prior to his death, Squier made one more cataclysmic contribution. Seeking a catchier name than Wired Radio, he played word games with *music* and *Kodak* and came up with the Jabberwocky jumble *Muzak*.

Please note: Much of the information about Squier's career appears in Paul Wilson Clark's *Major General George Owen Squier: Military Scientist.* Case Western Reserve University, Ph.D. dissertation, 1974.

5 / The Push-Button Ballroom

MOOD MUSIC AND EARLY RADIO

These oscillations, as well as the radio waves of space, have been transposed into audible sound. The results, though interesting, cannot really be said to correspond with music as we know it. However, Saturn's magnetosphere produces waves which, when transposed into sound, have been described as a "slow, dreamy melody."

—David Tame, *The Secret Power of Music**

On a train headed for Saskatchewan, young Andre Kostelanetz looked out his compartment window at a montage of vast fields, farmhouses, town churches, and people scattered across America's cinematic hinterlands. Suddenly this freshly transplanted Russian émigré, who would one day be designated by *High Fidelity* magazine as "the prophet of classics for the masses," realized how thoroughly radio would transform this haphazard census into a mass audience galvanized by antenna wire.

The Kostelanetz intuition soon paid off when he became one of radio's biggest stars of what would become "light music"—a style of popular songs dolled up with a symphonic shimmer to please the largest audience.

By the 1920s, Radio Corporation of America CEO David Sarnoff had transformed the wireless from a person-to-person message unit into an entertainment altar. One-third of America's 1924 furniture budget was spent on radio receivers. Herbert Hoover offered crooner Rudy Vallee a medal for helping people forget the rigors of the Depression. In 1930, 40 percent of America's households had a radio; by 1938, the percentage had jumped to 82 percent.

Sarnoff once explained to a group of art students during the 1930s that the human voice had to wait for centuries before the supernatural conduits of electromagnetism could permit an individual to communicate with millions of people in different regions at one time. Sarnoff's colleague (and the inventor of the radiola), Dr. Alfred Goldsmith of the City College of New York, hailed radio as "the ultimate extension of personality in time and space."

Kostelanetz, as well, was aware that electronic communication was spinning life into "an age of fast tempo," decades before radio day-parting and the MTV soundbyte began pandering to the ever-diminishing attention span.

Born on December 22, 1901, in St. Petersburg (later, Petrograd), Russia, Kostelanetz was exposed to music from his earliest childhood as a member and later leader of the Petrograd choir. He arrived in the United States in 1922, working temporarily as a singers' accompanist before organizing radio orchestras, notwithstanding the ridicule of his peers and friends.

Kostelanetz made his radio debut in 1924. A decade later, he employed a sixty-five-man orchestra—the largest ever assembled for the popular airwaves—for his coast-to-coast broadcast *Andre Kostelanetz Presents. Radio Guide* magazine presented him with an award for providing "so much enjoyment" for so many; *Motion*

Picture Daily rated his program #1 among musical shows; and a 1943 poll conducted in the United States and Canada honored his promotion of both popular and "serious" music.

As with many light orchestra arrangers, Kostelanetz often followed in Victor Herbert's shadow, with modern adaptations of now classic operettas mixed with showtunes. He took Tchaikovsky's Fifth Symphony, superimposed modern lyrics over it, renamed it "Mood Love," and had the public loving it within three months.

Various reasons explain why Kostelanetz and his light music cohorts became an early radio success story. There is of course the good music. But there is another, more abstruse but no less relevant explanation that is intrinsic to radio's hardware.

With radio came a renewed belief in the physical existence of a universal medium termed *ether*. Lee De Forest referred to his invention as "those silent etheric voices, which seem often less of *nature* than of the *spirit* realm!"[*] Inspired by the Scottish physicist James Clerk Maxwell's conclusion that ether carried waves of electromagnetic energy, some engineers enjoyed fantasizing about the wireless as a cosmic conduit through which light waves, sound waves, electricity, and various other apparitions traveled into the ear from outer space. There were already hints of ghosts in the machine when electrical and radio pioneer Nikola Tesla credited his insights to the "appearance of images often accompanied by strong flashes of light." In his later experiments (according to Margaret Cheney's biography, *Tesla: Man Out of Time*), he reported getting messages from extraterrestrial aliens as well as telepathic instructions on electrons from pigeons.

Merging the languages of science and fantasy, we can infer that from ether came ethereal music—a style born out of radio's tenuous position with respect to the countermelodies emitted from stars and quasars. By trial and error, radio musicians and engineers determined that the sound of overlapping strings, preferably played at a high pitch, counteracted much of the static and buzzing that marred the early broadcasts. The light music style soon

[*]Tom Lewis, *Empire of the Air: The Men Who Made Radio* (New York: Edward Burlingame, 1991), p. 150.

evolved into an airwave onomatopoeia: lithe violins, harps, and chimes mimicked stratospheric echoes.

Ever since January 20, 1910, when De Forest attempted a live transmission from New York's Metropolitan Opera House of Caruso singing parts of *Cavalleria Rusticana*, high-brows had entertained serious doubts about "great" music's place in "De Forest's prime evil." In addition to the classical purists, many sentimental primitivists who clung to jazz as the antidote to urban neurosis were displeased with the prospect of hearing it on the radio.

Light music, on the other hand, inhabited a safer middle ground. Not quite classical, not quite jazz; not entirely showtune or waltz, it triumphed by eluding pigeonholes. An example was a particular contribution by Victor Young. This future movie composer, who conducted for radio in the 1930s, had performed a violin solo on a 1931 recording of "Stardust" that transformed it from a hot, jazzy number into a soft ballad. Young not only broadened the song's musical context (making it a tune for dreaming as well as dancing) but demonstrated how previously entrenched styles could be liberated for multipurpose packaging.

Morton Gould, another light music pioneer and an eventual star of what would later be called "easy-listening," remembers:

> The so-called serious musician turned up his or her nose at light music in any medium for many understandable reasons. It was a way of giving the serious musician more importance. If you could be in a private club, you could feel superior. There were a lot of psychological, physiological, and in some cases pathological reasons for these feelings. Oddly enough, the great artists of that time were experimenting with sound technology and early radio transmission—men like Leopold Stokowski. Stokowski subsequently did Fantasia in Hollywood; that was looked upon by the purists as the very last, final downfall of good music.

Gould is a fine example of a composer, conductor, and arranger struck by the "light" after years of "serious" music study. Born on December 10, 1913, at Richmond Hill, Long Island, he was considered a piano prodigy by the time he was four; graduated from New York University by fifteen, he was later chosen by S. L. Rothafel (alias "Roxy") to perform as staff pianist for Radio City Music Hall. He then joined the National Broadcasting Company and conducted "special arrangements" for New Jersey's radio station WOR in 1934, before becoming music director for the nationwide *Cresta Blanca Carnival* program.

Percy Faith, whose string arrangements were higher pitched and more poignant than most, hosted *Music by Faith,* which played on the Canadian Broadcasting Corporation from 1938 to 1940 and was simulcast in the United States. Born in Toronto, Ontario, on April 7, 1908, Faith began studying violin at the age of seven before switching to piano. He played regularly in silent movie houses and gave his first concert, at the Toronto Conservatory, when he was eighteen. His pianist career was abruptly handicapped after he burned his hands while trying to save his sister from a house fire. But the hotel orchestra's lure and radio's profits determined his unflagging career and reputation.

Due to the Canadian Broadcasting Company's budgetary restrictions and a creeping suspicion of his being the network's "token Jew," he left *Music by Faith* for a U.S. career in 1940. He started in Chicago, was naturalized in New York City, and soon hosted *The Carnation Contented Hour.*

Light salon, supper tunes, or midnight-hour "slumber music"—terms used interchangeably—stayed even as radio sound got better, and proud producers felt technologically proficient enough to broadcast the Great Masters. With an expanding marketplace of sponsors (including Chesterfield, Philco, and Firestone), radio was the hottest selling tool in the nation, with light music drawing in the largest listening market.

One of the first significant program innovations occurred when CBS head William S. Paley began competing with Sarnoff's NBC. Paley was much more intent on enhancing commercial revenues than on being "respectable." NBC preferred classical music, but CBS used Paul Whiteman's whitebread jazz band to promote products such as Old Gold cigarettes.

Paul Whiteman, often called the "King of Jazz" (a title that stirred considerable controversy), is another musician who took advantage of radio's power to introduce unexplored sounds to middle America. A native of Denver, Colorado, Whiteman had played both violin and viola for the Denver and San Francisco symphonies and was backup for a vocal quintet that included Bing Crosby on a version of "My Blue Heaven." Whiteman softened (and, in some respects, improved upon) jazz with soft strings, constraining it to little or no improvisation in order to appeal to a wider, more musically conservative audience.

Other light music radio stars would also go on to make easy-listening records. Gordon Jenkins, for example, performed as a multi-instrumentalist for NBC's Hollywood network from 1938 to 1944. The Mutual Network, in association with the Longines-Wittnaur Watch Company, had the Longines Symphonette; Enoch Light and the Light Brigade (popular in the hotel circuit) appeared on *Hit Parade;* Phil Spitalny and His All-Girl Orchestra played *The Hour of Charm;* Wayne King had *The Lady Esther Serenade;* and NBC presented Evelyn and Her Magic Violin.

Across the Atlantic, the BBC was nurturing its own breed of light orchestral radio stars. In fact, England would go on to perfect the genre of mood music. London-born George Melachrino (1909–1965) sang; composed; conducted; arranged; played the violin, oboe, and piano; and was the United Kingdom's biggest light music star. By 1927, he was broadcasting on the BBC and got top billing a year later when playing the Savoy Orpheans.

Morton Gould continues:

> *Other than the polarization of light and heavy music comes a very real fact. Radio was the great communicator, in terms of reaching millions and millions of people instantaneously: the equivalent of what television is today. If you were on radio, you were fairly well known—because you reached so many people. Therefore, because of the popular medium, from a commercial point of view, it was important to attract enough people to justify the cost of running or sponsoring these programs. The kind of music that would*

*please the most number of people and offend the least
became the norm. . . . The serious classical and Baroque
writers of the time may have actually written functional
music: themes like "Fireworks," Handel's "Water Music"—music to celebrate something with a million oboes
playing on a barge going up the river. This was all
functional music, in a sense."*

Before radio, millions of people could encounter a symphony
performance within a time frame of perhaps 100 years. But a
single radio broadcast could reach the same number of people in
one hour. The radio audience, cut off from the garrulous tuxedo-
and-gown crowds, had a one-on-one relationship with the musical
piece.

A common image of radio days depicts the family seated around
a room, listening to an installment of "The Green Hornet" or Jack
Benny. But while radio did house a great deal of drama and music
meant for active listening, it also presented light music (as one
more push-button appliance) designed to serve as background for
domestic scenes. There has been considerable celebration of radio's ability to unite people from great distances, but what about
the equally significant time–space transformation involving the radio, the listener, and the household chores (not to mention mood
music's longtime companion, the icebox)?

Without the imposed discipline of a symphony hall or opera
house, average listeners were at last free to select the music they
wanted to match the contours of their parlor and personality.
Brahms and Berlioz had to defer to Gould and Faith on radio's
home turf, where, to quote Kostelanetz, "every one is his own
master and, incidentally, master of the program."

6 / Ghosts in the Elevator

In hotels, office buildings, and many other places, one is perpetually awash in soft music, as in America. Plaintive arias leak from the walls in elevators, waiting rooms, bars, and lavatories; the music comes from nowhere, like a ventriloquist's voice.

—Luigi Barzini, *The Europeans**

Think of "elevator music," and the first sounds that come to mind are of "syrupy" strings, "homogenized" horns, and "whipped-cream" Wurlitzers languidly laboring to make us relax. Like all stereotypes, this one has some truth, but few critics appreciate why the music is purposely made this way and why, notwithstanding all the whining, griping, and cheap jokes, most people have welcomed its intrusion into their lives at one time or another despite themselves.

*Copyright © 1983 by Luigi Barzini. Reprinted by permission of Simon & Schuster, Inc.

Besides its significance as a musical innovation, elevator music is important for its literal meaning. Imagine what average turn-of-the-century urban dwellers (still stuck in a Victorian mindset) felt at the sight of a conveyance capable of lifting them multiple stories in a matter of seconds. Next to rollercoasters and airplanes, elevators were perceived by many as floating domiciles of disequilibrium, inciting thoughts of motion sickness and snapping cables.

Building proprietors and the rapidly growing lift industry dedicated part of their public relations campaign to allaying elevator jockey fears. Riders felt a little more assured when uniformed attendants were on hand to greet and guide them through their uncertain vertical passage. But following the first appearance of Otis' electric elevator in 1889, the flesh-and-blood attendant was eventually superseded by soft, comforting, angelic music luring and lulling the squeamish on board. By injecting ether and eliminating dross, elevator music became a style whose notes and harmonies sounded as if they were whipped up with air.

All of the monstrous visions of gargoyle-lined skyscrapers (perfected in Fritz Lang's 1919 film *Metropolis*) came to life on May 31, 1931, when New York City unveiled the 102-story Empire State Building. Music had to be piped into the elevators, lobbies, and observatories to give people at least some illusion of continuity amid the disorder.

One particular incident shows just how much elevator music became part of the historical record. On July 28, 1945, an Army B-25 bomber on a cross-country mission crashed into the Empire State Building's 79th story. Flames shot up the elevator shafts, damaging cables and threatening to engulf fifty people stuck inside of a glass-encased observatory on the 88th floor. The front-page article in the July 29th *New York Times* reported: "Even at this terrifying juncture, however, the 'canned' music that is wired into the observatory continued to play, and the soothing sounds of a waltz helped the spectators there to control themselves. There was no panic, but within a few minutes the heat and choking fumes from the fire below made the observatory uncomfortable."

Background music companies never considered elevators their biggest market, however. Their primary customers were places of work and recreation that used music as a mood boost, just as radio had orchestrated private homes. When it was still known as Wired Radio, Muzak® transmitted to grocery stores equipped with loudspeakers to announce such news items as reduced milk or egg prices. Restaurants and hotels played only music spun from the central Muzak studio's dual-phonograph turntables, running up to 17½ hours per day. To compete with Muzak, which would continue to lead the world in this trade, numerous other companies sprouted in both America and England. Popular journalists started discussing background music's role in our modern folklore as a changing economy stumbled through the Great Depression, recharged during the war effort, and burgeoned during the Cold War consumer blitz.

From the start, Muzak was not content to broadcast compilations of previously recorded material. It conducted its own studio sessions to produce custom-made "functional music" that resembled the breakfast marches (such as the Pan American Brass Band's "Star Spangled Banner") and lunchtime pipe-organs described in *Looking Backward,* with semi-classical filler in between.

Muzak's first 1934 recording was a medley of "Whispering," "Do You Ever Think of Me?" and "Here in My Arms," performed by Sam Lanin (brother of Lester Lanin) and his orchestra. Muzak's second band was Russ Morgan's midwest dance ensemble, whose star musicians included Fats Waller and Teddy Wilson (from the original Benny Goodman Sextet). The Dorsey Brothers Orchestra also contributed a 1935 version of "Solitude."

All Muzak recordings were pressed on vertically engraved 33⅓-rpm disks—forerunners of the LP, which became popular after World War II. Muzak was most likely the first company to press recordings on vinylite instead of shellac (which scratched too easily). Before using vinyl, Muzak engraved its music onto wax cylinders. According to sound engineer Irv Joel, who worked on Muzak's studio sessions in the 1950s, when it shared space at Capitol Records:

> *During the early thirties, Muzak's chief engineer invented the "gold sputtering process," which cut the*

original musical transcriptions onto wax; from the wax,
they made a "mother" recording which would be a neg-
ative of the groove. They sprayed a fine coating of gold
onto the wax, then parted the wax and got this im-
pression. The next step in the process was to electro-
plate it. From that was made a stamper and then the
record. Other record companies followed suit until sil-
ver proved cheaper.

By March 6, 1936, Muzak had completed its move from Cleveland to its New York studios on Fourth Avenue, where "Music by Muzak" emitted cover versions of "I've Got You Under My Skin" and "There's a Small Hotel" for such swanky clients as the East Side's Stork Club and the Chambord. That same year, when Franklin Delano Roosevelt defeated Alfred Landon in the Presidential election, Muzak was there to relay the results to its subscribers. The New Deal may have implemented a quasi-socialist program to bail the nation out of capitalism's hangover; but Muzak, in a more mercenary communitarian spirit, cultivated a franchise system that extended into Los Angeles; Boston; Washington, D.C.; Detroit; Buffalo; and Philadelphia.

Muzak was now getting closer to a bigger goal: to supply its clients with a program of tunes segmented by mood as a tonic for the times of day when the human spirit sags. This was an idea that Muzak President Waddill Catchings cherished. Catchings was a well-known investment banker who once bore the nickname "Golden Boy of Wall Street." Already boasting a record of profitable business schemes, he came up with the idea of assigning each song in the Muzak library a stimulus code that could be stored and transmitted according to rhythm, tempo, instrumentation and ensemble size.

Still in its formative stages, "Music by Muzak" served up a potpourri of classical, semi-classical, pop vocal, and quasi-Polynesian or Gypsy tunes, played by such prominent figures as Xavier Cugat, Clyde McCoy, and Harry Horlick. A more standard format was inaugurated in August of 1936 when Catchings ordered his programmers to target sequencing, timing, and vocal impact. No vocals could play between 9:00 P.M. and 12:30 A.M. After 12:30, no waltzes or tangos (except for an occasional "hit" song) were permitted. Slow music was usually avoided; if used at all, it had to appear either in the middle of a set or at the end.

A typical sequencing program for restaurants complemented the daily eating ritual. The breakfast hours (7:00–9:00 A.M.) offered cheery sunrise melodies and caffeinated rhythms. From 9:00 A.M. to noon, background filler whetted appetites until the official lunch diet of light classical and spicier strains was served. After more filler beginning at 2:00 P.M., cocktail tunes came on at 5:00 P.M. to mix with piano and such exotic condiments as vibraphone. The discreet and quietly classical dinner hours from 6:00 to 9:00 P.M. provided sustenance in anticipation of the evening dance protocol, which permitted increased volume and tempo the closer midnight encroached.

A March 1939 issue of *Newsweek* noted that Muzak's restaurateur clientele comprised at least 360 businesses. At least 1,000 new accounts were serviced in the next five years. Besides its regular functional music regimen, Muzak supplied interference-free transmissions of local New York–area radio stations WABC, WOR, and WEAF.

Muzak established four networks to meet varying demands and budgets. The "Purple Network," available for a monthly lease premium of $35, served restaurants from 10 to 3:30 A.M. In addition, it offered special requests, the most popular being a "wedding sequence" that included strains from Wagner's *Lohengrin* and Mendelssohn's *Midsummer Night's Dream.* Reportedly, twenty-seven requests for this sequence alone were made during one day in June 1940.

The "Red Network" offered news reports, weather, sports updates, and time signals; it was intended mostly for modest-sized bars and grills. The "Blue Network," on the other hand, serviced mostly department stores. The "Green Network" reestablished Muzak's early commitment to providing service to private residences, with transmissions beamed exclusively to apartment buildings for a landlord's fee of at least $25 per month.

Following an early Stevens Institute of Technology study in the

1930s (which found that "functional music" reduced absenteeism in workplaces by 88 percent, with a 53 percent reduction in early departures), industrial psychologists started taking Muzak very seriously and conducted similar, more elaborate tests. Dr. H. C. Smith demonstrated that 75 percent of the workforce favored not just good but well-programmed music. Joe Coco, a Muzak engineer for over forty years, recalls that "Muzak was never meant to be played loudly, just subdued like wind playing between the leaves of trees."

Muzak received further impetus from an unexpected source. In 1937, the Medical Research Council's Industrial Health Research Board of Great Britain published *Fatigue and Boredom in Repetitive Work* by S. Wyatt and J. N. Langdon. Twelve young English women employed in making paper firecrackers apparently worked better and harbored less of a resentful attitude when exposed to morning music. This, more than any previous study, demonstrated music's boost to worker production and, according to subsequent observations by Muzak programmer Jane Jarvis, "proved conclusively that the use of music in an ever-rising stimulus curve to combat fatigue was very desirable." Work music became so well regarded in England that, in 1940, British composer Eric Coates wrote "Calling All Workers," a pep-melody that his wife requested while she was making wartime supplies for the Red Cross. It soon became a signature tune for the BBC's *Music While You Work* program.

A few years later, the Frankford Arsenal in Philadelphia released a study linking background music to a reduction in on-the-job accidents. This information was augmented by even more tantalizing news that farmers in McKeesport, Pa., had reported how their cows gave more milk to the "Blue Danube Waltz."

Muzak was catapulted into bigger ventures when Warner Brothers purchased it in 1938. Warner combined Muzak with Associated Music Publishers, a transcription library that, in turn, got to use Muzak's recording studios. But a year later, Warner Brothers sold these acquisitions to a triumvirate of ambitious and slick entrepreneurs: Waddill Catchings, Allen Miller, and William Benton. Miller (an American "soldier of fortune") had helped form England's Rediffusion, Ltd., which, like Muzak, transmitted music over telephone lines. The big star was Benton, a public relations specialist who was destined for a U.S. Senate seat in Connecticut.

William Benton acquired full controlling stock in Muzak in 1941 for just $100,000, on the advice of economist Beardsley Ruml, whose famous book *Pay as You Go* helped inspire our federal withholding tax. Not long after graduating from Yale in the early 1920s, Benton served as copywriter for the Lord & Thomas advertising firm, and soon he was the company's assistant manager. In 1929, in the wake of the Wall Street crash, he joined Chester Bowles (later governor of Connecticut) to start the Benton & Bowles Advertising Agency. Benton & Bowles secured success during the Depression years precisely because it perfected radio advertising as an art. Shows like Fred Allen's *Town Hall Tonight* and Maxwell House's *Showboat* helped pioneer the blurring of entertainment and product promotion that is so much a fact of life today.

It should be noted that Benton later took the post of Assistant Secretary of State for Public Affairs in 1945 to promote the American propaganda machine Voice of America. His ideas about knowledge dissemination eventually led to creation of the United States Information Service. He was also active in the formation of UNESCO (United Nations Educational, Scientific and Cultural Organization), an agency that would later decry the use of background music in public places.

Despite its future battles with Muzak regarding the mechanical royalties conundrum, ASCAP had been instrumental in pushing Muzak into wartime military arsenals. A 1944 ASCAP pamphlet entitled *Music in Industry: Principles of Programming* offered advice on how to make full use of background music's utilitarian advantages with such tips as avoiding "tricky instrumental effects, prolonged vocals, or changes of key in the middle of a chorus." The literature, compiled by U.S. War Production Board member (and future Muzak research director) Richard (sometimes Richmond) Cardinell, recommended starting each day with military marches and a fox trot or polka "to wipe the gloom off the faces of the incoming employees and perhaps to instill a little esprit de corps into the whole group."

Muzak became an American institution through its wartime clout. Besides supplying arsenal music, it helped the Office of War Information circulate training instructions. The 17½-hour programming day increased to 24 hours by January of 1942. If necessary, the lilting tones of "You Stepped Out of a Dream" or "Do I Worry?" could be interrupted by "on the line" reports of enemy bombs. Muzak headquarters took civil defense precautions by encasing itself in windowless plywood and stayed abreast of news with its own United Press International ticker. It felt compelled to add a brand-new program of air-raid music whose songs could never be disclosed ahead of time for fear that listeners hearing a regular broadcast would recognize one of the air-raid program songs and start a panic by running for cover.

As Muzak spread, musician licensing grew more complicated. It became difficult to keep tabs on when, where, and how often a song was broadcast or played for any kind of public function. Establishments that wished to play music used Muzak to avoid legal tangles with musician and composer unions. North American had already acquired the music publishing company Breitkopf Publications, Inc., and formed Associated Music Publishers, Inc., when Warner Brothers united the latter with Muzak, giving Muzak the American rights to many compositions: classical, semiclassical, and popular.

Muzak's Associated Music Publishers was ASCAP's sole competitor before a group of about 256 radio broadcasters formed BMI (Broadcast Music, Inc.) in 1939. Merritt Tompkins, a former president of Associated Music Publishers, was BMI's first president. Anticipating the 1940 ASCAP strike against the broadcast industry, BMI sought legal coverage for songs not under ASCAP's rubric and bought Associated Music Publishers out by 1947. All of this finagling led Muzak to play an indirect role in recent music-licensing history.

Muzak had mounting problems with the American Federation of Musicians—primarily its notorious president James Caesar Petrillo. This former pianist and bandleader shook the music business cage with his stern demands. Argumentative and litigious, with an alleged deathly fear of germs that made shaking hands with others unthinkable, Petrillo led a long and bitter fight against permitting any kind of "canned" music into Chicago establishments, reasoning that it would deprive working performers of their livelihood.

In 1940, Judge Learned Hand of the Federal Circuit Court of Appeals wrote an opinion for the court, ruling on a suit brought by RCA, that playing a record over the radio posed no copyright infringements. Petrillo disagreed with the ruling and commissioned Ben Selvin (a former orchestra leader from the 1920s, a broadcasting expert, and supposedly the first recording artist to sell a million records) to prove that recordings and broadcasts put musicians out of work.

To Petrillo's chagrin, Selvin concluded in a report to the 1941 AFT convention that union action was not the answer, since mechanized music was unavoidable and because record labels compensated by paying back millions of dollars to studio musicians. Selvin's presentation elicited support from the AFM members and many bandleaders, as well as a standing ovation.

Ben Selvin's role in dismissing the political maneuver he had been commissioned to defend is only part of the irony. The other twist is that Selvin was Muzak's chief programmer in its early years; he supervised its first New York City transmission in 1936 and had helped the company devise its first standardized programming.

Despite the consensus against him, Petrillo was committed to preventing record companies from catering to any background music services, not to mention radio stations and jukeboxes. On August 1, 1942, he ordered a strike, barring all musicians from studios. It took record companies four years to cave in to Petrillo's demands. Some music historians (such as Donald Clarke in *The Penguin Encyclopedia of Popular Music*) speculate that this strike tolled the Big Band era's death knell by silencing many promising players.

Muzak entered Chicago's market in 1946, forging a franchise

with Boom Electric & Amplifier Company, which provided sound systems for Wrigley Field and Comiskey Park. Petrillo, learning of Muzak's invasion, threatened to establish a boycott by live orchestras of any hotel establishment that used piped music. His ire was directed at both Muzak and Boom Electric because he felt they had entered his turf surreptitiously. In October of 1949, Muzak filed a complaint with the National Labor Relations Board, accusing Petrillo and the AFM of violating the Taft-Hartley Act (which Congress had passed over President Truman's veto in 1946). In the meantime, another union, the Electrical Workers' Local 134, which installed the Muzak equipment, became irate over Petrillo's threat—a situation all the more muddled because both unions were members of the American Federation of Labor. Petrillo was tenacious and managed to pressure ten businesses into discontinuing their Muzak lines for four months. Finally, however, the NLRB ruled in favor of Muzak in its case against Petrillo, ending the impasse.

All of the industrial know-how Muzak had put into the war effort soon got rechanneled into the postwar era's prolific private economy, which social scientists characterized as heralding the arrival of the "Organization Man." Although it was a private corporation, Muzak constituted one of the most intricate federal–private mergers in America's history, with civil defense, public service, and entertainment issuing from the same source in the service of profit and public welfare.

The mainstream press meanwhile doled out reports confirming Muzak's efficacy. The March 1946 *Reader's Digest* reprinted a *Forbes* article titled "Have You Tried Working to Music?" Its author, Doron K. Antrim, informed middle America that "music is now being piped into banks, insurance companies, publishing houses and other offices, where brain workers find that it lessens tension and keeps everyone in a happier frame of mind."

Among Muzak's most notable customers were the Federal Reserve Bank, National City Bank, Prudential Life Insurance Company, Bell Telephone, and McGraw-Hill Publishing Companies. Muzak surveyed workers with in-house questionnaires and found that a meager 1.6 percent considered background music distracting on the job; meanwhile, 83 percent preferred the music to a music-free environment, and 60 percent reported experiencing a definite reduction in fatigue following introduction of the music.

Dr. Harold Burris-Meyer and Richard L. Cardinell, both Stevens Institute of Technology alumni, made a significant impact on Muzak's applications. Cardinell conducted a 1947 study of eight divisions of the Army Map Service in Washington, D.C., and obtained even more favorable results. Among supervisors, 44.5 percent saw a boost in production efficiency; and 88.7 percent of employees claimed "Muzak helps me in my work." The study's summary: "As Muzak relieves monotony and makes the time go faster, conversation decreases and employees invariably take a kindlier view of each other."

Cardinell received corroboration from a Dartmouth University probe showing that music helped to enhance reading speed and comprehension. Researchers at De Pauw University gathered evidence that waltzes helped students with arithmetic. Expounding on his research efforts, Cardinell spoke the lingo of a sonic interior decorator:

> *Factors that distract attention—change of tempo, loud brasses, vocals—are eliminated. Orchestras of strings and woodwinds predominate, the tones blending with the surroundings as do proper colors in a room. The worker should be no more aware of the music than of good lighting. The rhythms, reaching him subconsciously, create a feeling of well-being and eliminate strain.*

Cardinell reached one more stunning conclusion: "In some cases, it is possible to achieve a direct production increase by playing a program which completely ignores employee preferences and concentrates on the functional aspects only."

"Stimulus Progression," Muzak's most elaborate program, premiered in the late 1940s. It was implemented by Burris-Meyer and Cardinell but masterminded by Muzak executive Don O'Neill, who had toyed with the idea since he joined the company in 1936. Stimulus Progression was a method of organizing music according to an "Ascending Curve" that worked counter to the "Industrial Efficiency Curve" or what some authorities called the average worker's "fatigue curve." Subdued songs progressing to more stimulating songs in fifteen-minute sequences throughout the average workday yielded more worker efficiency and productivity than did random programming. Programs were soon tailored to workers' mood swings and peak periods as measured on a Muzak mood-rating scale ranging from "Gloomy—minus three" to "Ecstatic—plus eight."

Muzak literature claims: "The idea was to combat monotony and offset boredom at precisely those times in a work day when people are most subject to these onslaughts." Although several years passed before the Stimulus Progression program began to work efficiently, Muzak's quarter-hour programming had remained its trademark innovation for decades.

Ben Selvin, among Stimulus Progression's earliest engineers, devised a 45-hertz tone that could automatically turn the music off in factories that requested fifteen minutes of silence for every quarter hour of music. At the time, the music was divided into four blocks; the softer first and third segments were programmed for the offices, while the louder and brassier selections for factories were included on segments two and four.

Over the years, Muzak compiled a digest of jagged graph studies conducted by Lever Brothers, Fairfield University's language laboratory, and the U.S. Army Engineering Labs to show how Stimulus Progression increased office output, reduced stress, lessened costs, enhanced worker concentration, and improved personnel morale.

By 1948, "Travel Muzak" was disseminating wistful arrangements like "I Want My Mama" and "I'll Be Seeing You" on trains, passenger ships, and planes. Entering the 1950s, Muzak became the biggest consumer of phone lines in the world.

But another, far more pesky bugaboo was gumming up Muzak's ointment: the notion that piped-in music somehow interferes with an individual's right to privacy and even brainwashes listeners. The question of whether music alone (without subliminal messages) constitutes an infringement on protections guaranteed by the Bill of Rights or a mind-manipulation technique received close judicial scrutiny in the early 1950s. The precipitating event was Muzak's effort to transmit a program called "Transit Radio," consisting of local radio programs and announcements (including commercials) from a Washington, D.C., radio station (WWDC-FM), into the District's public buses and trains.

The District's Capital Transit project began in March of 1948 with a pilot study using a "music as you ride" format on selected streetcars and buses. The speakers were laid out so that passengers could hear the music and announcements no matter where they sat or stood, at a volume level that did not inhibit chitchat.

Capital Transit signed an agreement with Washington Transit Radio, Inc., for exclusive installation, maintenance, and use rights in all Capital Transit vehicles, including office headquarters, terminals, and waiting rooms. The program consisted of 90 percent music and 10 percent public service announcements and commercials. Because of the District of Columbia's peculiar status as, in effect, a federal territory, the United States Congress granted a franchise to Capital Transit alone, challenging the distinction between public and private utilities. Matters were complicated by the fact that D.C. Transit was perceived as being a federally monitored monopoly that permitted the city's residents no competing transit alternative.

Although 92 percent of the passengers polled after the pilot study wanted the program to continue, protests poured in when "music as you ride" was formally instituted on at least twenty vehicles. The D.C. Public Utilities Commission investigated the complainants' claim that the music and announcements violated their constitutional rights to privacy and free speech.

The Commission's hearings started in July of 1949. According to U.S. Supreme Court Reports of October 1951, two disgruntled passengers, Pollak and Martin, who led the complainants, were initially thwarted when the Commission ruled that the "transmission of radio programs through receivers and loud speakers in passenger vehicles . . . does not violate the free speech guaranty of the First Amendment, where the programs do not interfere substantially with the conversation of passengers and there is no substantial claim that the programs have been used for objectionable propaganda."°

Citing train and bus operator observations, the Commission concluded that vehicle music kept riders "in a better mood" and further ruled that "The Fifth Amendment does not secure to each passenger on a public vehicle regulated by the federal government a right to privacy substantially equal to the privacy to which he is entitled in his own home."

On March 3, 1952, after the dissenting passengers lost again in a hearing before the United States District Court, the case of *Public Utilities Commission of the District of Columbia* v. *Franklin S. Pollak* came before the United States Court of Appeals of the District of Columbia, taking almost three months for a decision. The Court reversed part of the Commission's judgment because it concluded that the use of commercials and announcements "deprive[s] objecting passengers of liberty without due process of law." But the court found no such violations with the playing of music alone.

With the Court of Appeals refusing a second hearing, Capital Transit, Transit Radio, and the Utilities Commission took the case to the Supreme Court. This was followed by Pollak's and Martin's cross petition, which sought to prohibit music as well as announcements. But the Supreme Court reversed the Court of Appeals decision, finding neither an equation between music and mind control nor any constitutional reason to ban announcements.

Justice Harold Burton, writing for the Court's majority, stated that no First or Fifth Amendment rights were in jeopardy and that broadcasting the music was "not inconsistent with public convenience, comfort and safety and 'tends to improve the conditions under which the public ride.' " He also cited Edward G. Doody & Company's 1949 public opinion survey which revealed that 93.4 percent of those polled voiced no opposition to the music, and 76.3 percent gave an outright approval.

Burton went on to counter the arguments of Pollak and Martin

°Public Utilities Commission v. Pollak, U.S. Supreme Court Reports (October 1951), vols. 342–343, pp. 1069–80.

by showing fundamental differences between privacy in the home and privacy in public places:

> *This position wrongly assumes that the Fifth Amendment secures to each passenger on a public vehicle regulated by the Federal Government a right of privacy substantially equal to the privacy to which he is entitled in his own home. However complete his privacy may be at home, it is substantially limited by the rights of others when its possessor travels on a public thoroughfare or rides in a public conveyance.*

Justice Felix Frankfurter had chosen to recuse himself from participating in the judgment of the case because of his strong feelings against such "aural aggressions." Justice Hugo Black concurred with the Court of Appeals decision against non-musical broadcasts but showed no variance toward music alone. Justice William O. Douglas filed the only resolute dissenting opinion, in which he objected to D.C. Transit's compulsory listening policy and offered his memorable quip that "The right to be let alone is indeed the beginning of all freedom."

Most intriguing about Douglas's opinion is his ethical distinction between machine-imposed and human-imposed noise: "One who is in a public vehicle may not of course complain of the noise of the crowd and the babble of tongues. One who enters any public place sacrifices some of his privacy. My protest is against the invasion of his privacy over and beyond the risks of travel." Is it possible (or sensible) that low-volume music (intended to help mask noise) should be more deserving of censure than loud passenger cackle? (Perhaps urban crowds were more containable when the judge wrote these sentiments in 1951.)

Muzak and Transit Radio may have stemmed the tide of some civil libertarians for a while, but the victory was short-lived. Transit Radio continued its program for only a few years more before being discontinued by the mid-1950s.

Muzak faced bigger challenges as its competition mounted and magnetic tape transmission and portable tape players made background music installation easier and cheaper. By 1955, RCA and

Capitol records started making arrangements with companies like Magnecord, Inc. and Magnetronics to provide music for restaurants, offices, factories, and funeral chapels.

Magne-Music, a tape-reel service operating out of Tulsa, Oklahoma, recorded some of its music at New York's St. Patrick's Cathedral for use in devotional religious observances. One selection, consisting of "pipe organ, symphonic carillon and vibraharp" was cataloged as "Music for Mortuaries." Magne-Music had a total of eight commercial categories, including music for cocktail lounges, hotels, luncheons, dinner, and after-dinner, with instrumental renditions of favorites such as "Laura," "Begin the Beguine," and "Sophisticated Lady."

Among the biggest background music suppliers aside from Muzak was J. P. Seeburg, a jukebox manufacturer in Chicago that maintained a library of up to 7,000 recordings. Seeburg had the advantage of adding private houses to its customer roster: 570 new homes erected in the Detroit suburb of Westchester Village were equipped with Seeburg's Select-O-Matic units specially made for high-fidelity use. Seeburg transmitted its "planned sequence of selections" from "self-contained" machines, dispensing with phone lines and dependence on a central broadcasting studio.

Muzak met the magnetic competition as early as 1953 with its M8R System, among the first electronic tape playback units to allow full automation for functional music relays. Described as an "electric brain," the M8R responded to inaudible signals and adjusted music transmissions with little human intervention. This technology allowed Muzak, for the first time, to have franchises in communities with populations of 25,000 or fewer people.

Muzak was installed in the White House during the Eisenhower years. Lyndon Baines Johnson owned Muzak franchises in Austin during his early senatorial days. By 1955, the company ventured into broadcasting its music through FM multiplexing on side channels known in broadcasting parlance as SCAs (sub-carrier authorizations). The number of Muzak franchises swelled to at least 150, including offices in Canada and elsewhere abroad. The Jack Wrather Organization, which already owned the *Lassie* TV show, the Disneyland Hotel and Monorail, and the Gilbert Toy Company, bought Muzak in 1957. The attendant excitement was orchestrated to the sounds of such newly acquired Muzak melodies as "Gigi" and "The Hawaiian Wedding Song."

As each new study validated the benefits that the company claimed to provide, detractors were stymied by the dearth of counterstudies. Harold Burris-Meyer, looking proudly on his Muzak accomplishments, had already stated in the 1946 *Reader's Digest* article: "If people who claim they require absolute silence were placed in a near vacuum . . . they would probably go nuts. We are conditioned to sound, but our present need is for more that soothes and less that frays the nerves."

During the brief recession of 1958, Muzak's aggressive marketing kept the company in the black. Stevenson, Jordon & Harrison (a consulting firm) established that "Music by Muzak" was a most effective and least costly management tool. Howard Taubman, a *New York Times* reporter, would soon write: "Electrical appliances have taken the drudgery out of getting the laundry done, and now music turns it into enchantment."

7 / Emotional Archives

BACKGROUND MUSIC IN THE MOVIES

Easy-listening music (at least in theory) helps the consumer buy, the patient relax, the worker work; its goal is to render the individual an untroublesome social subject. Film music, participating as it does in a narrative, is more varied in its content and roles; but primary among its goals, nevertheless, is to render the individual an untroublesome viewing subject; less critical, less "awake."

—Claudia Gorbman, *Unheard Melodies**

Toward the finale of *Grand Hotel*, Greta Garbo (playing the temperamental ballerina Grusinskaya) laughs and prances in her suite. Her countless bouts with manic-depression give way to fevered joy as she anticipates a rendezvous with her newfound lover Baron Von Geigen (John Barrymore). Yet even while swooning, Garbo senses something is awry: "The music has stopped. How quiet it is tonight. It was never so quiet in the Grand Hotel. . . ."

*From *Unheard Melodies* by Claudia Gorbman, p. 5. © 1987, published by Indiana University Press and the British Film Institute. Reprinted by permission.

Greta has every reason to feel ill at ease. Throughout the film, her mood swings have been counterpointed by Rachmaninoff's romantic Second Piano Concerto piped into her hotel suite. Now, with the musical buttress pulled out from under her, she is on the verge of gazing at life unadorned. What lousy timing, considering that her beloved (a jewel thief in disguise) has just been murdered. With neither paramour nor soundtrack, Garbo leaves the hotel as dizzy as she was when she entered.

Released by MGM in 1932, *Grand Hotel* complicated the debate about music's new role in the talkies. Audiences, still new to the sound film, were known to deride a phantom symphony of violins, harps, and horns coming out of thin air whenever characters were in distress or succumbing to a kiss. Directors and producers likewise used music only if it had a narrative source, whether that source was a phonograph, a radio, or a live orchestra written into the story.

Grand Hotel played it safe by having things both ways. It was one of the first and few situations where both a movie's source music and background music were inextricable. With the exception of a live jazz band in "the funny yellow room where they dance," music blares from invisible speakers, the volume rising and falling as doors open and close—an antiphony for characters wandering in a place where "people come, people go and nothing ever happens."

From its inception, the science of film scores helped to articulate the background music industry's needs. Early movie soundtracks in general and the soundtrack to *Grand Hotel* in particular most likely inspired Muzak's arrangements of the scores of our lives. Music by Muzak,® like Hollywood film scores, provides seamless segues between waking and dream life in the service of what Claudia Gorbman calls a "bath of affect." Background music on both sides of the movie screen minimizes discontinuities of space and time and draws subjects into suspended disbelief.

Movie music had its first incarnations in the days of *The Beggar's Opera,* when magic lantern spectacles at carnivals and fairs used balladeers to narrate picture stories. By the time Thomas Edison, Louis Lumière, and Oscar Messter brought us the cinematograph, sideshow venues continued to be the natural place for talking pictures. Edison presented the first "sound-film" on October 6, 1889, as a kind of peep show. The first theatrical silent films, shown in spaces that lacked sound-absorbent walls, used barrel-organs, phonographs, and music boxes to mask the grating din emitted by early projectors.

In 1896, long before World War I spurred advances in electroacoustic science, Charles Pathé introduced the Berliner gramophone, with longer-running records and a mechanical "Joly" allowing for some kind of synchronization between film strip and record. That same year, Oscar Messter made a similar experiment. Messter, trying to correct the problem of recorded sound's low volume, would run several gramophones at once, with giant horns attached.

Edison's movies were often distributed with written "suggestions for music" in the early 1900s. New York's Sam Fox Publishing Company released *Sam Fox Moving Picture Music*, consisting of classified "mood music" volumes by J. S. Zamecnik intended for silent movie pianists.

In 1908, while in Germany, Italian composer Giuseppe Becce published *Kinothek*—the first definitive book on cinema music compilation. Becce set the standard for many film libraries throughout the world by transmuting the works of many renowned composers into functional mood units. Often, stylistically contrary pieces were juxtaposed according to the logic of the film narrative. The opus proper lost its autonomy in favor of what Kurt London, in his book *Film Music*, calls "the melting pot of compilation":

> *Here we have, for the first time in the history of modern music, a systematic tabulation of music according to its uses. . . . It contained, if we follow the romantic conception of programme music, all the moods of men and the elements, every kind of reaction to human destiny, musical drawings of nature and animals, of peoples and countries: in short, every sphere of life, well and clearly arranged under headings.*

In James L. Limbacher's *Film Music: From Violins to Video*, Max Winkler, another early film composer, summarized the cinema's art of mood control:

> The immortal chorales of J.S. Bach became an "Adagio Lamentose for sad scenes." Extracts from great symphonies and operas were hacked down to emerge again as "Sinister Misterioso" by Beethoven, or "Weird Moderato" by Tchaikovsky. Wagner's and Mendelssohn's wedding marches were used for marriages, fights between husbands and wives, and divorce scenes: we just had them played out of tune, a treatment known in the profession as "souring up the aisle."

Another movie music guide appeared in 1924: Erno Rapee's *Motion Picture Moods for Pianists and Organists: A Rapid Reference Collection of Selected Pieces Adapted to Fifty-two Moods and Situations.* It offered a wide selection of motifs, including "Wedding," "Sinister," "Orgies," "Sea-Storm," "Chase," and "Oriental."

As Kurt London contends: "The silent film without music had no right to exist." When this same maxim proved true for most sound films, it began to seem that, without something like Muzak® to enliven our off-screen tragi-comedies, neither did we.

Background music companies like Muzak must work with "real" instead of "cinematic" time. The hyperexplicit crescendos and diminuendos of a Max Steiner score are fine for an artificial narrative structure with a precise beginning, middle, and end. Philip Glass might be appropriate for a movie flouting conventional narration (such as Godfrey Reggio's *Koyaanisqatsi*). But for daily life's unpredictable events and mood shifts, the soundtrack gets more tricky.

Any coincidence between the content of a Muzak tune and the feelings or circumstances of people hearing it is aleatory, not synchronized. A pretty series of tremolo strings may evoke feelings of peacefulness or horror, depending on how a scene is shot and what the script demands. But in public places, the same music is open to as many interpretations as there are people. Nonetheless, moments of Muzak synchronicity do occur at different times of the day, from place to place, city to city, state to state, and country to country, when the music coming out of an elevator, office, airport, or department store seems suddenly to be playing our song.

By 1934, when people finally got used to music in the talkies, filmmakers began taking full advantage of a device known as "the up-and-downer," which automatically lowered the music volume when dialogue signals appeared on the soundtrack. When studios commissioned specially composed soundtracks, they rarely planned them in advance, leaving the pressure of concocting a last-minute score to the composers. Henry Mancini, in his autobiography, talked about his leaner days at Universal Studios when low-budget westerns and period pictures were churned out by several arrangers at once, all cribbing earlier scores from the studio library.

Leonid Sabaneev insisted that film music was the screen melody's "left hand," while the story proper remained the right hand. Writing in the 1940s, Aaron Copland described movie "background" music as "the most ungrateful kind of music for a composer to write. Since it's music behind, or underneath, the word, the audience is really not going to hear it, possibly won't even be aware of its existence; yet it undoubtedly works on the subconscious mind. The need here is for a kind of music that will give off a 'neutral' color or atmosphere. . . . To write music that must be inexpressive is not easy for composers who normally tend to be as expressive as possible."

It is only fair to note that some film composers flouted their self-effacing role by making scores rife with personality glitches. Dimitri Tiomkin's hands-on involvement with his movies gained him notoriety, due to the heavy accents he imparted to every scene. Edmund Meisel's leaden, expressionistic stamp became controversial with the soundtrack to Sergei Eisenstein's *Battleship Potemkin*. The European countries that allowed its release often censored the music, fearing that the aggressive rhythms would inspire their own proletariat to replicate the Russian Revolution of 1917.

The 1930s produced a slew of films with overwrought orchestrations, in which turbulent-sounding maestros called excessive attention to themselves. This tendency, known as "mickeymousing," might have worked for a Disney cartoon, but in *Of*

Human Bondage, when clubfooted Leslie Howard had the extra handicap of a limping leitmotif, the consequences were ludicrous. A classic story of how a film score can overrun its boundaries took place during the making of *Dark Victory.* When the dying Bette Davis made her ceremonial ascent up to her deathbed, she broke character and asked director Michael Curtiz whether she or Max Steiner would be going up the stairs.

Despite his reputation as a maker of sometimes obstreperous scores, Steiner composed "Theme from *A Summer Place*"—a song that not only elevated Percy Faith into the popular domain but that continues to be the most identifiable easy-listening soundmark. In fact, many famous movie scores later became mood music favorites. Mantovani got famous by reproducing "Charmaine," the theme song that emerged from Erno Rapee's synchronized score to Raoul Walsh's silent classic *What Price Glory?* Other movie themes turned easy-listening are "Diane" from Frank Borzage's *Seventh Heaven* (1927), "The Moon of Manikoora" from John Ford's *The Hurricane* (1937) (which plays incessantly whenever romance looms), "Fascination" from Billy Wilder's *Love in the Afternoon* (1957) (constantly counterpointing the love scenes between Audrey Hepburn and Gary Cooper with violinists hired to prod the seduction), and "Moon River" from Blake Edwards's *Breakfast at Tiffany's* (1961). There is, of course, also "Pachelbel's Canon," reborn from its 17th-century context into modern brunch Baroque for countless films, TV movies of the week, and commercials.

A fine example of a movie soundtrack leaping from the background to foreground is film composer Richard Addinsell's "Warsaw Concerto," used in the score for Brian Desmond Hurst's *Dangerous Moonlight.* This British film, released in 1941 (several months before the U.S. entered World War II), starred Anton Walbrook as Stefan Radetzky, a Polish composer and military pilot who is spared combat and sent to America to give fund-raising concerts for Polish refugees. Throughout the film, Radetzky faces an ethical dilemma: how to weigh the luxuries of art over the realities of war while his comrades risk their lives. In the film's opening, the Nazi air raid over Warsaw looks more like a *trompe l'oeil* behind Radetzky as he sits at the piano, inspired to write the

"Warsaw Concerto" while swooning over an American press correspondent (played by Sally Gray), whom he meets the very moment the bombs fall. From that point on, *Dangerous Moonlight* becomes a brilliant feat of narrative deception: the concerto plays constantly (both as a Radetzky performance and as film score atmosphere) while viewers are tempted to perceive the great military events as background to the music instead of vice versa. A few years later, the "Warsaw Concerto" would also become a fifties "mood music" favorite, variations of which appeared on albums designed for romance and dining.

Other films have used *Grand Hotel*'s caprice of mingling piped-in source music with the score. In Alfred Hitchcock's *North by Northwest* (1959), the music in the first scene—where Roger Thornhill (Cary Grant) receives his fateful telephone call at a hotel (before falling into the hands of kidnappers)—is provided by lounge musicians playing "It's a Most Unusual Day." In John Brahm's *Hangover Square* (1945), Laird Cregar is the twisted composer George Harvey Bone, so obsessed with his work that he falls into "blank little moods" at the slightest discordant sounds and discovers whole chunks of time missing from his life, during which periods he kills people. Throughout the film, Bone's composition in progress takes on the violent and tawdry noises around him. The street calliope, the angry chanting at a ritual bonfire, and the lurid songs of a dancehall all coalesce several murders later in his final concerto and fiery finale. We cannot always be sure which discordant notes come from Bone's piano and which are provided by Bernard Herrmann's background score.

In 1933, while writing the script for *The Power and the Glory*, director Preston Sturges was concentrating on making the story upbeat, but kept coming out morose. Sturges later realized that someone in an adjacent room was listening to a melancholy piece of classical music. This realization of music's subliminal effect on emotions and thoughts led him to explore the subject fifteen years later in 1948, when he got a new contract from Twentieth Century–Fox to write and direct *Unfaithfully Yours*, starring Rex Harrison as a symphony conductor driven to kill his wife, whom he believes to be adulterous.

While directing his 1971 lunatic masterpiece *The Devils,* Ken Russell was not content just to harass his actors into religious hysteria. He had to crank out Prokofiev's grating opera *The Fiery Angel* full blast while filming a coven scene rife with demented and horny nuns.

A 1991 cognitive psychology study entitled "Effects of Background Music on the Remembering of Filmed Events" has concluded that movie scenes can be more readily recalled with background music than without. The music seems to provide a setting by which viewers develop better schematic processing through memory cues.

Anyone growing up on movies carries a sound library of tunes and leitmotifs that, in turn, get superimposed on the "real" world. The twentieth century may have gone haywire, but cinema soundtracks have surreptitiously imposed a much needed order. Natural landscapes, the flight of migratory birds, sunsets, rippling shores, orphans running through war-torn streets, a Tokyo massage parlor, cattle roaming through vast fields, lovers ogling on a beach, big-city lights, Saturday afternoon at the rodeo, international travel— the infinite tableaux of set designs with their attendant tunes boggle the mind.

We are also likely to feel like strangers in strange lands after considering that the classic movie scores of the 1930s, 1940s, 1950s—the ones that linger in our minds most and affect our daily perceptions—were mostly invented by transplanted European Jews second-guessing what they supposed were WASP fantasies set to a musical style inspired by the anti-Judaic Richard Wagner.

Literary critic Georges Polti once reduced the possible number of dramatic situations to an exceedingly modest thirty-six. He was, of course, working under the academic assumption that drama is a fantasy world delimited by a stage for the purpose of enlightening audiences with archetypal clichés handed down from ancient religions and myths. Polti's limited and bleak perspective did not take into account mass media's power to extend the borders of make-believe and to superimpose technicolor terrain onto personal experience.

This extended musical palette does not end with movies alone.

Mood music, production music, and stock music libraries have adapted movie soundtrack principles to other media. The first major production music libraries thrived by the 1930s by providing themes, signature tunes, or "transitions and links" for newsreels, war propaganda, radio spots, and (later) television commercials.

Most of the big music libraries came out of England. Among the first were Phonographic Performances Ltd. and Synchrophone Ltd., dedicated to meeting the needs of movie theaters desperate for music to play during intermissions or during advertisements. Companies such as DeWolfe, Chappell & Co., KPM (Keith Prowse Maurice), Mozart, and H.M.V. (His Master's Voice) provided songs that were not easily recognizable but that, after frequent exposure, came to have a hypnotic and subliminal impact. These compositions could be stored, reprogrammed, shortened, extended, cross-referenced, and rearranged according to market demands.

Until the late 1960s, production music was issued on 78s and later on 33 rpm 10-inch disks. As the competition grew fiercer, with many music libraries cropping up, catalogs ceased to list tunes by artist or composer but increasingly adopted categories resembling those of today's new-age "environmental" companies. Categories such as "Industrial," "National Music," "Sea Atmospheres," and "Religious" identified and filled as many niches as possible.

Mood libraries, much like their predecessors in the early cinema, were challenged to classify tracks by their immediate visceral impact rather than by artist or musical genre. Self-descriptive titles like "Hurly-Burly" or "Hazy Morning" could alert broadcasters about what to expect before cuing up to an image. The players as well, divorced from any virtuoso role, consisted of ad hoc session musicians who were given temporary names like "The Tunesmiths" if they were named at all.

Production music, like Muzak, is heard so commonly by so many that it deserves a place among the twentieth century's most authentic folk arts. Terry Pavone, while working with a branch of the DeWolfe library in New York City, described the music as "a subjective product": "The music is not a final product. It's a piece of a final product that is intentionally designed to be incomplete." There has been a long-running tradition in production music to scrap a song if it becomes too easily recognized or grows too popular, since this would distract listeners from the movie, play, or advertisement the music was supposed to serve invisibly.

Yet the "accidental hit" was promoted from time to time, when its popularity could not be avoided—especially if it were the signature line of a much-loved television program like the theme from *Dragnet*, which was once a music library tune. Still, associating the words *art* and *stock music* strikes the average production music arranger as odd or ludicrous. Many people in the business are either frustrated musicians who hate what they do or people loosely associated with broadcast media who want to make the right connections or just earn some fast money. Still, the music triumphs for the average listener, who can enjoy it despite the contempt or misguided neglect with which the arranger or distributor treats it.

No musician better demonstrated the possibilities of the library tune as an art form than Robert Farnon. The Canadian-born Farnon once played lead trumpet for Percy Faith and the CBC Orchestra before repatriating to England after World War II. He composed the scores for the 1951 film *Captain Horatio Hornblower* (with Gregory Peck), *Gentlemen Marry Brunettes,* and the last Hope–Crosby road movie, *Road to Hong Kong.* He also arranged songs for Muzak, Tony Bennett, Frank Sinatra, Vera Lynn, and Pia Zadora. André Previn called him "the greatest string arranger in the world."

Farnon's greatest and least widely recognized contributions were his so-called hack melodies, commissioned by England's Chappell mood music library to evoke the romantic outdoors. Whether conducting the Royal Philharmonic Orchestra or arranging incidental music for BBC radio traffic reports, Farnon could convey plots, characters, and feelings with just a few quick musical phrases. At least four orchestral "miniatures"—"How Beautiful Is Night," "A Star Is Born," "Jumping Bean," and "Portrait of a Flirt"—became hits after library exposure.

In the 1950s, before television employed its own studio arrangers, production libraries offered unlimited musical combinations at minimal cost and with no copyright snags. Chappell, for instance, had a song in its collection called "Puffin' Billy" (written by Edward White) that was used for Britain's *Children's Favourites* television show at the same time that CBS used it as the opening theme for *Captain Kangaroo*.

The KPM library was inaugurated in 1958 and eventually became a dominant force in production music. Specialists in evoking light and busy activity, they offered tunes like "Shopping Street," "Workaday World," "Trafficscape," and "Screw on the Loose." One indelible entry called "Holiday Playtime" (ideal for the "Jolly family outing") has not only appeared on countless 1950s school films about good citizenship but currently plays on *The Ren & Stimpy Show* and on Nick-At-Nite's *Better Living Through Television* segments.

Just as an Eskimo thriving in a snowy environment could come up with dozens of words for colors ranging from white to light gray, the average American and West European consumer would soon be serenaded with countless musical variations to connote the magnificent sensations born from exposure to the smells of plastic wrap, perfumes, clothing textures, and other stimulants indigenous to mall culture.

Today, production music personnel can act as informal psychiatrists, coddling executives who wish to promote the right image with music but are not quite sure what image they want or whether they are really comfortable with the one they propose. To assist them further, companies like DeWolfe offer a library of compact discs with such easily classified titles as "Just Whimsical," "Work Force," "Power Struggle," "Space Adventure," "Rise Time," "Topsy Turvey," and "Wallpaper Music." DeWolfe has one Mozartian piano and orchestra number called "Blue Porcelain" that has played behind commercials for both a fancy European car and a feminine hygiene spray.

To this day, people who recoil at background music in a restaurant or office are more tolerant when similar sounding melodies show up in the movies or on TV. When film composers like John Barry or Danny Elfman add lush orchestral scores, they also supply a bridge between the elevator and the home entertainment center. Now, the movie itself is just one component in a complex marketing scheme that also includes the advertisement, the info-mercial, and the music video. From there, the soundtrack gets reused for other commercials, and even other films, until it is stamped indelibly in our cinememories.

8 / The Moodiest Years on Record

Have you ever thought of the possible connection between day-dreaming and progress in the science of electronics? Far-fetched as it may seem, they are unquestionably associated. It is now possible, if you so desire, to indulge in your favorite fantasy via the wonders of high fidelity.

—Liner notes to Wayne King's *Dream Time*

The aftershocks of World War II brought changes in American life that, by the summer of 1946, had altered the nation's music habits. Soldiers came back to a G.I. Bill encouraging them to invest in homes of tomorrow, lured by kitchens full of glistening appliances and mood-lit living rooms. The music too had to conform to these new surroundings. Muzak® may have comforted people during the first crucial stages of urbanization, but mood music on record brought the panacea home with different and much stranger results. Uncongenial to the babbling brass and jackhammer jazz of the earlier Swing Era, the postwar home required softer, subtler, more enchanting, and even haunting textures.

❀   ❀   ❀

In 1944, Westinghouse had already taken out a *McCall's* magazine ad preparing us for "living electrically." Monsanto's 1957 "House of the Future" opened in Disneyland, exposing us to the fortress home's synthetic treasures. The ideal American dwelling went from a quaint clapboard bungalow with a white picket fence to a microcosmic World's Fair of separate rooms with distinct themes. Cascades of mood music albums, likewise, offered sonic sprays for dens, patios, rec rooms, backyard barbecues, cocktail parlors, and bedrooms.

In *The Lonely Crowd* (first published in 1950), sociologist David Reisman wrote about the changing American character of "other-directed" men and women who were turning away from traditional mores and looking to the media for guidance about the parameters of "gracious living." With Madison Avenue propaganda selling everything from Frigidaires to air-conditioned bomb shelters, and with motivational researchers triggering consumer desires for thermostatic and stereophonic bliss, mood records supplied an important symbol of emotional security, romance, exotic travel, dining pleasure, intellectual serenity, and countless indoor adventures. The album jackets alone depicted bright, rich and bigger-than-life tableaux lifted from romance novels, movies, television shows, magazine ads, and lifestyle prescriptions from pop psychologists.

Another contributor to mood music was the LP's unique format. The phonograph record alternately waxed and waned in popularity throughout the 1920s and 1930s, but it was always upstaged by the radio. In the old Victrola days, the maximum time a recording could run was about four minutes and fifty seconds. The switch to 33⅓ rpm made the twenty-minute side possible, so records could play in the background longer without constantly nagging to be turned over.

What's more, the record industry did not thrive in mutual exclusion from Muzak and other background music services. Mood music became such a spreadable commodity that such composers, arrangers, and conductors as Robert Farnon, Lawrence Welk, and Frank Chacksfield played for Muzak and production libraries, scored movie soundtracks, arranged backup music for leading vocalists, and still had time to enjoy recording artist celebrity.

Is mood music on record different from Muzak? Yes and no. In the late 1950s, at a *Melody Maker* interviewer's prompting, British mood maestro Norrie Paramor sought in vain to grasp mood music's elusive definition, ultimately finding no difference at all:

> It's very difficult to define. . . . I imagine it's meant to entertain without being obtrusive, to put you in an easy frame of mind. In other words, perhaps it is music to be heard, but not necessarily listened to. . . . Victor Silvester's Ballroom Orchestra played gently as a background to a cocktail party could be classified as mood music. Though when you turn the volume control up, it becomes music for dancing.

Mood music on record had one important distinction: it functioned as Muzak's id. Muzak was confined mostly to moderate tempo arrangements with few if any distractions. But mood music indulged in volatile mood swings forbidden in the workplace: happy to grim, frantic to narcoleptic, sexy to robotic. Records abounded with outrageous themes, dissonant styles, and risqué suggestions.

Still, mood music's essential ingredient was as unmeasurable to the recording industry as ether was to radio. The common properties of mood albums? Slower, more hypnotic time signatures; massed strings treated with echo-reverberation; background vocals that sounded more angelic (or in some cases, demonic) than human; and often well-conceived philosophies about music's utilitarian function.

Columbia Records released a *Quiet Music* series of instrumentals performed by the Columbia Salon Orchestra that were meant to calm the nerves and alleviate the strains of daily travail. In 1955, Columbia followed with a four-album series called *Music for Gracious Living* that included the arpeggios of Peter Barclay and His Orchestra, along with back cover recipes for buffets, bridge games or barbecues.

Capitol, an important mood music laboratory, had an early

1950s series simply called *Background Music*—four albums consisting of an eclectic mix of light swing, polka, showtunes, and semi-classical romance songs (all without vocals). *Light and Lively* had "Rhythmic, bubbling melodies with a soft, sparkling beat." *Songs We Remember* was "especially good if anyone is in a singing mood." *Bright and Bouncy*'s "happy music to accent lighter moments" included "Isn't This a Lovely Day" and "It Had to Be You." The fourth record was a Broadway revue of *Show Tunes* "done in tempo." All of these selections were intended to "never dominate, yet always be pleasant and listenable." According to the prescriptive liner notes: "Early in the evening, when the hostess is struggling to get the party off the ground, the music will fill those embarrassing lulls."

Mood music is perhaps the twentieth century's most authentic music, tailored exclusively for the electronic revolution. These recordings fully exploit the intended use of the hi-fi and stereo as domestic appliances with all of the environmental controls of thermostats, air-conditioners, and security systems.

Mood records have been ideal sonic showcases. Their acoustical forays into advancing sound technologies allowed record producers and engineers to accrue stardom along with the musicians. "Musical motion" or the "elaborate system of charting each and every instrument for proper stereo placement" came about at roughly the same time that the cinema attempted to expand visual and audio perception with Cinerama and other wide-screen novelties. According to freelance engineer Robert Oakes Jordan, RCA Records' Stereo-Action claimed to be "a conscious and deliberate effort to set music in motion by actually moving the sound of various instruments from one speaker to the other, and, at times, suspending it in the space between." Other recording advances were packaged with similarly evocative appellations: RCA's "Dynagroove," Somerset's "Dynacoustic," Liberty's "Visual Sound Stereo," Mercury's "Living Presence Series," London's "Phase Four Stereo," Columbia's "360-degree Sound," and Capitol's "Full Dimensional Stereo."

What follows is a review of several categories that I feel best summarize the plethora of records from mood music's golden era and the personalities behind them. To sustain their mood-specific designations, I have included biographies only when appropriate to the music. I will also take moments to describe the music that captured America's heart and soul with a sensual language more in keeping with fabric catalogs than music textbooks. So come with me into a walk-in dream showroom where all you ever wanted, hoped to be, or perhaps dreaded being unfolds like a parallel world. These mood records are the closest America has ever come to creating a genuine, home-grown surrealism. A mood music appreciation may propel Surrealism's next phase. Now that our fantasy media have colonized and drained the mind's dark regions to the point where they've become horror novel and splatter-movie pap, these records (and their attendant artwork) can enchant us with exaggerated dreamscapes of order and happiness.

Mermaids After Midnight

Red velvet sheets, gossamer drapes, scented rooms, and martinis pouring from a bottomless shaker: just the foreplay to this soundscape of misty evenings, postcard-perfect sunsets, and aquatic paramours . . .

Featuring: *The Orchestras of Frank Chacksfield, Jackie Gleason, Nelson Riddle, and Paul Weston.*

At their San Simeon castle in the late 1940s, William Randolph Hearst and his darling Marion Davies spent their evenings having dinner in the refectory before retiring for a movie in their private theater. Before each picture started, the theater projectionist had to play in its entirety a remarkable new album called *Music for Dreaming.* This collection of elegantly conducted sentimental favorites was the perfect anodyne to get the Hearsts "in the mood" as they lounged among their menagerie of Egyptian statues and museum bric-a-brac. The man who made the album, Paul Weston, only found out about this historical tidbit in 1986 from Roland Dragon (brother of classical conductor Carmen Dragon), who had served as Hearst's private secretary. The news strengthened Weston's self-image as mood music's progenitor.

Weston was born Paul Wetstein on March 12, 1912, in Springfield, Massachusetts. A onetime economics major at Dartmouth, he started playing with college bands to a beat that was anything but relaxing. This was certainly incongruous with his image: a modest-sized, bespectacled man who projected the reserve of a university professor.

Weston garnered a reputation in show business by arranging for Rudy Vallee, Phil Harris, and Tommy Dorsey, with whom he had worked from 1935 to 1940. Backing singers such as Bing Crosby, Dinah Shore, and soon-to-be wife Jo Stafford, Weston always had a predilection for music that jarred the senses. When he became A&R director in 1944 for the fledgling Capitol Records, his musical life was still immersed in free-form jagged tempos, screeching brass, and the likes of Buddy Rich and Gene Krupa tom-tomming at breakneck speed. Weston recalls:

> It was like a social club more than a record company. Johnny Mercer got upset when he found out he had to have regular releases. With the Tommy Dorsey band, we hardly ever did a ballad in slow tempo. It was always considered danceable. Then, as Frank Sinatra and Doris Day became more famous than the bands, the tunes got slower and slower. Jitterbugging went out, and my albums stepped into the gap.

Detecting the mood change, Weston recorded *Music for Dreaming* in 1945. This decidedly subdued first album shocked most fans with its gentle Swing with slackened tempo, moderate volume, and strings mixed with piano to muffle the brass. The songs, too, were balmier: "I'm in the Mood for Love," "My Blue Heaven," and "I Only Have Eyes for You" executed in a style Weston describes as "underplayed" and "underarranged." It worked. *Music for Dreaming*'s record sales boasted a then-astronomical 175,000 copies.

Weston wanted assurance that the public's taste for "creamy-on-the-melody" was not transitory. While at Capitol, he gauged the demand by sending a representative to ten major U.S. cities for interviews with record company salesmen and record-shop proprietors. He also corresponded with at least 200 record distributors. The findings were consistent; and so were his subsequent album titles: *Music for Memories, Music for Romancing, Music for the Fireside,* and *Music for Reflection.*

By 1950, *Coronet* magazine hailed his "smooth, shimmering arrangements" and dubbed him "Master of Mood Music"—a sobriquet with which he had trouble coming to terms. "I was the first person the term mood music was applied to," Weston reflects, "but afterward, a lot of other people snuck under the tent."

That same year Weston left Capitol for Columbia. Seeing mood music branching out into various styles (not all of which he liked), he continued with *Dream Music by Paul Weston, Music for a Rainy Night,* and *Melodies for a Sentimental Mood.* While at Columbia, he decided to write several arrangements to pay tribute to the jazz musicians he had worked with in his radio days. The results were *Mood for Twelve* and *Solo Mood*—two albums that maintained a virtuoso veneer against background music that nonetheless crept into the foreground.

Other former bandmen turned sandmen included Wayne King, whose album *Dream Time* used his smooth sax and a lushly padded orchestra to showcase "most requested" movie themes such as "Fascination," "An Affair to Remember," and "Tammy," along with such standards as "Stardust," "Till," and Leroy Anderson's "Forgotten Dreams." Known as "The Waltz King," King had already whispered sweet melodies into many a feminine ear on his *Lady Esther Serenade* radio show in the 1930s, sponsored by Lady Esther Cosmetics for older women less prone to shimmy.

Weston admits that his mood albums walked a narrow line between respectable jazz and wallpaper music. That is why he looks back on the mood genre as any Frankenstein would regard the monster that made him rich:

> *I had instrumental solos and countermelodies; the framework of a dance band but with added strings. Robert Farnon would operate in the classic form of or-*

chestra, not jazzy at all. Percy Faith was the same, and Kostelanetz more so. I believe this reliance on strings without the jazz feel that I brought even to my ballads was the reason the term "elevator music" came to symbolize most of the later mood music attempts.

By 1959, Weston and Stafford returned to Capitol. As the *Music for* series was being re-pressed into stereo, Jackie Gleason's Orchestra had already taken over the label's mood music helm with more histrionic packaging.

A man of girth, mirth, melancholy, and alleged tippler tendencies, Jackie Gleason added wider meaning to the term *"lush* moods." As the liner notes to his *Night Winds* album attest: "This man who has given the nation some of its warmest humor has also given it favorite musical backgrounds for its gentlest dreaming."

His involvement in the *Jackie Gleason presents . . .* series remains a matter of controversy. Some say the connection was nominal only or minimal at best. Gordon Jenkins, who composed such classy mood suites as *Seven Dreams* and *Manhattan Tower,* described Gleason as the studio's shadow figure who "sits in the control room puffing at a fat cigar while his arrangers do the conducting."

Others maintain that Gleason was *too* involved. With no formal musical training, his efforts to convey what he called his "plain vanilla music" were constant exercises of frustration. William A. Henry III's *The Great One: The Life and Legend of Jackie Gleason* explains how his instructions to the orchestra flouted academic terms like "syncopation" and "arpeggio" in favor of such analogies as "the sound of pissing off a high bridge into a teacup." To evoke that sensuous, floating effect, Gleason conjured this scenario: "It's five a.m. and you see her body outlined through her dress by the streetlight and you get that 'Mmmmmm, I want to come' feeling."

Gleason's records catered blatantly to the common man's lusts. The album jackets depicted silk-and-lace-dishabilléed vixens reclining on sofas; hopeful sirens leering with come-hither lips; jeweled femmes fatale straddling bar stools; and nordic nymphs lurking in dark forests. This was mood music for men who may not have been up on the latest Kinsey findings but appreciated a good trollop on the pages of *Cavalier*. As William A. Henry III notes: "If Gable on the wide screen needed background music to help him pitch and woo at the critical moment, then surely the poor slob in Brooklyn did too."

Gleason reportedly had to raise much of the investment to produce the records before Capitol assented. His first album *Music for Lovers Only* sold a then-surprising 500,000 copies. Between 1952 and 1955, *Jackie Gleason presents* . . . enticed Americans to spend at least $2 million.

Music, Martinis and Memories provided musical accompaniment to countless cocktail parties, while *Lover's Portfolio* ("music for listenin', sippin', dancin' and lovin'") included a bartender's recipe manual. This, like most entries in the series, suggested an orchestra gone tipsy, with a soused saxophone.

One of Gleason's main trumpeters was Bobby Hackett, a former player with Glenn Miller, who was revered in jazz circles for his Dixieland flair but never scoffed at a chance to (at the right price) take a break from improvisation dementia and indulge in a more subdued formula. He reportedly met Gleason while working with Miller on the 1942 movie *Orchestra Wives,* at which point Gleason promised that he would one day record Hackett in a string-filled room.

Twenty-four subdued trumpets helped flesh out *Opiate d'Amour*'s airy selections, six of which (including "Melancholy Serenade," "Pink Lace," and "Pale Blues") Gleason composed himself. The star instrument was Romeo Penque's *oboe d'amour*. Here, as in other albums such as *The Gentle Touch* and *Lazy Lovely Love*, there is a "band within a band"—a "sometimes lazy, sometimes lively" jazz ensemble played against the regular strings.

Lonesome Echo (with a cover designed by Salvador Dali) stands out for its foray into the unconscious. Mandolins, cellos, marimbas, and guitar are deliberately paced, and each track is barely distinguishable from the others except for varied melodies weaving in and out. This is a musical Rorschach blot inviting many moods yet leaning toward "nostalgic" and "sad"—an atmosphere only to be expected from the "comedian" who composed "Melancholy Serenade" as a signature tune.

The listening instructions to *Lonesome Echo* appear to be advice from a sound psychoanalyst: "This is the music that says relax . . . close your eyes . . . remember. . . . " But the spooky renditions of "I'm Always Chasing Rainbows," "Dancing on the Ceiling," "I Wished on the Moon," and "How Deep Is the Ocean?" threaten to drag us into the mind's less hospitable regions. The back cover photo of Gleason and Salvador Dali shaking hands hints at a deeper motive. Describing his cover art, Dali puts the Freudian clutch in overdrive:

> [The] first effect is that of anguish, of space, and of solitude. Secondly, the fragility of the wings of a butterfly, projecting long shadows of late afternoon, reverberates in the landscape like an echo. The feminine element, distant and isolated, forms a perfect triangle with the musical instrument and its other echo, the shell.

For *That Moment,* Gleason contributed his own oil painting called *The Kiss*—an angular, extremely abstract answer to Edvard Munch's much more explicit depiction of lovers smooching into one another's abyss. Gleason claimed to have a deliberate notion of this album's mood down to the painting's color scheme: "I chose the colors for their psychological value. Pastels are *simpatico* with music. The pink of the girl's face is the flush of love, and the blue of the boy's face is the azure of emotion."

Like *Lonesome Echo,* most of the *Jackie Gleason presents . . .* oeuvre implies the musical equivalent to Dali's desert mirages. This is music with a distorted "persistence of memory," where time distends, clocks melt, and landscapes assume the contours of love goddesses one moment, decaying carcasses the next.

A bit more sobering but no less romantic, Frank Chacksfield offered the British counterpart to Gleason's "gentle touch." Among the brightest stars in the "music-for-leisure technique," Chacksfield had a predilection for songs about tactile reverie. Consider some of his original composition titles: "Seamist," "Web of

Dreams," "My Blue Dream," "It's Just a Daydream," "On the Smooth Side," "Clouds," "Silk and Gold," and "Rather Shy."

One of his early albums, *Velvet*, explains that "Softness in music is not only a matter of volume . . . it means that there must be no jarring notes, that the playing must be smooth, controlled and sophisticated." But Chacksfield's music was also presented in a deeper sociological context:

> The musically aware hostess no longer allows the but-
> ler, or her husband, to sling records on to the turntable
> in a haphazard way. She no longer risks the dangers
> of the soup being spilled by Haydn's "Surprise" Sym-
> phony, of Mrs. Alias-Jones choking over the fish be-
> cause an ill-timed bit of jazz trumpet has frightened
> her. She now supplies a ready-made background of el-
> egant and suitable music to smooth the evening into one
> long feast of pleasure and unshattered nerves.

Born in Battle, Sussex, England, Chacksfield courted his muse in boyhood as deputy organist for the local parish church. His parents pressed him not to pursue music, but Chacksfield turned away from a dreary solicitor's day job to moonlight at the piano.

Once war started in 1940, he enlisted in the Army, took con-valescent time after a service-related illness, and soon sang at pi-ano for a BBC broadcast from its Glasgow studios. His major break came when he became staff arranger for the War Office's "Stars in Battledress" show. His taste for layered arrangements did not surface until he signed onto Decca and, in 1953, released his first gold record, "Limelight," the title song from the Charlie Chaplin film released the same year. In a time when few British nonvocal recordings became hits across the Atlantic, Chacksfield won the #2 spot on the U.S. charts with the first popularization of Robert Maxwell's "Ebb Tide." It prompted *New Musical Ex-press* to recognize him with its "Record of the Year" award, and a 1953 nationwide jukebox operators poll voted his orchestra the most promising newcomer.

While Chacksfield's romance reveled in lakeside melodies whose inspiration might have come from tasteful postcards, and

Gleason's land-based fantasies took frequent dips in a sea of vermouth, Nelson Riddle's mood music made full-scale ocean probes on two of his best albums, *Sea of Dreams* and *Love Tide*.

By the 1950s and early 1960s, images of the sea dominated popular culture. Movies like *The Creature from the Black Lagoon*, Bobby Darin's hit "Beyond the Sea," and the craze for scuba gear invested oceanic life with an allure that Riddle, in turn, treated as a sensual descent.

Riddle's place in the easy-listening pantheon is somewhat complicated to delineate. A prolific contributor to film and television scores, he had dabbled in many styles. As a trombonist for Tommy Dorsey's band and as an arranger for NBC radio, he had developed an affection for playful jazz and skip-happy rhythms set to flute and piccolo. This became obvious with his 1962 theme song for the television show *Route 66*, which shot up to #3 in *Billboard* and was one of the first television themes to be released commercially. He is most widely remembered for his musical director days on *The Smothers Brothers Comedy Hour*, as well as for his presence at the Kennedy and Reagan inaugurations.

Riddle achieved fame as a background arranger for Frank Sinatra in the 1950s, making melodies that one *New York Times* journalist described as hovering "between a swinging celebration of bachelorhood and more introspective ballads." This style inspired Linda Ronstadt decades later to abandon MOR rock for pillow-soft Riddle collaborations on her Grammy-winning LP *What's New?*, as well as on *Lush Life* and *For Sentimental Reasons*.

Riddle's *Sea of Dreams* offers songs of time-travel into amniotic bliss. The cover depicts a heavily cosmeticized sea nymph, seductive and sinister, inviting updated visions of the ancient association between the ocean and feminine mystery. The songs too are about dripping enigmas: "My Isle of Golden Dreams," "Tangi Tahiti," and "Easter Isle." *Love Tide*, the sequel, continues with a full orchestra complemented by harp, vibes, guitar, and celeste—all in the service of a standard easy-listening formula of melody and countermelody. Obscured by the thumping of an acoustic bass paired with harps, a rustle of jazz lies submerged somewhere in the deeper currents, barely surfacing in Riddle's version of "Caravan."

Riddle's seascapes were also a reflection of his home, situated on the Southern California coast overlooking the Pacific, where he has been photographed seated on a rock, gazing wistfully westward, sketchbook in hand. But unlike the turbulent orchestrals on Les Baxter's album *Midnight on the Cliffs* (where the suggested clangor of waves summons cliff-dwellers to their doom), Riddle's music is more focused on the calm before the storm. This is music in suspension, where drowning is only a sensual slumber. No other arranger of his time (other than Baxter) gave "the deep" such fervent attention; and his sea reveries have since been equaled only by later generations of new-agers obsessed with "space."

Cathedralized Classics

What better way to discover or rediscover the classics? A snippet of sonata here, a morsel of aria there, mixed with pop melodies, then blended with echo-reverberation to re-create the vaulted acoustic grandeur of cathedrals, concert halls, and shopping malls . . .
Featuring: *Andre Kostelanetz, the Living Strings, Annunzio Paolo Mantovani, and George Melachrino.*

In his book *The Influence of Music on History and Morals,* British musical historian Cyril Scott predicted "a new species of violin" and a sound where "floods of melody will be poured forth from the higher planes, to be translated into earthly sound by composers sensitive enough to apprehend them."° This was in the 1930s, after radio had already put live orchestras in limbo but before the postwar recording studio fulfilled Scott's prophecy by merging violin with microphone to create a new instrument.

Plucked, layered, processed, and pampered, lush string arrange-

°Cyril Scott, as cited in Joscelyn Goodwin, ed., *Music Mysticism and Magic* (New York and London: Arkana, 1987), pp. 286–87.

ments seemed to be everywhere by the 1950s. Though many people today might take it for granted or even ridicule it, the use of massed strings for popular melodies (instead of symphonies) was a stylistic and audio breakthrough when it first occurred.

Of all such string arrangements, none were more rich and mellifluous than those of Annunzio Paolo Mantovani. Many adjectives have described or lampooned Mantovani's style: "cascading strings," "honeyed, caressing tones," "pseudo-symphonic," "the gush of lush," and the "Niagara Falls of fiddles."

Many in the emerging light music field took advantage of the new studio technology to create sound tapestries with innumerable strings, but Mantovani championed the art. The sustained hum of Mantovani's reverberated violins produced a sonic vaporizer foreshadowing the synthesizer harmonics of space music.

Born in Venice, Mantovani followed his dad, Benedetto Paolo, who was a concertmaster (first chair, first violin) for Toscanini and a professor at music conservatories in Venice and Milan. While Annunzio was still a child, the family moved to England. Annunzio got his first job performing in a Birmingham restaurant when he was fifteen; by the time he became a professional, he had taken his mother's maiden name, Mantovani, as his surname.

Mantovani claims that his musical style was indelibly influenced in the mid-1920s by violinist Fritz Kreisler. He explained to *High Fidelity* magazine in 1957 that, after hearing Kreisler's encore performance of "The Girl with the Flaxen Hair" at Albert Hall, he suddenly understood "how some music had been neglected. How the lighter side of music has always been thrown about and never received its proper dignity."

Combining his classical violin with Kreisler's stylistic populism, Mantovani adapted many tunes for performance in hotels and eventually worked for the BBC in 1927. He toured the British Isles with his Tipica Orchestra before conducting for London's Monseigneur Restaurant in Piccadilly from 1935 to 1939.

The early Mantovani made a few instrumental recordings (including a version of "Red Sails in the Sunset") before serving as Noël Coward's musical director in the 1940s. But his truly "cascading" sound did not emerge until 1951, when London Records (the American arm of Decca) requested an album of waltzes from him. Unwilling to settle for the expected, Mantovani sought a gimmicky yet innovative formula that would permit him to sell a lot of records without tiring his fans.

"I wondered what I could do to make an impression in America," he once recalled. He employed a forty-piece orchestra (with twenty-eight string players), ran them through Decca's enhanced studio system, and brought the medieval use of church acoustics into the twentieth century.

Mantovani himself never shied away from the religious analogy: "Strings were not being used as they are now . . . I wanted to get a classic string sound with plenty of violas and cellos. I wanted to use close harmonies. I wanted an effect of an overlapping of sound, as though we were playing in a cathedral."°

His first attempt at cathedralized classics was a treatment of Ruggiero Leoncavallo's "On with the Motley," a *Pagliacci* excerpt that composer Ronald Binge had arranged with "a scoring effect that would sustain the melody line with reiterated waves of sound." After Mantovani applied more embellishments, London Records was impressed enough to order twelve more tracks.

One of those waltzes, called "Charmaine," was an American hit by 1951. We can thank Bill Randle, an enthusiastic Cleveland disk jockey who played it constantly over the airwaves to the rhythm of switchboards flashing with calls of support from equally zealous listeners. Randle became so enamored with the song that he used the first sixteen bars as a teaser to open his show. Finally he corralled the necessary support to get it released as an American single.

It was natural for Mantovani to derive his initial hit from a movie theme. From its first high-frequency flutter, "Charmaine" connotes Christian heaven remade into a Hollywood soundstage. Listening to it with eyes closed, one can imagine a soft-focus descent of sequined angels wielding magic wands over dancers who float from the ballroom floor in a slow-motion version of waltz time turned dream

°George T. Simon (& Friends), *The Best of the Music Makers* (Garden City, N.Y.: Doubleday, 1979), p. 381.

time. Pastoral woodwinds offer a bit of earthly assurance, but the incessant violins lift us back into the melody unmoored.

"Charmaine" was just one of the tracks on Mantovani's *Waltz Encores* album, a collection that included similar soft-focus treatments of "Greensleeves," "Dream, Dream, Dream," and "The 'Moulin Rouge' Theme," another hit that secured the U.S. #8 spot in 1953. All in all, Mantovani amassed "a million-dollar musical empire" by playing what many nonaficionados dismiss as "dentist's office music."

Mantovani was the first musician to sell 1 million stereo records in the United States. Between 1953 and 1972, fifty-one Mantovani albums (a deluge of Strauss waltzes, movie themes, and romantic standards) reached Top 50 lists for sales. *Continental Encores* took us on a European pleasure passage "Under Paris Skies" before spending an "April in Portugal" and bidding "Arrivederci Roma." Some of the most romantic moments in the cinema were recaptured in *Film Encores,* including "Unchained Melody," "Three Coins in the Fountain," and (one of Mantovani's signature tunes that he used to open his live concerts) "Love Is a Many Splendoured Thing." With exceptions like his 1964 album *Kismet* (which featured vocals by Robert Merrill), most all of Mantovani's work was instrumental and was considered by many observers to be a musical "halfway house between jazz and the classics."

Arthur Lilley, who was Mantovani's studio engineer from the early days, deserves a great deal of the credit for Mantovani's success. If Decca's studios had to lay down carpet to contain the ear-splitting frequencies of a rock-and-roll session, Lilley would be the first to tear it out again when Mantovani was getting ready to record, in order to heighten the echo effect. Lilley would assign at least nine microphones to the strings alone to get a level of echo equaled only perhaps by Phil Spector's "wall-of-sound." Mantovani also benefited from Decca's "FFRR" (Full Frequency Range Recording), which was developed during wartime research. Part of that research is traceable to Berlin's Jesus Christus-Kirche cathedral, whose acoustics were used extensively by Deutsche Grammophon. When the United States established RIAS (Radio in the American Sector) during the German reconstruction, one of its engineers discovered the church and helped bring its "sacred sound" into the world of modern recording.

Adding to the Mantovani mystique, *Billboard* magazine featured a multiple-page info-advertisement in 1967 entitled "Mantovani: A Mirror of His Time." It provided correspondences between crucial historical dates and the subject matter of many Mantovani releases.

In 1947, for instance, Mantovani had released "Beyond the Sea" as a single just as America began its Marshall Plan to rebuild postwar Europe. Mantovani helped christen the Cold War with his 1948 release of the "Warsaw Concerto" from his first 78-rpm album *Music for the Films.* When Edmund P. Hillary scaled Mt. Everest in 1953, *Mantovani Plays Tangos* included "Blue Sky." The famous Soviet Sputnik satellite, launched in 1957, coincided with *Mantovani Film Encores Vol. 1* and its featured song "Over the Rainbow." "Unchained Melody," on the same album, fit in perfectly with Strom Thurmond's record-breaking filibuster on the Senate floor that same year.

Mantovani synchronicity got scarier in 1959 after Nikita Khrushchev was turned out of Disneyland and *Mantovani Film Encores Vol. 2* included "When You Wish upon a Star." Three years later, he may have paid tribute to freshly elected President Kennedy with the song "Mr. Wonderful" on *Great Theme Music,* but his version of "Turkey in the Straw" seemed a jaundiced joke on the American U2 reconnaissance plane shot down by Soviets. Mantovani helped inaugurate the Space Age in 1961 with "Come Back to Sorrento" on his *Italia Mia* album in honor of Alan Shepard's record Mercury launch 116.5 miles above the earth. He paid equal tribute to John Glenn's first American orbit with the albums *Stop the World I Want to Get Off/Oliver,* and *Moon River and Other Great Film Themes.* Then, in 1965, when a Soviet cosmonaut stepped out of his orbiting space craft, the album *The Mantovani Sound* included "Who Can I Turn To?"

Despite its reputation for excessive sentimentality or (less charitably) "schmaltz," the Mantovani sound is emotionally ambivalent—warm one moment, distant the next. The reverberating stereophonic spectrum seems to come from an unknown source yet

floods the listener's geography at all points. A good example of what
Morton Gould called the "hangover effect" was Mantovani's take
on "Ebb Tide," which begins with a slow, slightly threatening low-
register buildup of overlapping violins approximating an aquatic
ebb and flow; then suddenly we are once again thrown a melodic
lifeline. Although Mantovani allowed the strings to dominate the
melody in most of his songs, he retained subdued interludes of
mandolin, acoustic guitar and accordion (an instrument *High
Fidelity* magazine claimed he loathed).

"It is all very well for critics to dismiss my music airy-fairily as,
say, sugary," he once commented to *Billboard* in 1967. "But far
more effort and thought and know-how go into it than any critic
would dream."

Once described as "The man who could make a hymn out of a
rock number," Mantovani was not impressed by the Presley generation. He identified his audience in *High Fidelity* as "that fan-
tastically large group of people who like music but can't appreciate
the masterworks—and who can't abide anything like rock n' roll."
He later clarified his position as follows: "Perhaps 25 percent of
the people like the classics, and about 25 percent like the Beatles . . . I aim to please the 50 percent in the middle." It is a maxim
he lived by until March of 1980, when he died at age 74 in a
Tunbridge Wells nursing home.

With Italian genes and a British passport, Mantovani exhibited
the personality extremes of both cultures. Journalist Murray Schumach distilled his character as "a mixture of English restraint and
Italian sentiment. His clipped speech and well-tailored dark suit
mirrored England. . . . But his sudden, intense gestures, his im-
pulsive humming, his bowing of imaginary violins reflected the
Latin heritage evident in his complexion, eyes, and hair."

Arthur Jackson, a one-time head of Chappell's production music
library, had rubbed elbows with the biggest names in light orchestral music. He recalls Mantovani as "A friendly man to talk
to, but with delusions of grandeur. Even after 35 years I can recall
every word of a conversation I had with him. 'You've given me
some nice reviews, Arthur, but you . . . haven't got through to your
readers that I'm better than everybody else.' "

Though he worked best as a studio craftsman, Mantovani gave lots of successful live performances. He had a light-hearted and humorous stage presence, a "disarming nonchalance," making jokes and funny baton gyrations in a bid to dissuade audiences from taking him and his art too seriously. Robert Sherman in the *New York Times* paid him a most fitting compliment when reviewing a Carnegie Hall performance in 1966: "as the sumptuous sounds filled the auditorium, you could almost close your eyes and imagine yourself back home listening to the hi-fi."

Despite being light music's patron nation, Britain did not catch the Mantovani fever as quickly as did the United States. Russian émigré Andre Kostelanetz went further than Monty by giving "pop classics" a distinctly American character. His death in 1980 inspired President Jimmy Carter to give a eulogy reaffirming Kosty's view of America as "a great music hall with the roof lifted off."

Hailed by *High Fidelity* magazine as "the prophet of classics for the masses," Kostelanetz believed that the proper orchestra should consist of at least 50 percent strings. He also had the savvy to recognize music as an assembly-line commodity and praised the phonograph record for exposing average Americans to more music than the most professional composers could have heard a century ago.

While Walter Benjamin's famous essay "The Work of Art in the Age of Mechanical Reproduction" lamented that the mass-produced object "substitutes a plurality of copies for a unique experience," Kostelanetz had an enthusiasm for simulacra equaled only by Andy Warhol:

> *I don't know if one can compare this amazing discovery of music by millions of people over the past quarter century to the invention of the printing press, but perhaps a better analogy would be the also recent development of the color off-set process that enables millions to see, enjoy and own fine reproductions of paintings by Renoir and Degas.* °

°"Kostelanetz Constructs Bridges for Audiences," *Down Beat*, 12 January 1955, p. 10.

Like many other easy-listening arrangers, Kostelanetz appreciated the importance of the sound engineer. In 1980, *Village Voice* critic Leighton Kerner cited him and famed Boston Pops conductor Arthur Fiedler as "marvelous combinations of market appraiser and orchestral technician." Recalling his impressions of watching Kosty in concert, Kerner also says: "The main matter of his radio programs were show tunes dressed up for symphony orchestra and acoustically sequined, satined, and laced by special mikes and sound reflecting panels."

Kostelanetz proved his technical wizardry when the United States entered World War II. While volunteering to conduct serviceman ensembles in war theaters from Germany to Burma, he had introduced a mechanical gadget that let musicians know whether they were in proper pitch without having to listen to themselves. The Massachusetts Institute of Technology adapted his machine to their sonar system for locating submarines. The British Admiralty later praised Kosty for his contribution to winning the Battle of the Atlantic.

Besides being the guest conductor for the New York Philharmonic longer than anyone else, Kostelanetz did backup arrangements for Perry Como, Beverly Sills, and Lily Pons (whom he later married). His success in selling at least 52 million records kept him living well in a New York penthouse apartment, surrounded by precious European and Oriental objets d'art. Astronauts reportedly listened to his music on moon journeys.

Even for marketing purposes alone, however, mood records had to be much more than just "high-class pop." The blurred boundary between the classics and pop may have been a welcome change in some quarters, but many opponents of light music scoffed at the trend. Average consumers with no preestablished opinion on the matter were, in turn, cajoled with novel twists on the theme.

Years ago, if you told someone you were in a Melachrino mood, they would have been puzzled *precisely* because they knew what and whom you were talking about. George Melachrino's *Moods in Music* series on RCA supplied an audiologue of varying tempers and situations: studying, romancing, dining, working, courage and inspiration, or just daydreaming.

George Miltiades Melachrino was born in 1909 in London. This perennially happy man made "Music by Melachrino" famous all over Britain. One of Great Britain's most popular orchestras, the Melachrino Strings became a household favorite in both the United Kingdom and America.

Melachrino was the British third of the World War II Allied Expeditionary Forces triumvirate that included Robert Farnon representing Canada and Glenn Miller representing the United States. This perhaps explains his penchant for lively marches and steady up-tempo beats, which lingered throughout his career in compositions for film, radio, television, and the stage.

In the spirit of other mood music pros, Melachrino took much of his inspiration from movies and their power to reinforce image and atmosphere. He exhibited his cinema music talents with the score for the British film *House of Darkness* in which he abridged "First Rhapsody" (a tune he used to open and close his AEF broadcasts) from seven and one-half to four minutes for use as a theme song.

The *Moods in Music* series of albums, likewise, had an unmistakably cinematic character. Just as they suggested that daily life could have a soundtrack, their album covers also included Hollywood-inspired scenes and poses connoting ideal worlds where clothes fit just right, fixtures are color-coordinated, the food and fruit are waxed to perfection, and the people are beautiful enough to fit into a museum diorama on affluent life in the 1950s.

The liner notes to *Music for Dining* promised to "add that little bit of extra seasoning that turns an ordinary supper into an adventure." The repast begins with a martini, a cocktail glass of vermouth, or some other aperitif to accompany "Diane." Next the pâté de foie gras is served up with truffles and the "lush treatment" of "Too Young." To keep matters in their proper seasonal and climatic perspective, a chilled plate such as lobster mayonnaise or vichyssoise is recommended for "September Song." The entrée, always warm and full of stuffed relics from the upper end of the food chain, starts out with "Clopin Clopant" for the side dish; then, by the time the brandied duck arrives, listeners are eager to let the "deep tones of a nine-foot grand announce the lovely strains of the 'Warsaw Concerto' and overcome the discreet tinkle of silver and crystal (and perhaps a slight loosening of the belt) as the waiter presents the pastry tray."

Melachrino continued with several other records for specified activities: *Music for Reading, Music for Relaxation,* and *Music for Daydreaming.* There was hardly a lifestyle that Melachrino did not address. *Music to Help You Sleep* includes the soporific harp strings of "Soft Lights and Sweet Music," "Beautiful Dreamer," and "Goodnight Sweetheart," with quotes from Proust, Shakespeare, Nietzsche, and Ovid on the art of dozing.

"Now that modern science has come out in favor of it, everyone agrees on the good sense of listening to music while you are otherwise occupied." So claimed the liner notes for *Music to Work or Study By.* This particular album offers cover notes that address many key points of background music philosophy: "The privacy of the listener's mind is never invaded, so that it may range freely over the most involved manual or intellectual problems without disturbance despite—or perhaps because of—the song that is on the lips."

Songs like "Heigh-Ho," "Whistle While You Work," "Scrub, Brother, Scrub," and "Waltz in Water Colours" not only motivate us to move but suggest that we do so as cartoon characters. The lead-in song, "Can't Help Singing," is a theme for worker compulsion in up-tempo pizzicato, with brass and orchestra. These are slightly speeded-up waltzes, premised on the idea that the energy and inspiration that go into dancing could be diverted into work, shopping, or sports events. (Muzak, too, often labeled its programs in the 1950s "Dancing," even though they were never piped into a ballroom or sock hop.)

At the production end, the *Moods in Music* series had William Hill Bowen as Melachrino's primary arranger, along with Robert Sharples and Robert Armstrong. But the true *Moods in Music* mastermind was Ethel Gabriel, among the first female record producers. Gabriel was inexhaustible in her efforts to provide optimum easy-listening with the finest technology and no skimping on the orchestra.

Growing up in suburban Philadelphia, she was one of few girls with ambitions to play the trombone; by the age of thirteen, she was already leading a dance band. Her first significant career move was to pose as a living advertisement while conducting a pseudo orchestra in a window display at a music store in Chester, Pennsylvania, called Caruso's. Gabriel claims: "When I did Melachrino, he had a full bottom-string section, a fat and wonderful warm sound. I used Bob Armstrong, who could make a fat chord out of five instruments, a bass tone with high piccolo, spreading all the frequencies of bottom, mid-range, and high."

But these technical considerations were just part of the optimum mood equation. Gabriel was equally meticulous about nurturing the listener's frame of mind:

> In between each band, there is a spiral on the record which takes the stylus from track to track. I would worry about someone going off one mood and into another. If the standard spiral lasted three seconds, I would make it five seconds. I felt that it takes time to breathe, exhale, and get into the next mood. I didn't jerk you from one mood to the other. The sequence was very important. I had a lot of little tricks like fade endings. I would make the studio technology fit into the concept of the album. From the beginning to end, it had a flow.

Gabriel carried the *Moods in Music* idea over to the *Living Series* on RCA's economy Camden label. Anyone looking through the easy-listening section of a rare records shop will be staggered by the profusion of Living Strings, Living Voices, Living Guitars, Living Marimbas, and Living Brass selections. Using many of Melachrino's BBC musicians, the Living Strings set out to prove once again that "the strings of music are the most effective key to the strings of her heart."

The early Camden sessions used such outfits as the Oslo Symphony, with mostly classical adaptations. But Gabriel sensed that the style was not working, so she leaned more toward pop. She remembers: "During the fifties, RCA had commissioned a study to help determine the most preferred concert act. The questionnaire results revealed that the first choice was the Living Strings and the second was Elvis Presley."

LPs by the Living Strings were among the first records to play on airplanes—primarily on American Airlines flights. They were also marketed as sales premiums and giveaways at places like gas stations. Later, when most of the music syndicators for easy-listening radio used them, the Living Strings' version of "If I Were a Rich Man" became one of FM's most loved instrumentals.

Many Living Strings members were from the BBC and London Symphony Orchestras. Most of the early Living Strings titles were recorded in England and packaged with classy aluminum foil covers. The music was processed by what Gabriel describes as a "room sound" effect, obtained through natural ambiance. They, like many other recording artists at the time, used a church on New York's 19th Street as their recording studio. Gabriel recalls:

> Echo was important back then. Before we got the German echo chambers in the early 'sixties, we found that the best echo was through the men's room on RCA's studios on 24th Street. When Toscanini recorded at places like Manhattan Center, they would channel his music through it and pipe the sound into the studio.

The Living Strings Plus Two Pianos attempted to add a Latin flavor, conducted by Geraldo, a British leader in dance bands whose Gaucho Tango Orchestra played the Savoy Hotel in the 1930s. Born Gerald Bright, he took on the Spanish nickname, wore pseudo-Latino costumes and proceeded to make tunes whose style was a hybrid of mariachi and Guy Lombardo. The Living Brass (starting just before the emergence of Herb Alpert's Tijuana Brass and the Baja Marimba Band) attempted to make what would be, in Gabriel's words, "a version of how mariachi would sound through American ears."

Gabriel sees the Living Series as "geared for a person who loves music, but at the very moment you get too classy with them, it's over their head. Between the Living Strings and Melachrino, I controlled at least 95 percent of easy-listening music on the radio."

Broadening her horizons, Gabriel produced an album called *Music to Stop Smoking By,* which predated new-age sonic therapy. It was engineered for what Gabriel and many others in the trade would designate as "the comfort zone." To avoid being cast as an audio manipulator, Gabriel is modest about these efforts:

> *I was not a psychiatrist, just a music major. I was better as an A&R person. But I know we need the support of a stabilizing mood to calm us all down. Nowadays we know too much, and the average person doesn't have guarded information. The news is reporting everything in a high pitch. We cannot cope with the stresses and strains switching with every moment. We grew more technologically than we did emotionally, so the strings are going to be the emotional crutch. Music is a brain- wash; some have learned this. The mind control is where pressure is put on, where it is forced. The music's going to come back that holds you and caresses you.*

Sizzle & Suds

Music that tingles, then massages, with dashes of spicy rhythms and ethnic percussion marinated in catchy melodies. These songs keep leaping into the foreground but always return to the brain's back burner when the listener chooses. Imagine summer places, Canadian sunsets, and string-scored holidays . . .

Featuring: *Percy Faith, Morton Gould, David Rose, and Hugo Winterhalter.*

The music and musicians in this section have a much bristlier relationship to mood music. Many of the artists had broader am- bitions and managed to maintain their ground with an occasional AM radio hit. Their tenacity in fighting against the mood music label and their inevitable surrender to it make them among the most fascinating studies in musical politics.

The best example is Percy Faith. His popular rendition of the Max Steiner classic "Theme from *A Summer Place*" may epitomize the sentimental background wash, but it was never Faith's favorite. In fact, he could only regret its evolution as a signature tune when his previous hit "Delicado" packed the Latinized punch he favored. But he made the "Theme" an international sensation almost in spite of himself. Besides winning him a Grammy, it never left the charts during the whole year of 1960.

The "Theme from *A Summer Place*" shocked a lot of older Faith enthusiasts who saw alien signs of Fats Domino in its pounding triplets. This propensity to easy-rock explains why the Ventures later adapted it to their repetitive guitar licks with ease and how Faith helped assemble a disco version called "Summer Place '76," recorded just before he succumbed to cancer.

Faith's delicate balance between being too mellow and too raucous was both a musical gift and a career scourge. On the one hand, he was a champion of sweet strings; but on the other, he always grew skittish when his reputation got too caught up in them. He never alluded to this angst in 1950, however, when he described his goal as being that of "satisfying the millions of devotees of that pleasant American institution known as the quiet evening at home, whose idea of perfect relaxation is the easy chair, slippers and good music." These were cozy sentiments from someone who never wanted to get *too* comfortable.

No wonder Faith wanted to be more than just a practitioner of weepy music for the lovelorn. As a backup arranger, he had worked with almost every major Columbia vocalist. He helped launch Johnny Mathis's career, wrote "My Heart Cries for You" in 1950 for Guy Mitchell, and helped Tony Bennett win three gold records: "Because of You," "Cold, Cold Heart," and "From Rags to Riches." Faith's score for the James Cagney/Doris Day film *Love Me or Leave Me* gained him an Oscar nomination, before he went on to compose for lesser efforts like *Tammy Tell Me True, The Oscar,* and a documentary about women in the movies called *The Love Goddesses.*

Nevertheless, Faith's obituary in *The New York Times* saluted: "A composer who specialized in turning the simple melodic line supplied by other composers into full-scale orchestrations." His string soprano section gave listeners the impression that the songs played just for them.

Some of Faith's more important records consisted of selections he arranged and recorded to highlight his string players. The best of these are *Bouquet, Bouquet of Love,* and *Country Bouquet.* On *Bouquet,* the first Faith album to showcase the strings alone, Faith divided his forty-five-piece orchestra into four sections, with "two banks of violins, one section of low strings, and one section of piano, harp, guitar and vibraphone."

Faith perfected his sprightly style in *Themes for Young Lovers,* a 1963 release that alienated some previous devotees yet led the way for other mood musicians to adapt rock and pop melodies for larger audiences. With orchestrated versions of songs like "Go Away Little Girl" and "Our Day Will Come," Faith indulged in his favorite method of pairing a soaring background violin with pizzicato and percussion counterpoints. This was particularly effective when used for sound effects on his rendition of "Rhythm of the Rain."

Like Faith, Morton Gould was anxious to keep out of the "mellow" music rut and was attracted to exotic rhythms. He pursued them with fervor on his *Jungle Drums* album, mixing classical structures, popular melodies, and exotic sound effects. He also constantly revitalized his act by incorporating the newest of pop and rock into it with what one critic called "his infectious contemporary pulse."

But long before he became president of ASCAP, Gould engaged in higher-brow projects—composing symphonies, suites, a flute concerto, and ballets. He also maneuvered his orchestra into adaptations of Calypso melodies and sailor folk songs on his soundtrack to the 1958 wide-screen "Cinemiracle" film *Windjammer.*

Hugo Winterhalter was another "soft" arranger always hunting for an edge. He demonstrated that he shared Faith's love of Iberian percussion with *Hugo Winterhalter Goes . . . Latin,* reprising the Faith hit "Delicado" along with the "Ecstasy Tango," "Granada," and "Vaya con Dios."

Winterhalter was an important arranger for bandleaders Tommy

Dorsey, Vaughn Monroe, and Benny Goodman, as well as for such singers as Perry Como, Dinah Shore, Kay Starr, and the Ames Brothers. He bolstered Eddie Fisher's career with a lush backing for the standard "Wish You Were Here." He also conducted the Milwaukee and Washington symphony orchestras, proud that his key influences were Debussy and Sibelius.

But Winterhalter found himself increasingly summoned to provide albums with an easy touch, often with themes of wistful nostalgia (*The Eyes of Love*) or ocean-cruise wanderlust (*Wish You Were Here*). *The Eyes of Love* came out in 1957, just as the Gleason albums were getting popular. Here, Winterhalter took a Gleasonish fantasy probe through a dreamscape of "green eyes, dreaming eyes, flashing eyes and fluttering eyes"—an entire collection dedicated to proving that love is not blind, with "I'll Be Seeing You," "I Only Have Eyes for You," "Smoke Gets in Your Eyes," and "I See Your Face Before Me."

Winterhalter would take risks, such as using French horn against strings, a technique that also worked well for Faith. His dynamic interplay between violins and rhythm sections triumphed in "Canadian Sunset," thanks mostly to Eddie Heywood's piano and a melody catchy enough to earn the song the #2 spot on the charts in 1956.

David Rose is among the few orchestra leaders in the sizzle-and-suds game who seemed to love every minute of his work. He is the true author of the *holiday shopper's jubilee* style. As a conductor, arranger, and composer, Rose's mark of distinction was his brilliant pizzicato. His "Holiday for Strings" (where a phalanx of plucked violins mimic hysterical laughter) was a hit in 1943 and got borrowed and reinterpreted by many production music libraries for use in commercials, industrial films, and cartoons. This and several other Rose songs, like "Holiday for Trombones," inspire scenarios of ecstatic bargain hunters in motion: from middle class mall-hoppers to bedecked dowagers exiting their limousines to purchase jewelry or hats. "Holiday for Strings" was also a theme song for *The Garry Moore Show* and *The Red Skelton Show*.

Rose's career as a classical popularizer started at nineteen when he was a standby pianist for NBC before joining the network in 1941 to assist in the music for Tony Martin's radio series. He soon formed the David Rose Orchestra through the Mutual Broadcast System and conducted the *California Melodies* program. Also in 1941, he became a musical director for MGM, scoring background arrangements for Doris Day and Esther Williams films. He also arranged for such stars as Don Ameche, Dorothy Lamour, and Martha Raye (whom he married and divorced within a year). He backed her on her only hit "Melancholy Mood" in 1939. He also composed the "Waukegan Concerto," inspired by Jack Benny's queasy violin playing and conducted by Leopold Stokowski at the Hollywood Bowl.

Eight of Rose's most memorable and perky ditties—including "Holiday for Strings," "Manhattan Square Dance," and "One More Time"—were all written in a single week for broadcast use. He is also responsible for the bucolic orchestrals of *Bonanza* (another theme song grafted onto the collective memory), *High Chaparral*, and (later) *Little House on the Prairie*. His work won him four Emmys, five Grammies, and one Oscar nomination. Muzak liked "Holiday for Strings" enough to commission Rose to do a special elevator version of the song.

Not content to linger in department stores and product showrooms, his style moved on to strip clubs. "The Stripper" replaced "Holiday for Strings" as his signature hit in 1962, with its foxy drum beat mixed with sashaying horns to spark thoughts of floozies flashing their gams in a "pink room."

Keyboards by Candlelight

Piano and organ arrangements to lend any home the trappings of a cocktail lounge or hotel bar. From frolicking to funereal, these selections evoke urban sophistication, happy hour, casual dining, nostalgia, or that undefinable misty moment . . .

Featuring: *Floyd Cramer, Lenny Dee, Ferrante and Teicher, Dick Hyman, Horst Jankowski, Liberace, Peter Nero, and Roger Williams.*

Many urbane establishments owe their mystique to the·phantom keyboardist who plays compulsively in the background. In recent years, he has shown up on television ads as a shadow wrapped in candlelight while a voice-over intones the 800 number needed to order your double-disk collection of anonymously arranged oldies.

Solitary, always smiling, paid to please, and ready for requests, he has been the Chopin of cocktail lounges, the Schubert of saloons, and, in recent years, the Bach of bank lines. Such on-location pianists and organists are among mood music's most intriguing sociological flukes—canned soundtracks on salary, prone to ego bruises. A chosen few are scooped up from obscurity and dropped into the recording studio to cut a hit record or two, but these must contend with the knowledge that their music will probably end up as a matching aesthetic to private dinners, parties, seductions, and other "real" events.

Betraying an affinity with interior design, their notes and arpeggios match architecture, scenic decor, and tableware. Liberace's glissando approximates the tinkling of chandeliers; Ferrante and Teicher can sometimes suggest coffee percolating; Roger Williams's cascading keys conjure images of simulated waterfalls; and Dick Hyman's brisk fingerwork sounds like tumbling ice cubes and clinking martini glasses.

The candlelight keyboardist's flirtation with the scenery stems from his progenitors in old movie houses. There his presence was mandatory yet resented by viewers who wanted a more elaborate orchestra to accompany the show. Not only did the pianist or organist need to maintain the movie's rhythm (or to simulate one when none was present), he had to improvise with a repertoire ranging from symphony hall to burlesque. His artistic predicament invites the same ennui Erik Satie must have felt when his vaunting ambitions were pinioned at café-concerts.

The gin-joint pianist became a cliché with the film *Casablanca,* thanks to Humphrey Bogart's browbeating "Sam" into playing "As Time Goes By" as a backdrop for brooding. François Truffaut's

Shoot the Piano Player later cast Charles Aznavour as the man at the ivories and chronicled his fall from the concert hall arena to a Parisian honky-tonk and finally to the criminal underworld.

Peter Nero's career, though nowhere near as melodramatic as that of Truffaut's piano player, perfects this identity challenge. Born Bernard Nierow in Brooklyn in 1934, he started his musicianship as a child on a 28-cent toy xylophone before becoming a "semi-prodigy" at piano. By eleven, he was playing Haydn's "Piano Concerto in D Major."

Nierow, described by the press as impatient by nature, grew tired of the classical regimen and, by eighteen, sought fleeting gratification through Art Tatum and Oscar Peterson. After obtaining a Bachelor of Arts degree from Brooklyn College, he became a jazz pianist "much to the bewilderment, chagrin and pain of those around me." He admitted that classical music was less appealing because it demanded too much practice. His habit of retaining classical influences in every jazz exertion made him a leading figure in the movement toward their fusion. Among the first and best examples of this is his study in syncopated Baroque called "Scratch My Bach."

But when it came time to perform these hybrid gems, Nierow was working as a saloon pianist at New York City's Hickory House. He got flustered because he wanted audiences to pay attention to his playing. A faltering stint in Las Vegas forced his return to the saloon, this time demoted to the role of intermission pianist.

Not until 1960 did his decision to please the masses pay off. Stan Greeson, Roger Williams's manager at RCA, heard Nierow play at a musician's hangout on 52nd Street and was immediately convinced that he had a new star. Soon Bernard Nierow became Peter Nero and began playing renditions of "Over the Rainbow" and "Autumn Leaves." His first album, *Piano Forte,* launched him on a coast-to-coast tour in 1961. He later became musical director of the Philadelphia Pops Orchestra, lending classical forms to popular songs. His biggest-selling album was *Hail the Conquering Nero* in 1963.

The restless Nero, torn between two musical worlds that many people considered irreconcilable, received an apt description from Sidney Fields of the *New York Daily News* in the early 1970s, just after Nero's version of Michel Legrand's "Theme from *The Summer of '42*" became a hit: "When Peter Nero plays his own compositions on the piano, some jazz people say he's too classical. When he conducts a symphony orchestra or performs with it, he's too jazzy."

Whereas Nero used orchestral arrangements with brass backing, other, more minimalist keyboardists employed the bare essentials of a bass guitar and drummer. This "cocktail sound," like all mood music, became distinct precisely because it eluded existing musical categories.

Some cocktail pianists fit much more snugly in the jazz idiom, with a minimum of fence-straddling. Carmen Cavallero was classically trained and performed in big dance-band ensembles in the late 1930s before adapting to the "cocktail set." Frankie Carle, a one-time bandleader who wrote the Glenn Miller anthem "Sunrise Serenade," considered himself a jazz musician, but he played enough functional supper music to waver into easy-listening territory. Dick Hyman, who became a Muzak favorite with his version of the Kurt Weill–Bertolt Brecht tune "Moritat" (later "Mack the Knife"), was also jazz-identified, but he got moodier when backing John Gielgud's Shakespeare recitations or playing organ for the TV game show *Beat the Clock*.

Germany's Horst Jankowski received a dubious accolade in 1965 when *Melody Maker* described his first album, *The Genius of Jankowski*, as "inoffensive background music for tea and scones." Jankowski emerged as a postwar youth with a concert pianist degree from the Berlin Music Conservatory. He had already assembled his own jazz combo by the time he was eighteen. After touring Europe backing vocalist Caterina Valente and directing Miles Davis and Oscar Peterson, Jankowski came into his own with his memorable instrumental "A Walk in the Black Forest." Formerly called "Black Forest Drive" when consigned to a production music library, it was later released as a single and gave pop piano a new lease on life.

No discussion of the creative rewards inherent in mass appeal is complete without reference to Arthur Ferrante and Louis Teicher—the childhood prodigies of Manhattan's Juilliard who progressed from being avant-garde hellions into one of the most successful and prolific easy-listening institutions in modern music history.

In an article for *Music Journal* in 1965, Ferrante and Teicher summarized their ascent from art-noise to elevator bliss: " . . . it was while teaching that we began experimenting and creating new material for two pianos. For novelty numbers we stuffed wads of paper, sticks, rubber stops, masonite strings, cardboard wedges, and sandpaper into the pianos conjuring up weird effects (à la Cage) resembling gongs, castanets, drums, xylophone, and harpsichord. Though we have gradually dropped many of these gimmicks, we feel that we have developed a musical style, and undoubtedly play in a manner that makes some former colleagues at Juilliard wince a bit."

After releasing several of these avant-garde albums with titles like *Blast Off!* and *Heavenly Sounds in Hi-Fi,* they took an abrupt change of course by 1960 when they got signed to United Artists. For the first time, they began incorporating large orchestral backing, from the accomplished conductor Nick Perito (who also had an influential role in many of Muzak's arrangements). From there, success was inevitable as their duo-piano act provided lush interpretations of theme songs from such films as *West Side Story* (the song "Tonight"), *The Apartment,* and *Exodus.* Ferrante and Teicher went on in their essay: "With the much appreciated success of recordings of movie music, and simplified versions of popular Chopin, Tchaikovsky, and Rachmaninoff classics, we decided to drop the classical repertory for concepts and change the billing from 'duo-pianists' to 'a two-man show.' "

Eleven of their songs made the "Hot 100" between 1960 and 1970. "Midnight Cowboy" (which was released in 1969 and climbed to *Billboard*'s #10) is among their most striking efforts, with Vincent Bell's "water sound" guitar paired with a combination harpsichord and piano, along with an orchestra and chorus rising and falling at strategic moments. They did retain a flair for experimentation with shades of prepared piano in their versions of "What Now My Love?" and Bob Dylan's "Lay Lady Lay," featuring an unorthodox mixture of pianos, with reverberated electric guitar and horns.

Ferrante and Teicher never felt compelled to justify their fruitful romance with the market mean: "There are no regrets about having 'deserted' the classics. We are just as good now as we were in our 'serious' days, only then we were known to a very small segment of the concert-going public. In changing to the lighter side of music we no longer have to teach to make a living."

Although Percy Faith is now immortalized for his string arrangements, he was also (and originally) a pianist; his "Kitten on the Keys" arrangement may have inspired Bent Fabric's "Alley Cat"—a tune so popular that Fabric was commissioned to record a custom-made Muzak version.

Floyd Cramer represented a more unusual piano-playing hybrid. He was a Nashville sessions man for RCA starting in 1955 and had played on Presley's "Heartbreak Hotel." Around the time that "countrypolitan" brought the music of the Deep South into mainstream suburbia, Cramer developed a unique style called the "slip-note" or "whole-tone slur" that gave the piano a slat-key twang.

Far from offending jazz or classical bluenoses, Cramer rubbed his fellow country aficionados the wrong way with his decidedly more "Yankee" leanings. "Countrypolitan" music established once and for all that the Grand Ol' Opry was susceptible to mass marketing's airbrush. In 1960, Cramer's single "Last Date" was a slip-note sensation, reaching Cashbox's #10 ranking, followed by "On the Rebound" in 1961. Bill Pursell, another Nashville pianist, followed Cramer's success into the Top 40 in 1962 with a similar mixture of piano, strings, and background vocals with "Our Winter Love."

The art of shimmering keys spilled over into organ music, with manifestations ranging from cathedral pipes to lounge Wurlitzer. Ethel Smith offered swing favorites played on her Hammond on albums such as *Galloping Fingers,* while Earl Grant (who was also a vocalist) mixed organ with piano for moody and often lugubrious instrumental interpretations of otherwise wistful tunes like

"Tammy," "Till," and a heavily *organic* "Ebb Tide," which reportedly sold 1 million copies as a single.

Lenny Dee's organ, much like Earl Grant's, managed to sound
festive while retaining a moody edge. He could turn a version of
the Leo Sayer hit from the seventies "When I'm With You" from
a playful to a contemplative melody. Discovered by country singer
and musician Red Foley sometime in the fifties, Dee soon proved
his knack for reinterpreting many popular tunes in what can be
likened to a kind of easy-listening decoding process. Though his
only hit single was the 1955 "Plantation Boogie," he had a more
indirect pop impact through the late sixties and early seventies
with his exposure in easy-listening radio formats and a stream of
MCA albums.

Liberace was the saloon player's antithesis. He made up for
the inattention every other candlelight keyboardist received by
cultivating flamboyant costumes, candelabra, and dancing fountains. His passion for showmanship was reinforced by his 1950s
television show, his role in a soapy movie called *Sincerely Yours*
as a concert pianist gone deaf, and his repeated appearances on
talk shows and game shows for decades to come. More than the
others, he took great pains to keep the classical touch in his many
arrangements. When Liberace was only seven, Ignace Paderew-
ski had praised his playing; he later performed with the Chicago
Symphony.

But Liberace's courtship of what many consider "schlock" was
already consummated when he classically manipulated "Mairzy
Doats" and "Three Little Fishes," turning his instrument into a
high-camp prop. His original composition "Rhapsody by Candlelight" went well with the candelabra, ermine capes, kitsch hairdos,
and sequined jackets.

Roger Williams bagged the theatrics but cultivated a flair for
making dramatic sweeps from classical to jazz to country to soft
rock-and-roll. His early career was less shaky than Nero's but just
as categorically ambiguous. He became one of the most prolific
and successful of mood pianists with his "clink-clink-plunk-plunk"
arpeggios that virtually transformed the piano into a harp.

Born Louis Weertz, this "preacher's kid" from Omaha, Nebraska, displayed his musical penchant at age three. After breaking his nose repeatedly during high-school boxing matches, he decided to do something better with his hands and at sixteen became a piano major at Drake University. Here Roger's irreverent blending of supposedly distinct genres got him expelled when a conservatory official overheard him playing "Smoke Gets in Your Eyes" in one of the practice rooms. After getting a B.A. in engineering while in the Navy, Williams reentered civilian life, marched back to Drake for a post-graduate exam, and reenrolled. Roger finally went to Juilliard, where he received jazz tutelage from Teddy Wilson and Lenny Tristano.

After agreeing to accompany a Juilliard vocalist for an appearance on *Arthur Godfrey's Talent Scouts,* Roger was lucky enough to snag the first of his many featured solos when the vocalist did not show up. Soon Dave Kapp of Kapp Records took him in, changing Louis's name to the ultra-American "Roger Williams" in honor of Rhode Island's founder.

According to Williams: "I would start playing jazz in the studio, and Dave used to drag in a cigar store Indian. The Indian looked like he was saluting with a sign on his head saying 'Where is the Melody?' I resented this at first, but it forced me to play melody and arrive at a style."

Williams's first arpeggio hit came in 1955 with "Autumn Leaves," whose trademark key cascade was partly due to the fact that he thought it was called "Falling Leaves." It made #1 on the charts for four weeks. Up through 1969, Williams had twenty-two *Billboard* hits, and by 1972 he boasted a total of thirty-eight LPs. His later hit "Born Free" was another example of how he excelled by playing the melody "straight," with very few pyrotechnic flourishes.

Williams eventually earned two of the entertainment world's highest accolades: he became the first pianist to get a Hollywood Walk of Fame star, and he had his likeness placed in the Movieland Wax Museum. He has also been hailed as the "Pianist to the Presidents," since he had played for every Oval Office holder since Truman. Today, his influence is conspicuous in such candlelight torch-bearers as Richard Clayderman, Carl Doy, and Johnny Pearson. Williams insists:

I would rather call easy-listening "in-depth listening."
It means respecting the wishes of the composer more
than other pianists. I memorize the lyrics to every song.
When it says I hate you my tone gets very cold. Nobody
phrases like a singer does. Pianists usually take short
breaths, play jazz and chop things up. To have long
phrases as you play requires breathing, relaxing. I milk
it. I play the arpeggios beautifully. Chick Corea said
he'd give anything to have my left hand.

Supermarket Symphonette

Step lively to a kinder and gentler Swing, elevated and swathed in
a moderate tempo to keep you energized but never distracted. More
to the beat of drum majorettes than jam sessions, this is heartland-
of-America music, touching even hearts that have long been cold or
broken . . .

Featuring: *Ray Conniff, Bert Kaempfert, and the Champagne Music of*
Lawrence Welk.

American supermarkets and department stores built in the
1950s were meticulously constructed, reverberant temples of al-
loy and glass. Their reflective surfaces (and in some cases, their
curved "space-age" roofs) had proved capable of sustaining echoes as intoxicatingly as a medieval church. Of all the easy-
listening maestros in the Cold War landscape, Ray Conniff comes
closest to furnishing music that is "to the supermarket born."
Conniff's music connotes the mystically metallic clanking of shopping carts trailing down aisles, the rustle of cash registers, the
tinkle of loose change, and the grunt of chromium doors automatically opening for the next phalanx of shoppers. Conniff's meticulous, up-tempo, and regimented beat has a chilly innocence—
the perfect soundtrack for patrons traipsing under Safeway or
A&P klieglights.

Born in Attleboro, Massachusetts, Conniff was always bemused by his dad's piano playing. He took to the trombone and became an arranger after learning the trade from a mail-order transposer. When school ended, he journeyed to Boston; then in 1935 he joined Bunny Berigan's Orchestra en route to New York, where he worked with other "society" orchestras conducted by Bob Crosby and Artie Shaw.

Conniff did a stint in the Army before joining Harry James as a staff arranger in 1945, contributing his light touch to such tunes as "September Song," "The Beaumont Ride," and "Easy On." But because of his discomfort with the emerging "Be-Bop" sound and James's fascination with it, Conniff left the band to roam Hollywood, badly in debt.

"I filed an income tax with a gross earnings of $2,600," Conniff recalls, "with a wife and three children to support and foreclosure notices on the house. In despair, I went out and took a job on a housing development as a pick-and-shovel laborer."

In 1949, faced with $30 a week in take-home pay and wondering if he had buried his musical career in the process, Conniff conducted a private study to determine how to make a hit song. The flutter of money is as fundamental to the Ray Conniff success story as is his music. Conniff did not glean his musical formula by hanging out in coffeehouses or nicotine-drenched nightclubs, but from studying radio and television jingles:

> I tried to figure out a hit solution. I bought eight or ten records like Artie Shaw's "Begin the Beguine" and Glenn Miller's "In the Mood," listened over and over, looked for a trend running through, listened for a week; nothing registered. Then after work one day, something hit me. In 80 percent of the records, either the song or background score had recurring patterns. At that time the advertisers would punch "I'd walk a mile for a Camel," "Ivory soap, it floats!"—repetitious stuff.

On other occasions, Conniff has waxed more metaphysical over his discovery, claiming: "There was always a pattern in the background. You could call it a ghost tune behind the apparent one. And there was another pattern, a pattern of tempo. All I can say is that it's a sort of pulsing. The average persons like to hear a pulsation, not obvious, but reassuringly there in the background."[*]

Conniff proceeded to knock on the doors of every record producer he knew, getting the same patronizing responses until Mitch Miller got interested in this "ghost tune." The 1950s dawned. Conniff was at Columbia Records working again with Harry James, this time as a chief engineer. By July of 1951, Conniff was part of Harry James's backup for three Frank Sinatra songs, one of which, "Castle Rock," he arranged. He formed "Ray Conniff and the Rockin' Rhythm Boys" in 1953, the same year he had a cameo appearance as a trombonist in Universal's *The Glenn Miller Story*.

As the specter of television loomed and musicians looked to make a fast buck scoring shows, Conniff arranged "Tiger Rag" and "Moments to Remember" with bandleader and pianist Raymond Scott for Lucky Strike's *Hit Parade*. Then, in October of 1955, Mitch Miller, still haunted by the ghost tune, asked Conniff to arrange the song "Band of Gold" for singer (and star golfer) Don Cherry. This allowed Conniff to experiment with a chorus for the first time.

As the chorus sang in the background throughout the recording session, Mitch Miller reportedly rushed out of the control booth shouting, "Ray, this is a great sound, this is tremendous!" Hence, the Conniff formula of instruments and vocals was born, with "Band of Gold" hitting #5 on the U.S. best-seller charts.

Conniff's first solo recordings were two singles, "Begin the Beguine" and "Star Dust," which did not achieve hit status but nonetheless got plenty of airplay. When Hal Cook of Columbia's marketing department suggested that Conniff was more of an album artist than a singles artist, he had sown the seeds for Conniff's first LP in 1956, called *S'Wonderful*. It was recorded in monaural sound and produced at New York's 30th Street studio, an old church whose high ceiling produced what Conniff called a "natural echo." Conniff's "chorus invisible" of four women and four men joined eighteen musicians, including Billy Butterfield and Doc

[*]Serge Elhaik, "The New Ray Conniff Story," *S'Conniff (The Ray Conniff Newsletter)* #3 (1991), p. 8.

Severinsen on trumpet, with occasional piano by Dick Hyman and guitars by Tony Mottola and Al Caiola.

Suddenly the Conniff sound sent ghosts floating throughout the Columbia studios. The style was so vibrant, yet so relaxing; so haunting, yet so comforting—a formula so singular and precious that no one else to this day has been able to copy it. This pure alchemy was achieved by combining the base metals of brass with the Conniff choir's golden throats. Conniff acknowledges:

> *I wasn't the first to use voices as instruments. That was done in early classical symphonies. But I believe I was the first to put voices right alongside instruments until you couldn't tell them apart. Trumpets and girls go together, because they operate on almost identical frequency ranges. Male voices blend better with tenor and baritone saxophones.*

Recording *S'Wonderful*'s other ten songs, Conniff needed to reproduce the church echo. He and his sound engineer Fred Slaut created a "stairwell echo" by piping the ten studio recordings from a speaker at the bottom of the Columbia building's stairwell up to the sixth floor.

His debut album guaranteed him a fruitful solo career, but he still lent his enchanted echoes to such recordings as Frankie Laine's "Moonlight Gambler"; Johnny Mathis's "It's Not for Me to Say," "Wonderful, Wonderful," and "Chances Are"; Guy Mitchell's "Singing the Blues"; and Johnny Ray's "Just Walking in the Rain." Conniff also wrote twelve arrangements for Tony Bennett, including the hit single "One for My Baby."

S'Wonderful retained obvious influences from Conniff's bigband days with "I Get a Kick Out of You," "Dancing in the Dark," and "That Old Black Magic." But by the time he followed up with *S'Marvelous* and *S'Awful Nice*, Conniff had begun to play more and more with technical effects until his style got so singular that he permanently altered any song he chose to cover.

Consider Conniff's reworking of the Sonny James ballad "Young Love." He transforms the rockabilly style into a mystical chorus of girl trumpets and boy saxes swooning to muted brass, an acoustic guitar, harp, and metronomic drum brushes. Baby-boomers enamored with the original can listen to this version with a queasy sense of déjà vu, imagining themselves as toddlers being wheeled along retail shelves and bopping to the tunes that mother loved.

Among Conniff's most intriguing arrangements were his special takes on the classics. *Concert in Rhythm* gleaned ghost tunes out of the great masters—from Tchaikovsky's "Swan Lake Ballet" to "Schubert's Serenade." He had an ingenious method of transforming something as idiosyncratic as Tchaikovsky's First Piano Concerto into a vaporous *danse macabre* that, in some ways, surpasses the original's blaring egotism.

Conniff's singers were mostly noted for their background "do-doos," "ba-baas" and "da-da-daas," but he gave them several albums on which to go foreground. On *Somebody Loves Me*, he relayed his singers through a "three-channel pick-up": the left channel had the male singers, piano, and percussion; the right carried the females and the harp; and the center channel contained the rhythm section's guitars, bass and drums. This allowed a left-and-right vocal exchange that mixed spatial with aural motion. Besides being heard at the opening and closing of the 1968 Dean Martin movie *How to Save a Marriage and Ruin Your Life*, the Ray Conniff Singers appeared regularly in four-second radio station identification spots, performing with the AM dial's familiar single-note-per-call-letter flair.

Conniff's disarming candor deflects all of the scorn that jazz and big-band purists have heaped on him through the years:

> *Instead of playing trombone solos that other musicians liked, I made an about-face and wrote my arrangements with a view to making the masses understand and buy records. From that point, I became very successful. I use the word* success *both financially and as a person. I felt much more fulfilled seeing a record like Johnny Ray's "Walking in the Rain" go to number one in* Billboard. *I could have gone on as I did with the big bands and be a little over the heads of the general buying public, but this is a better way to go.*

Bert Kaempfert was another brass man who successfully converted the sound of commerce into art. Born in Hamburg, Germany, this only child was pampered through his early years as a musical prodigy and proved a model student at the Hamburg School of Music. He acquired a working knowledge of clarinet, accordion, piano, and saxophone, lending his talents to Germany's popular Hans Busch band and the *Radio Danzig* show before World War II. Kaempfert adapted Swing to the "strict tempo" dance style popular among Germans.

After the war, Kaempfert became an arranger and A&R man for Polydor Records. While still in Hamburg, he indirectly altered pop music history by introducing the original Beatles to singer Tony Sheridan, an association that led to the group's first studio recordings. In 1960, Kaempfert's single "Wonderland by Night" peaked America's "Hot 100" charts and was a million seller. A *Cashbox* poll voted the Bert Kaempfert Orchestra the "Number One Band of the Future."

Kaempfert's most famous composition, "Strangers in the Night," was included in the score for the 1966 spy-comedy film *A Man Could Get Killed* and jump-started Frank Sinatra's flagging career. The same year, he had a hit on the British charts with an inventive arrangement of "Bye Bye Blues," a song that typifies the Kaempfert mystique: an electric bass guitar line thumping like a merry cadet to a muted trumpet and echoing background chorus. He also wrote "A Swingin' Safari," "Spanish Eyes," and the Wayne Newton hit "Danke Schoen." Herbert Rehbein, Kaempfert's main arranger, established his own smoother, slower take on the Kaempfert style in the album *Music to Soothe That Tiger*.

The keynotes of supermarket swing—relaxation, fun, and a storybook ideal of happiness—were never better celebrated than in the Champagne Music of Lawrence Welk.

"Light," "sparkling," "effervescent," and "bubbly" were only some of the enthusiastic terms his fans used to praise Welk in the stacks of letters he received after his Honolulu Fruit Gum Orchestra made an auspicious New Year's Eve appearance at Pittsburgh's William Penn Hotel. Performing at the hotel's "exclusive"

Italian terrace, Welk felt an instant, almost vertiginous, synaesthesia between the players and the luminous atmosphere. Welk's own descriptions of that night in his autobiography *Wunnerful, Wunnerful!* reveal how his music followed the landscape's logic: "There were toasts of champagne and we played lots of waltzes and romantic dance music, while the lights from the chandeliers reflected in all the mirrors and the whole room seemed to sparkle and glow."

Welk's announcer Phil David looked through the fan mail and coined the term "Champagne Music," realizing that "bubbly" was the adjective most frequently used to describe the music. From that moment, the Honolulu Fruit Gum Orchestra became Lawrence Welk and his Champagne Music Makers. The style was official: bouncy and steady with lots of accordion, violins, clarinets, flutes, organ, and soft trombones for a potpourri of pop, polka, swing, country, Dixieland, Latin, and some inspirational.

Welk had previously written "a sweet legato ballad" on the birth of his daughter called "You're My Home Sweet Home." He speeded up the tempo, held a contest to give it the best name, and turned it into "Bubbles in the Wine"—the Champagne theme song.

But according to Welk, the Champagne style came about by chance and duress. Not able to employ adept musicians all of the time, he had to settle for itinerant players who in some cases could barely stay in key, let alone maintain the correct pitch on the longer notes. Welk wrote arrangements suited to their limitations. The pairing of "short, light, delicate musical figures" with the lively accordion led to the accidental but subsequently profitable fizz effect.

During the late 1950s, Welk contributed several arrangements under Muzak's "Dance" category. Among them: "I Get Up Every Morning," "Million Miles Away," "Stormy Weather," "Lullaby of Broadway," "There's a Small Hotel," "Moon over Miami," and "Hurry! Hurry! Hurry! (Back to Me)."

His television show started regionally in 1951, then went national on ABC-TV in 1955 (the same year Disneyland opened). *The Lawrence Welk Show* eventually became the longest-running program in TV history. Watching reruns today, we can see how the show's entire look anticipated the disco ambiance of the 1970s: the purple background lighting, the soft-focus contours, the sequined outfits, and the rhinestone chandeliers anticipating the cotillion ball.

Welk earned the distinction of becoming the second-wealthiest performer in show business. He garnered more than twenty hit singles from 1956 to 1965, including "Calcutta" in 1960, with Frank Scott on harpsichord. *Billboard Music Week's* 14th Annual D.J. Poll named "Calcutta" the "Favorite Instrumental Record of 1961."

Raised in a heavily ethnic German community in North Dakota, and the child of immigrant parents from Alsace-Lorraine, Welk was imbued with strong Catholic values that stressed good works and frugality. He thrived in the shadow of religious tenets that, like his humorous German accent, he could never relinquish.

This probably explains his very simple remedy for what he saw as the growing level of stress in American life: "Champagne music puts the girl back in the boy's arms—where she belongs." His prescription also consisted of a friendly smile, pretty colors, "family values," and an unflagging willingness to steer toward the middle of the road. Champagne music was bound to connote conservative politics—a stereotype that only got reinforced when Welk performed at President Eisenhower's second inaugural ball in 1957. Still his stunning visual and aural phantasmagoria can suit anyone magnanimous enough to enjoy it, regardless of their social convictions. Take, for example, the androgynous (and far from conservative) k.d. lang, who basks in the "Champagne" luster in one of her music videos.

Ray Conniff had also won the silent majority's seal of approval, when Pat Nixon revealed that she was one of his fans. During one White House concert for the Nixons in the early 1970s, the ghost tunes managed to smooth over an embarrassing incident that can only be done justice in Conniff's own words:

> *Nixon's office called and wanted me to appear for the fiftieth anniversary of DeWitt Wallace, who founded Reader's Digest. I did a repertoire that went back 50 years, five or six songs for every year. We used 16 sing-*

ers and the Air Force Rhythm Section from D.C. One of the girls that was a substitute was sympathetic to the anti–Vietnam war cause, and we found out later that she was living in a commune of other people against the war.

First she said she wouldn't be seen in the White House, but she called back, and we took her in. She came on stage with the singers before I did. I came on to start the show and announce the singers. She was one of the first out. I suddenly hear this voice on the mike which was not the announcer's but hers. Nixon is sitting right in the front row and she starts saying: "Mr. Nixon, you go to church on Sunday; so how can you let all this killing go on in Vietnam?!" She held a sign that she wore as a piece of cloth on her dress that said something like "Stop the Bombing."

The incident was covered on local television and went all over the world. I struggled to get the sign from her but couldn't. The thought then came to me: when the ship's sinking, start the music. During the first tune, I was so mad. It dawned on me that the President was insulted in his own home with 500 or 600 people in the room. They thought I might be in on it. One newsman shouted "Throw the bum out." I talked to the girl and asked her to stay, but the Secret Service wheeled her off. I told the President it was as much a surprise to me as it was to him. Nixon said "Don't worry about it. If it hadn't happened, no one would have known you were at the White House. Now all the world will know!"

Gregorian Cocktail

Tired of singers screaming into your eardrum? Fight those prima-donna doldrums with a Gregorian cocktail! This blend of soft, subtle, mysterious, and not-in-your-face vocals is the sonically secular answer to yesterday's Gregorian chants, cathedral choirs, and the Sirens of classic lore . . .

Featuring: *The Alan Copeland Singers, The Anita Kerr Singers, The Living Voices, The Norman Luboff Choir, The Ray Charles Singers, The Ray Conniff Singers, The Sandpipers, and The Swingle Singers.*
In the synthetic music machine the sound-track roll began to unwind. It was a trio for hyper-violin, super-cello and oboe-surrogate that now filled the air with its agreeable languor. Thirty or forty bars—and then, against this instrumental background, a much more than human voice began to warble . . .

—Aldous Huxley, *Brave New World*

In his early 1970s hit 'If You Could Read My Mind," Gordon Lightfoot sang the line "You know that ghost is me" with the folksy cry of a lovelorn innocent. But his earthy style fit incongruously with a song shrouded in otherworldly images of dark castles, old-time movies, haunted wishing wells, telepathy, and encounters with poltergeists. That is why it took an ectoplasmic transfusion from the Ray Conniff Singers to liberate the ghost from Lightfoot's body and let it float through the echo-chamber unscathed.

Conniff's technique of pairing voices with instruments conferred a stunning afterlife on popular songs. But by 1972, when the Ray Conniff Singers performed their Lightfoot séance, such shadow choruses were already in their waning days. Gone would be the Johnny Mann, Anita Kerr, Ray Charles, and Enoch Light Singers, the Norman Luboff Choir, the Living Voices, the Swingle Singers, the Cascading Voices of the Hugo and Luigi Chorus, and other acts that crooned in a utopia where girls went "la-la," boys went "ba-ba," and the human voice impersonated waterfalls, rustling breezes, hives of swarming insects, and electronic resonators.

Shadow choruses were so common by the late 1950s and early 1960s that few instrumental artists prospered without featuring them on at least one album, and hardly any pop singer could decline to enlist their powerful background magic. The singing style went completely counter to the sweat-passion of jazz, soul, rock, and folk. When not voicing wordless choruses, these singers practiced subdued lyricizing with a willingness to be as self-effacing as the quiet, dreamy fiddles sharing their space.

If T. S. Eliot was right to equate the cocktail party to a modern-day holy communion, then surely the shadow chorus loomed in the cathedral loft. The connection is not incidental, since the vocal delivery of the mood music chorus bears many similarities to Gregorian chants and to polyphonic choral music.

R. Murray Schafer's *The Tuning of the World* describes how the architects of Norman and Gothic cathedrals had stone walls and floors engineered to produce an exceedingly long reverberation time of about six seconds. The power of chants and polyphony lay in their disembodied echoes—an enveloping aural massage that came from nowhere and everywhere.

Modern ensembles like the Ray Conniff Singers re-created the Gregorian style in the service of commercial pop. And like all mystical disciplines, it worked best as an applied science. Conniff got so precise that he wrote "Da-Da," "Ba-Ba," and "Do-Do" right on his arranger score sheets.

Leon Theremin, on the other hand, created an Ether Wave device that evoked the sound of the ancient Sirens when its operators moved their arms and legs around a magnetic field. The Theremin machine's alien twang became a familiar science-fiction soundtrack in the *One Step Beyond* television theme and in the movie *The Day the Earth Stood Still.*

The ability to send the human voice into technological reverberations was discussed as far back as in Francis Bacon's *New Atlantis:* "We have also divers strange and artificial echoes, reflecting the voice many times, and as it were tossing it, and some that give back the voice louder than it came, some shriller and some deeper; yea, some rendering the voice differing in the letters or articulate sound from that they receive."

Capitol Records in the early 1950s was the Studio of Sirens. Les Baxter's album *Music out of the Moon* was purportedly mood music's first attempt to use the "choir invisible," with singers and Theremin playing simultaneously. According to Baxter, Capitol's studio (under Paul Weston) was worried because normally voices were never recorded that high. The record was destined to be a cult favorite, and it impressed astronaut Neil Armstrong so much that he reportedly requested hearing it through NASA's speakers during his Apollo moon excursion.

Capitol Records also offered *Oooo!*, Jackie Gleason's holy cocktail hymnal. Artie Malvin, a vocal arranger who had worked with Ray Conniff and organized background vocals for many singers, assembled Gleason's voices and remembers that "Gleason told his producer Jack Philbin that he wanted to do an album with choir as orchestra." *Oooo!* turned out to be Gleason's most gorgeously perverse and memorable romp into the mood-control funhouse. Demure piano and guitar whisper on one end of the stereo spectrum; a half-saintly, half-possessed antiphony broods at the other. The results: standard love plaints like "Willow Weep for Me" sound at times like choirs at a coven.

Though many background vocal selections became markedly more modern and only vaguely resembled their medieval predecessors, others were near duplicates. Bert Kaempfert's version of "Sweet Maria" leads in with his signature bass line, followed by a beautifully anachronistic Gregorian send-up.

In 1960, Horst Jankowski put sixty-five voices through an informal audition for his Jankowski Choir. He assembled six individuals from diverse backgrounds, including a mechanic, a model, and a teacher. Jankowski describes the music as "somewhat like a motion picture sound track: On the screen you see one man seated at the piano in his lonely apartment. As he plays, from out of nowhere a full string section and choir add drama to the scene."

In the early 1960s, RCA's A&R chiefs Hugo Peretti and Luigi Creatore formed "The Cascading Voices of the Hugo and Luigi Chorus," which featured strings, occasional brass, and enchanting arrangements of popular songs redone with a rippling soprano background and a foreground chorus of male tenors and baritones. Norrie Paramor took full stereophonic advantage by having "modern-day Ariel" Patricia Clark's "in-and-out" soprano voice weave through thirty-three stringed instruments on his Capitol album *Autumn*.

The Norman Luboff Choir also set a high vocal standard. Summoning tender memories of remote times and places, the Choir took listeners through the wild west, the Caribbean, the sea, and the grandeur of Broadway. Weston, who had worked with Luboff's choir when it backed Jo Stafford on *The Railroad Hour*, recalls:

> *I took seven singers, three girls and four guys, and made a series of records. One of them, called "Nevertheless (I'm in Love with You)" was a hit on my first year in Columbia. I said to Norman, "I'm gonna let you make an album with your choir." So we decided to call it* Songs of the West. *It was a gigantic hit, despite the fact that Columbia's president always called him "hopalong Luboff." Luboff's singers were the best in Hollywood.*

The Living Voices also thrived in those halcyon days when many studio vocalists could secure contracts from one ensemble or venue to another. These background singers were as adaptable as quicksilver, moving through albums, television performances, movie soundtracks, and commercials. One of the Living Voices, Linda November, was later hired by Henry Mancini to help with some of his movie themes. Mancini's title song for *Breakfast at Tiffany's* illustrated the wordless chorus at its most pristine and evocative. Males "do-do" across the soundtrack like guardian seraphim, gently quelling one of Holly Golightly's frequent "mean reds" spells.

The wordless chorus also got a boost following James C. Petrillo's notorious American Federation of Musicians recording strike of the early 1940s. He permitted no orchestras to play, forcing choirs to replace instruments. Since vocalists were excluded from the union, they attained prominence over instrumental bands—especially since they worked for less money. Although this may have been disastrous to big bands (which were doomed to extinction by the end of the war, anyway), the AFM strike enhanced the art of background vocals by giving many previously unheard singers exposure that they probably would not have gotten otherwise.

Shadow voices also dominated many of the nicotunes (cigarette jingles) that appeared on radio and television, up until the very last one to hit the airwaves on New Year's Eve of 1971, following a federal ban on broadcast media advertising of smoking tobacco. Among the best were the Brass Ring's chorus for Benson & Hedges 100's, the Singers Unlimited vocalization for Kent, and The Ray Charles Singers' spots for Chesterfield and Lucky Strike.

When Ray Charles was choral director for "The Perry Como Show," he fashioned a well-planned *mezza voce* guaranteed never to overwhelm. A native of Chicago, Ray Charles started as a singer in other people's bands. One of his earliest television jobs was for a show sponsored by Ford Motors where he arranged for Ethel Merman. But by 1948, he had gotten involved with Perry Como and was part of a vocal group called the Satisfiers. He also formed the Double-Daters, which consisted of a girl and three guys for an NBC show called *Million Dollar Band,* sponsored by Colgate Palmolive. He was also the Choral Director for the *Hit Parade* show from 1950 to 1957.

Charles's first recording dates with his Ray Charles Singers were for Essex Records out of Philadelphia. The albums were, as Charles claims, "really contrived to sell the suggestive pictures of naked women draped by large handkerchiefs on the covers." The graphics were randy, but the music was fuzzy and romantic, with very soft voices and album titles like *Faraway Places* and *Slow Boat to China.*

Charles himself is very exacting when describing his choral combinations:

> *My whole theory of singing is that you were singing to someone no more than 2 feet away, like a lover. Don't yell at me! Any choir is a multivoiced extension of myself. I had a big argument with the engineer on our first recording date because I wanted soft, almost whispering sounds. They kept arguing that you could not hear it through the surface noise on the record. I told them it was* their *problem. The New York singers were difficult because most of them studied to be soloists and were often under the influence of bad singing teachers. I wanted to get rid of their bad habits, to make the*

*voices blend and sound like one. The California people
didn't study voice, so the style came more naturally.*

After making two 10-inch LPs for Essex, Charles went to MGM
for an eight-album contract, then on to Decca to record five more.
But his breakthrough occurred when he got an offer from Enoch
Light at Command Records that was good enough to keep him
and his singers around for fifteen more LPs.

The Ray Charles Singers did many of the jingles for S&H Green
Stamps, Lipton Tea, Chesterfield, and Lucky Strike. They also
performed a well-remembered Robert Hall commercial that
played on radio throughout the Cold War's chilliest days and was
heard not long ago as background in Bob Balaban's movie *Parents.*
Charles won an award for his Cover Girl cosmetics radio spot,
which featured a then-unknown folk singer named Judy Collins.
On *The Perry Como Show*, he got to meet the *other* Ray Charles
in person and convinced the soulful singer to perform "America
the Beautiful" long before he did so at the 1984 Republican National Convention.

By the mid-1960s there was a craze for quasi-Baroque chorales
paired with modern pop accompaniment. Many singing groups
rushed in to try a hand at fugue fluctuations from baritone to
falsetto. The Alan Copeland Singers had proved their vocal revi-
sionism by turning Leadbelly's Deep South country blues "Cotton
Fields" into a sweet, suburban incantation. But their Baroque interpretations of Mason Williams's instrumental "Classical Gas"
and Simon and Garfunkel's "Scarborough Fair" crystallized the
late 1960s tension between styles that were simultaneously wacky
and severely ordered.

One of the most inventive and influential acts was the Swingle
Singers, popular during Wendy Carlos's *Switched On Bach* days.
The Swingle Singers were formed in 1962 by Fulbright scholar,
pianist, singer, and arranger Ward Lamar Swingle. Their original
intention was to vocalize big-band instrumentals, but they adopted
Baroque music for sight-reading exercises. Their first album *Jazz
Sebastian Bach* consisted of fugues sung by the wordless chorus
with added bass and drums. The record made it to America's Top

15 and was voted best 1964 vocal category LP by a *Downbeat Jazz* critics poll. Swingle's goal was to reinterpret the great composers chronologically, leading to the album *Anyone for Mozart, Bach, Handel, Vivaldi?* CBS Records later released *Love Songs for Madrigals and Madriguys.*

The Anita Kerr Singers, emerging from Nashville to tackle other aspects of the pop scene, produced such albums as *The Anita Kerr Singers Reflect on the Music of Burt Bacharach & Hal David* and *Velvet Voices and Bold Brass.* Memphis-born Kerr formed her Singers in 1949, with Chet Atkins producing their first albums. Kerr was one of the first women to produce country records in Nashville, including Skeeter Davis's album *The End of the World.* Her Singers also graced the background to Eddy Arnold's "Make the World Go Away"—the song Arnold's manager Gerald Purcell claims jump-started the subgenre of "countrypolitan" music.

Kerr got more specialized when she produced the Mexicali Singers. Here the "slightly Baroque" wordless chorus comprises "vocal instrumental impressions" replacing marimbas, violins, and trumpets. Legend has it that Anita Kerr discovered them by a mysterious coincidence. Making a wrong turn 3 miles beyond Prescott, Arizona, she came to a village square in Mexicali where she heard the alto, first tenor, baritone, basso, and two sopranos singing to the townsfolk. With skills honed in what the liner notes to their first album describe as "the Juilliard School of Doo-Wah," the Mexicali Singers switch from Bert Kaempfert to Beatles to Tijuana Brass—a progression highlighted by Kerr's phantasmal little-girl voice, particularly when she breaks out her trumpet impression on "Bye Bye Blues" played à la Kaempfert.

The Sandpipers, a vocal trio based in Los Angeles, continued the art of subdued singing, aimed at an intergenerational audience. Jim Brady, Michael Piano, and Richard Shoff started in the Mitchell Boys Choir, but teamed up to form their own group, and in 1966 they stunned the world with a rendition of "Guantanamera," which went up to *Billboard*'s #5. They followed with a smoky version of "Louie Louie" that same year and made another impression in 1970 with "Come Saturday Morning," from the film *The Sterile Cuckoo.* That same year, they managed an equally engaging, though seldom recognized, performance with their theme song for Russ Meyer's notorious cult classic *Beyond the Valley of the Dolls,* with dreamy lines like "Beyond the days of now and then/ Far above reality . . ." blending precisely with their vocal vapors.

They are also intriguing for their mystery guest, an elusive and rarely seen female who sang background on many of their tracks and who even toured with them. The woman, Pamela Ramcier, would appear as a human backdrop to the performance, often clothed in go-go boots and mini-skirt. A reviewer for *Variety* summed up a 1969 performance at Detroit's Elmwood Casino as follows: "The girl is kept in the shadowy background so there will be no mistaking her for one of the Sandpipers. Her wordless descants fit her in with the violins rather than the vocals. But they have never been able to keep her still. She moves on her own little darkened platform and the audience strains to see what the boys have hidden back there."

The wordless chorus has found a new mode of generation in the synthesizer. Brian Eno utilized some of the available synthesizer techniques in his angel-devil choir on *Music for Airports.* His chorus fulfills an ambiguous spiritual role, the secular answer to the Mormon Tabernacle Choir as the airport replaces the palace of worship, guiding our shadow voice as it evolves from Siren to medieval monk to cocktail crooner to programmable MIDI.

Mai-tai Melodies and the World of "Queasy Listening"

Pleasure ports beckon inside this mixed-tempo travelogue of songs and sound effects capturing the lusts of the Congo, mirages of Arabian sands, phallic festivals of the Orient, and electro-whiz slumber parties where the dream dates are from Venus . . .

Featuring: *Les Baxter, Martin Denny, the Electro-Sonic Orchestra, Enoch Light and the Light Brigade, and Robert Maxwell.*

In the 1950s, when conservatives and fundamentalists fought against rock-and-roll's "jungle" influences, the hypnotic beats of "real" tom-toms entertained many a cocktail lounge enthusiast, with nary an eyebrow raised. Just as we annexed Hawaii as a full-fledged state of the union, thousands of American and European tourists, never before exposed to the Pacific side of paradise, heard the best symphonies of conch shells, wind chimes, ukeleles, koto, bamboo sticks, and tropical bird-calls in the confines of hotel lounges, nightclubs, and shell bars. This was "exotica" music—an enchanting, teeming, intoxicating, and festering easy-listening sub-genre that vexed many an unsuspecting ear with the dark forces of "foreignness" while staying within the bounds of propriety.

Nothing better captures the exotica spirit than the now-legendary Tonga Room in San Francisco's Fairmont Hotel. This tropical-themed interior has an "Oriental" lounge act singing "authentic" island folk ballads in English, a cocktail menu of mai-tais and other paradisal drinks, and a simulated rainforest where showers descend at least twice every hour.

Exotica, like the Tonga Room, thrives as an environmental recreation, a musical whirlwind tour inspired by the notion that the entire non-Western world—from the dynastic palaces of China to the straw hut promenades of New Guinea—really is an assortment of devil-masks, radiant volcanos, coral reefs, stone gods, jungle rivers, and enchanted seas compiled from fantastic travel brochures.

Les Baxter, known for his impressive movie and television scores, is the exotica craze's initiator and tour guide. A former arranger for Nat King Cole, and one of Mel Tormé's original Mel-Tones, Baxter put our ear to the forbidden conch-shell with his *Ritual of the Savage (Le Sacre du Sauvage)* and its exotica anthem "Quiet Village." Described on the liner notes as "a tone poem of the sound and the struggle of the jungle," the album paired simulated Belgian Congo noises with symphonic strings, brass, and occasional kazoos.

Ritual of the Savage came with separate stories for each track: the frenzy of coastal traders on "Busy Port"; the soft romanticism of "Jungle Flower"; the ritual allure of a "Stone God" ceremony; and the incessant congas and chimpanzee wails of "Love Dance." The final cut, called "The Ritual," presents a thoroughly Baxterized version of African native ceremonies that the white man has rarely seen.

Baxter made most of these Afro-Caribbean–themed songs long before he ventured to Cuba. He never did make it to Africa, but his follow-up album *Tamboo!* attempted authenticity at the same time that it milked every "Dark Continent" stereotype. Putting it on your turntable is like stepping into a Tarzan or Mondo movie. The violin festoon on track three provides incontrovertible evidence that this is a genuine imitation of a previously fabricated wilderness.

The Sacred Idol (music from a film never released) came to Baxter as he stared out a window in Mexico. Alongside the "authentic" South-of-the-Border instruments, Baxter must have been hearing an after-echo of strings and choirs beckoning him from back home. This meeting of North and Central America (with North predominating) had proved salable enough for him to stray farther south, producing Yma Sumac's first album *Voice of the Xtabay*. Sumac, a Peruvian princess with a four-octave range, sang invocations to her people's ancient mountain gods—a show that had its worldwide debut at the Hollywood Bowl.

Earlier, Baxter made *The Passions,* a safari in vocal violence that attempts to capture a woman's emotional palette. Bas-Sheva (the consummate moanstress) was like Yma Sumac with fewer octaves. The recording, consisting of several 10-inch LPs, came with a complete reference guide explaining "Love," "Hate," "Lust," "Romance," and "Terror," and their mythical implications.

Baxter's music demonstrates how the most ancient tribal symbols had become fungible studio fixtures equally at home in the Gold Coast, the South Pacific, the Andes, and the Moon. It had much in common with Rodgers and Hammerstein's *South Pacific,* which was not so much a South Sea Island romance as a science-fiction celebration of America's power to mold the unknown with the image of reconstructed psychosexual fantasies of G.I.s who had been stationed in the islands during World War II.

While Baxter's pet sound was the full orchestra, Martin Denny preferred smaller-scale intoxicants. He manipulated xylophones, chimes, and jungle drums to sound like alien cradlesongs. Baxter's version of "Quiet Village" is a savage symphony of brass and cymbals; but Denny's is much slower, beginning with a dissonant low-frequency piano accompanied by the croaks and hoots of lurking swamp predators—a village far *too* quiet!

Denny owes much of his fame to industrialist Henry J. Kaiser, who owned Honolulu's Hawaiian Village nightclub—a shell bar famous for its coconut trees, pupu platters, and table lanterns. Denny's first combo consisted of Arthur Lyman on vibes, Augie Colon on bongos, John Kramer on bass, and Denny himself at the piano. Julius Wechter (who would later form the Baja Marimba Band after being a sideman to Herb Alpert) filled the gap when Lyman left Denny to form the Arthur Lyman Group in 1957; the latter's premier album *Taboo* sold close to 2 million copies.

Denny is remarkable for drifting into the strange while keeping close to the sweet, melodic shore. Among his chief fans was Alice Faye, who was reportedly mesmerized by Denny's band during the last five nights of a Hawaiian vacation.

James A. Michener, responsible for turning Hawaii into a volume of American folklore, praised Denny in the liner notes to *Hawaii*, a Denny album that included a piano rendition of the title theme and other tropical delights: "Why do I go for Martin Denny's type of music? It's professional and very expertly put together for the public. It uses instruments and rhythms most usually found in popular music. It's witty, and much to the taste of people who like a little humor for the long haul."

As a single, Denny's "Quiet Village" became a chart-topper in 1957. Denny got sublime compliments when many island visitors credited it for inspiring great bedroom "matinees." He invented his trademark animal sounds when some bullfrogs began croaking intermittently in a man-made pond by the bandstand. He put the sounds into the act, having his band members imitate birds while he duplicated the *ribbits* by grinding on a grooved cylinder. Denny became as much of a packaged tourist attraction as Diamond Head or Pearl Harbor.

Denny's first album, *Exotica*, was recorded in Honolulu, at the

Aluminum Dome, a part of Henry Kaiser's Hawaiian Village complex. The Dome offered a natural three-second reverberation, due to its half-sphere contour. "Quiet Village" was on the charts for thirteen weeks. Denny's idea of the ultimate Hawaiian sound was much different from what he encountered among the indigenous peoples. Disillusioned over the extent to which "genuine" Hawaiian music depended on steel guitar, Denny sought to superimpose a variety of international rhythms to get the "feel" of the South Seas.

Exotic Percussion made the best use of Liberty's "Visual Sound Stereo," with water; Japanese lutes; Hawaiian gourd; a miniature celeste; steel, wood, and wind chimes; Burmese gongs; and boombams tinkling from ear to ear. This album marked Denny's transition to focusing on the wonders of the Far East. His use of "tuned Burmese gongs" attempted to meld the charm of Buddhist temple ceremonial rites with the clatter of cocktail trays.

Associates who worked with airlines would bring Denny strange instruments from around the world. He believed that all sounds represented colors and once reconstructed a xylophone for a perfect glissando. He once stated that dissonance, not harmony, makes the most interesting music. Just listen to his koto version of "My Funny Valentine" to hear how he loved sounds grating against each other and thrown into improbable contexts.

Ironically, a generation of Japanese youth, among them Ryuichi Sakamoto and other members of the Yellow Magic Orchestra, were inspired by this Caucasian musical missionary. Denny knew the extent of Western influence on Japan after the war and recorded a Shogun–Elvis piece called "Sake Rock" that combined the magic of the koto with a rock-and-roll beat. This was, after all, the era when Disneyland brought us the Jungle Cruise in Adventureland and the Tiki Bird Room, and when engineers masterminding the Gemini rocket launches dwelled in a prefabricated "Tahitian Village" in Downey, California.

Everywhere, the combination of science and entrepreneurial ingenuity was introducing such wonders as the Vanguard satellite and Christine Jorgensen. So it is no wonder that the exotica ethic branched out into other vistas of sexuality and space exploration.

At the height of the Cold War, when American technology intimated that utopia was at hand, a new sound that was both easy-listening and unlistenable invaded hi-fi and stereo spectrums. Weird "outer-space" operas, electronic zithers and way-out harmonies form the category popularly referred to as "Space-Age Bachelor Pad Music."

Byron Werner, a Hollywood special effects man coined the term "Space-Age Bachelor Pad Music" and designated its patrons as "Lonely guys with too much disposable income who are nitpicky about their stereos." Here's how Jerry Nutter of New York's WNYC radio defines the genre: "Imagine what George Jetson would be like if he hadn't married Jane: 'Hubba-hubba!'"

Unlike the established Mantovani and Percy Faith, the space-age bachelor pad musician knew no predictable audience and no push-button sales formula. Werner goes on to say that these records are "not any good for dancing, like Latin music, or seducing, like Jungle music, or anything else, *but* showing off that new hi-fi set." The music arrived just when feral man was going soft, pampered by urban technology and dainty white-collar duties. His greatest pacifier was the stereophonic incubation chamber, where proper speaker placement became as essential as air vents.

The space-age bachelor pad aesthetic is best summed up on the jacket of *Presenting a New Concept in Sound,* by the Electro-Sonic Orchestra: "This *is* electronic music. Not the weird machine-made sounds usually associated with the term, but music based on popular melodies, and played on conventional instruments that have been ingeniously electrified."

The album's conductor Dick Jacobs made this unique contribution through a device called a *transducer* that attached directly to six violins, two violas, a bass violin, a piano, a drum, an electric bass, an organ, an ondioline, and a cello. Each transducer also had its own *potentiometer* for volume control. Transducer output was put into a premixing unit and was, in turn, fed into a multichannel console. Without using any conventional open mikes, the Electro-Sonic Orchestra got sharp audio separation effects while applying its electrified outlander sound to such standards as "Tammy," "Vo-lare," and "Itsy-Bitsy Teenie-Weenie Yellow Polkadot Bikini."

Another characteristic of space-age bachelor pad music is its tendency to use otherwise conventional and tame instruments for maniacal purposes. Besides the Ferrante & Teicher experiments with prepared piano, there was Ruth Welcome, a zither enchant-ress who kept New York audiences spellbound. Albums like *Hi-Fi Zither* and *Zither Magic!* promised "sheer sorcery" in her interpretations of "It Might as Well Be Spring," "Wunderbar," and "Memories Are Made of This."

Robert Maxwell mixed his hellion harp with whimsical saxo-phones, banjos, and electric guitars. He also had a supper club stage act for places like New York's Persian Room, where he adorned his harp with multicolored lights that blinked to the pres-sure of a foot-pedal.

Maxwell's major contribution is the song "Ebb Tide," recorded by many easy-listening legends. He is also remembered for com-posing two of the most formidable themes from the Golden Age of Television: "Shangri-La," which appeared regularly on Jackie Gleason's variety show to usher in Reginald Van Gleason III; and "Solfeggio," the jungle theme for the *Ernie Kovacs Show* that played during the infamous Nairobi Trio sketch.

Dean Elliott, who had recorded soundtracks for the animated feature *The Phantom Tollbooth* and such low-budget Albert Zug-smith epics as *Sex Kittens Go to College* (with Mamie Van Doren), is best known in space-age bachelor pad circles for his *Zounds! What Sounds!* album. In addition to his big band, Elliott utilized such high-tech extras as automobiles, axes, coffee cans, dog barks, frog croaks, mechanical teeth, and underwater detonations.

Jack Fascinato's *Music from a Surplus Store* offered a sound-scape by which "a collection of seemingly un-musical implements, such as trowels, putty knives, and crowbar, sound out melodically from all points across the stereo stage." Each original composition included a star implement. "Oily Boid" paired a center stage trum-pet with the rhythmic squeezing of two needle-nosed oil cans. "Sweepy Time" adorned its pizzicato string quartet with "a real drone of a GI scrub brush that's dashing furiously from side to side." "Latin Hardware" was an orchestration of loose-jointed pliers, "soprano crowbar," and a "putty knife gone Latin," with the semblance of electric guitar, flute, and vibes attempting some form of jazz rhumba.

There was a mixture of neurotic big-band spoofs and blissful babes babbling on Bob Thompson's *Mmm Nice!*. The depth-of-sound got perfected in *Riot in Rhythm* and *Music for the Weaker Sex* by Henri René and His Orchestra, along with Kenyon Hopkins and the Creed Taylor Orchestra's *Lonelyville: The Nervous Beat* and *Ping, Pang, Pong, The Swinging Ball.*

Command Records had put out a series of *Persuasive Percussion* albums full of more stereo gimmicks masterminded by Enoch Light. Between his stints with the Grand Award and Command labels, he produced such albums as *Big, Bold and Brassy, Persuasive Percussion,* and *Provocative Percussion,* and later the Project 3 ("Total Sound Stereo") series recorded on stereo 35mm film instead of on tape. Between 1957 and 1970, the Enoch Light series produced over thirty chart-making albums.

Many different names traveled through the Enoch Light recording sessions. Terry Snyder and the All-Stars, Command All-Stars, the Light Brigade (from Enoch's radio days), and Enoch Light and the Brass Menagerie. Light's most prominent musicians were Doc Severinsen on trumpet, Tony Mottola and Bucky Pizzarelli on guitars, Stan Freeman on electric harpsichord, and Phil Bodner (who would go on to form "The Brass Ring") on flute.

Light, had wanted originally to be a physician but ended up playing in early radio broadcasts. Tony Mottola remembers: "Enoch was one of the few people who gave the working musician a chance to become a recording artist in his own right. Stereo was just a concept, just a thing with two speakers. He was the first guy to utilize it, first to do it brilliantly, with percussive effects, coming out of left, to right, to center."

Jean-Jacques Perrey and Gershon Kingsley are responsible for bringing the Moog synthesizer into easy-listening pop. Both had disciplined backgrounds before their foray into zany futurism. Perrey, born in the north of France in 1929, pursued music after leaving his ambitions for medicine. Kingsley was educated at the Los Angeles Conservatory of Music, Columbia University, and New York's Juilliard. He was musical director for several Broadway shows and received two Obie awards and two Clios for commercial music before organizing the First Moog Quartet.

Vanguard Records set Perrey & Kingsley up in an experimental New York City laboratory to apply their "electronic sonosyntheses." One CD compilation describes them as "The first music for easy-listening ever recorded on the Moog." Many of their compositions—including "The Unidentified Flying Object," "Electronic Can-Can," "Jungle Blues from Jupiter," and "Girl from Venus"—suggest "Baroque Hoedown," the theme song to Disneyland's Main Street Electrical Parade, which they also composed.

Despite their vaunted weirdness, exotica and space-age bachelor pad music are almost invariably placed in the murky miscellany with the Mantovanis and Winterhalters. They took mood music as far as it could go but, in turn, provided a flashy doorway into the larger easy-listening manse that may seem less "cool" at first but gets equally (if not more) beguiling on closer listen.

That Sex-Behind-the-Gauze Sound

Airport intrigues, groovy discothèques, eroticism of the European cinema . . . these lava-lamp love themes merge easy-listening with Baroque, jazz, bossa-nova, and soft rock, for a timesweep back through the days of the late 'sixties and early 'seventies . . .
Featuring: *Caravelli, Raymond Lefevre, Antonio Carlos Jobim, Francis Lai, Michel Legrand, Paul Mauriat, Sergio Mendez, and Franck Pourcel.*

Once upon a time in 1969, the noises of a simulated orgasm set to music caused an international incident. The song "Je T'Aime . . . Moi Non Plus," recorded by French composer Serge Gainsbourg and British actress/model Jane Birkin, became an instant pop culture classic precisely because, at the time of its release, few people were allowed to hear it. Ears burned around the world as the Vatican denounced it; police in Milan seized it from customs; and the airwaves of Boston, San Francisco, New York, the BBC, and Denmark banned it.

Gainsbourg had previously recorded the song with Brigitte Bardot, but that version was withheld, due to Bardot's after-the-event disapproval. Birkin (who had already shocked middle-class sensibilities only a couple of years earlier with her role in a simulated ambisexual "paper" orgy in Michelangelo Antonioni's *Blow-Up*) had no qualms about joining Gainsbourg for an effusive recording session. With a driving rock bassline and romantic strings, Birkin and Gainsbourg provided the French poetics and slurps, culminating in *her* orgasm and hints of a sequel made possible by *his* endurance. Hard on the heels of all this publicity money couldn't buy, "Je T'Aime" sold well internationally; sales were propelled further through the song's exposure in after-hours clubs, discothèques, and boutiques across Europe and North America. It made #1 in Portugal and inspired subsequent covers by artists as diverse as Ray Conniff and Donna Summer.

This randy contribution from Paris is important for another reason: it demonstrated how creative and outrageous the union of mood music with pop had become by the end of the 1960s. "Je T'Aime" 's popularity parallels that of Claudine Longet, who had used a similar style on her version of "A Man and a Woman." Longet's whispering voice was more of a contour that blended perfectly with her surrounding strings and accordian. The "Je T'Aime" style proved once again that mood music and easy-listening were downright sexy.

The previous year, Paul Mauriat's "Love Is Blue" combined the Percy Faith spirit with European panache and hit #1, selling over 2 million copies within a year. Written by André Popp and Pierre Cour, it started out as an entry in the 1967 Luxembourg Eurovision Song Contest but was destined to be America's first bestselling instrumental since 1963.

With Caravelli, Raymond Lefevre, and Franck Pourcel, Mauriat was among France's four major instrumentalists. He was the "Je T'Aime" era's most intriguing success story. An alumnus of the Marseilles Conservatory, he altered his childhood dream of being a concert pianist at 17 when he got more interested in modern styles from rock to jazz. He formed his own orchestra and toured France and other parts of Europe, before finally settling in Paris, where he soon became Charles Aznavour's arranger.

By adding light classical touches to pop and rock songs, Mauriat revealed a latent musical conservatism that managed to thrive throughout the 1960s. Songs like the Beatles' "Penny Lane," Procol Harum's "A Whiter Shade of Pale," and Herman's Hermits' "A Kind of Hush" contained easily recognizable and often complex melodies that could be adapted to Baroque stylings with little difficulty. This explains why so many different musical charts declared "Love Is Blue" #1 in the United States for seven consecutive weeks.

This French–Baroque pop influence (helped by the novel sound of the Swingle Singers) spread to many radio and television commercials. With it came those late 1960s and early 1970s images of foppish playboys donning ascots, frilly dress shirts, paisley blazers, long sideburns, and an arsenal of syrupy poeticisms.

It also reflected an international mood born of unprecedented travel industry growth. People flew between America and Europe more than ever, and teenagers had the advantage of airline discounts offered to anyone between the ages of 12 and 21. France, in particular, enjoyed most of the glamour. With Charles de Gaulle's political bipolar disorder, the slapstick of the May 1968 student unrest, the media-contrived scandals involving Jean-Luc Godard's "Maoist" cinema, and the semi-grounded fears that the French now had a nuclear weapons arsenal, the country exported a more fun-loving self-image to ward off potential critics.

The sex-behind-the-gauze sound varied from the orchestral majesty of Raymond LeFevre's "Âme Câline" to the discothèque guitars of "No Matter What Shape (Your's Stomach's In)," recorded in 1965 by the T-Bones from a hip Alka-Seltzer commercial jingle. Such catchy styles helped smooth out the rough edges of 1960s and early '70s counterculture (which soon looked remarkably dated, anyway). It was a sound premised on the salability of pretty locales, beautiful people, complicated yet never kinky sexuality, the studied urbanity of international fashion shows and style magazines, and the prevailing rhetorical atmosphere of constant profundities that threatened to change our lives but never materialized.

Aside from the musicians and some crafty record producers, the greatest proselytizer for Franco-Brazilian seduction music was filmmaker Claude Lelouch. This renegade free-spirit obtained a movie camera the day after he failed his college exam and proceeded to make anti-capitalist documentaries and low-budget erotic thrillers, before winning worldwide respect in 1966 with *A Man and a Woman.* This film tells the story of a love affair between a widow and a race-car driver who struggle to find each other in a labyrinth of montages, pregnant close-ups, and the general ambiance of an existential television commercial. Lelouch's film would never have been such a success, however, without Francis Lai's never-to-be-forgotten score.

Francis Lai began as a songwriter for Yves Montand and a piano accompanist for Edith Piaf, for whom he wrote such songs as "The Right to Love," "Take Me With You," and "The Dirty Little

Canal." His main *A Man and a Woman* theme (co-written with Pierre Barouh) combined Electravox piano, and a constant yet bewitching volley of Gregorian cocktail la-la-las. Lai's entire score was built on the ever-present strings, with additional support from organ, horns, electric bass, pop percussion, and an occasional acoustical guitar. But *A Man and a Woman*'s imitation of Antonio Carlos Jobim's Brazilian beat had just the right amount of ethnic anomaly to render it disturbingly alluring and ambiguous. This became the ideal music for representing international jet-setters who, like the film's protagonists, sleep then fight one moment, conduct soul-searches the next, but always manage to catch the next racing car or plane on their itinerary.

The Franco-Brazilian charm of songs like "Theme from *A Man and a Woman*" and "Love Is Stronger Far Than We" surfaced again and again in such popular permutations as the theme song for Yardley of London cosmetics (heard regularly in commercial breaks during episodes of *The Monkees*), the Brass Ring's "The Disadvantages of You" for Benson & Hedges 100's cigarettes, and the Mason Williams–Nancy Ames theme for *The Smothers Brothers Comedy Hour* (sung by the Anita Kerr Singers during the first shows). Sergio Mendes's collaborations with Jobim on such albums as *The Swinger from Rio* prepared us for his Brasil '66 group and their Euro-bossa-nova covers of songs like Burt Bacharach and Hal David's "The Look of Love" and the Beatles' "The Fool on the Hill."

The follow-up Lelouch and Lai collaboration, *Live for Life*, cast Yves Montand as a media reporter in love with a kittenish model played by Candice Bergen. Here again, the film score stresses musical images that suggest but never commit, with all metaphysical hunger sated by airy yet filling layers of *l'amour*.

Lai's transition from Franco-Brazilian sophistication to the more sentimental *Love Story* period was rewarded when he was nominated for an Oscar for his composition of the 1971 film's main song. In 1977, Lai teamed up with director David Hamilton (who had made a name for himself with soft-focus nudie coffee-table books) to score the film *Bilitis*. At this juncture, Lai attained his sex-behind-the-gauze perfection.

Sex-behind-the-gauze music and movies became an ongoing market by the early seventies. Serge Gainsbourg composed the score for Claude Berri's 1972 film *The Sex Shop* while Pierre Bachelet and Hervé Roy gave us the haunting and hypnotically repetitive soundtrack to Just Jaeckin's *Emmanuelle* in 1974. This movie followed the picaresque adventures of a ravishing French tart who traipses from France to the night clubs and opium dens of Thailand. Gainsbourg went on to work with Jaeckin in scoring the 1977 film *Madame Claude* and one of several *Emmanuelle* sequels, *Goodbye Emmanuelle* (directed by François Leterrier) that same year.

Another influential Frenchman was Michel Legrand. A pianist, composer, and one-time Swingle Singer, Legrand wrote music for the films *The Umbrellas of Cherbourg*, *The Go-Between*, and *The Thomas Crown Affair*. His "The Windmills of Your Mind" won an Oscar for best song. He is probably most remembered for his best score Oscar in 1971 for *Summer of '42*. The Lai–Legrand presence is obvious on the Barry DeVorzon–Perry Botkin collaboration for the music to *Bless the Beasts and Children,* later known as the theme song to both the soap opera *The Young and the Restless* and the background score for Romanian gymnast Nadia Comaneci.

Credit for easy-listening's excursion into the pop market does not go only to France and Brazil. Back in 1962, Riz Ortolani and Nino Oliviero's score for the Italian cult documentary *Mondo Cane* gave birth to "More." The Italians also gave us Nini Rosso's melancholy but gorgeous trumpet ballads and the music of Ennio Morricone, who paired spaghetti westerns with melodies so Esperanto and eclectic that they appeared to have been composed on another planet in "the Earthling style."

Sex-behind-the-gauze continued with Gato Barbieri's theme to *Last Tango in Paris* and even slipped into some of Giorgio Moroder's Euro-disco mannerisms. Disco was the last bastion of gauzy eroticism, with its track-lit dancefloors, spinning ball of mirrors, layered orchestrations, and the choral backings of Donna Summer and former porn star Andrea True of the Andrea True Connection—not to mention the millions of stray voices mouthing "Love To Love You Baby" and "More, More, More."

Brigadier General George Owen Squier, the father of Muzak.® (Courtesy of the National Archives, Washington, D.C.)

This Muzak® ad (ca. 1950s) is from an earlier time when the company focused on psychological programming. Decades later, Muzak changed its emphasis from psychology and science to a multichannel music menu that stresses what it refers to as "Audio Architecture—the art of capturing the emotional power of music and putting it to work for clients." (Reprinted with the Permission of Muzak LLC) (Special thanks to Louise Milmann.)

THEY SHALL HAVE MUSIC.

Want to have your spirit elevated too? Then ride in an
elevator that plays music by 'Muzak'. Something new? Quite.
In the Beggs Building in Columbus, Ohio; and in the Palmolive
Building in Chicago, among others, the cares of the business
day are now wafted away on the notes of a lilting melody.

This section of a 1947
Otis Elevator ad
shows how elevators
and Music by Muzak
were matching
aesthetics in a
technologically
changing world.
(Courtesy of the Otis
Collection, Otis
Elevator Company/
United Technologies
Historic Archives.)

Annunzio Paolo Mantovani, along with his arranger and fellow composer Ronald Binge, devised a method of having a 40-piece orchestra simulate studio reverberation, with one violin section's melody note overlapping the next for an effect he compared to the acoustics of a cathedral. As a result, his layered strings brought Heaven to vinyl. (Photo reproduced by Permission of the Music Division, New York Public Library for the Performing Arts, and the Astor, Lenox, and Tilden Foundation.)

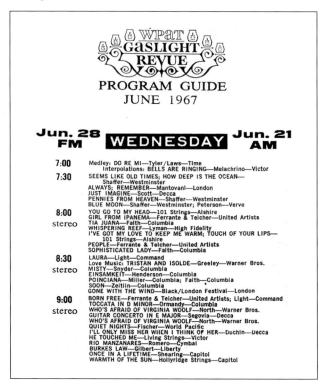

Courtesy of the Jed Hacker Collection

MUSIC FOR NIGHT PEOPLE

WGAY STEREO

(Stay with us after the clock strikes twelve. We promise you won't turn into a pumpkin)

WGAY-Stereo plays beautiful mood music, twenty four hours a day. It's always nice to hear, but somehow it's especially beautiful once the clock strikes twelve. You can work, play, dream with it—and do a little wishing too. Late nighters stay up with us. All nighters live with us. Early risers wake up with us. Some people we know couldn't make it from midnight to dawn without WGAY.

99.5 FM   50,000 WATTS

A Connie B. Gay Station

Some of the most cherished Beautiful Music memories are reserved for WGAY, which served the Washington, D.C., area. Its story began in April of 1959, when, under the call letters WQMR (Washington's Quality Music Radio), the 1,000-watt daytime AM channel began broadcasting back-to-back mood music. Live announcers spinning real turntables had to follow closely scripted guidelines so as not to interfere with the acoustic spell of instrumental Broadway, Hollywood, and standard Tin Pan Alley tunes, not to mention the harps that played short wisps of the "WQMR Concerto" between every record. The call letters WGAY returned in April of 1961, with the christening of a brand new 20,000-watt FM station located securely at 99.5. This static-free and (at least for a while) sponsor-free fare ran from 6:00 a.m. to midnight with dream themes by such artists as Frank DeVol, Percy Faith, Andre Kostelanetz, and Henry Mancini. In 1966, Bob Chandler became the operations director of what would soon be touted as "Washington's ONLY 50,000-watt stereo station." Chandler helped the format move on by the late sixties and early seventies from tried-and-true older songs to nice, custom-made instrumental interpretations of what were then "current" pop and rock favorites. After Chandler retired in 1990, WGAY, like many stations playing similar formats, submitted to "adult contemporary" intimidation. (Courtesy of the Bill Halvorsen Collection.)

Ideal moods from the Mystic Moods Orchestra. (©Mobile Fidelity Sound Lab, reprinted with permission.)

Is this sincere promotion or smug parody? Regardless, this pastiche of an ad, which appeared in the March 1996 issue of Britain's *Record Collector* in a special feature on "Easy Listening and Space-Age Pop," proclaims mood music's physical and psychological advantages. (Courtesy of *Record Collector*, design: Val Cutts.)

THANK YOU FOR THE MUSIC

film about **MUZAK**

Finnish director Mika Taanila was partly inspired by this book when in 1997 he made *Thank You for the Music*, a short documentary about Muzak, Philips Background Music Services, and easy-listening in general. He was aghast when, after its premiere screening in Helsinki, several snobs complimented him on such a philosophically and gratifying movie despite "that awful, soft music." Taanila recounts another priceless moment: "A representative of the Finnish Musicians' Union pointed out to me on that occasion that 'the film is absolutely great, but why did you use such tasteless music on the soundtrack?' I was speechless, of course. I guess he was sleeping through the 24 minutes of the film. Or maybe he could not read the subtitles." (Courtesy of Mika Taanila and For Real Productions Ltd., poster designed by Timo Mänttäri.)

9 / World Music Originals

THE 101 STRINGS AND THE MYSTIC MOODS ORCHESTRA

The 101 Strings and the Mystic Moods Orchestra stand as two lustrous American institutions unsurpassed in the arts of *packaging* and *atmospherics*—the vodka and tonic of every good mood music concoction.

Responsible for what is essentially the *original* world music, the 101 Strings capture the global aspirations of today's "world" sound but without any pretense to ethnomusicological "accuracy." Theirs is a *wider*, more overtly American world view—a macrocosm incarnate, now gobbling up nations and cultures; now regurgitating them into readily recognizable sounds and symbols; now grooming, duplicating, and selling them in the discount racks of Woolworth's, K-Mart, and other mainstream emporia at budget prices.

The 101 Strings do not practice any tongue-in-cheek exotica game. The Martin Dennys of yesteryear may have fooled around with ersatz jungle beasts and cultural cartooning, but the 101 Strings concentrate earnestly (and consequently much more successfully) on giving Middle America an exact replica of the world it wants.

Niceties of history, anthropology, and (of course) musicology became as moribund and dusty as mummy tissue exposed to oxygen when the 101 Strings released their first hit album *The Soul of Spain*. This Iberian "tapestry of emotional colors and contrasts" features dashes of Flamenco and folk song overwhelmed by an ever-present orchestra that lingers from the "Malagueña" opener to the "Sunday in Seville" finale. What we hear is the true Spain of Don Quixote and Ferdinand the Bull—a wish-fulfillment fantasy that thrives in storybooks, the cinema, and restaurant menus.

The 101 Strings' *Soul of . . .* series captured Les Baxter's "feel" for foreign lands as culled and reassembled from Hollywood/ Broadway stockpiles of color-treated sunsets, papier-mâché pyramids, and polystyrene Parthenons. Yet the Strings went much farther, by exoticizing Europe: letting it stand out in all the theme-park charm imagined by its second- and third-generation immigrant offspring.

With their practiced hands on the market's pulse for orchestral porridge and ethnic spice, the 101 Strings proceeded to capture the souls of Mexico, Greece, Russia, Scotland, and Israel on vinyl before pursuing more domestic themes such as *Hit Sounds from Hit Movies* and *The Sounds of Love*.

All of the so-called authentic instruments and rhythms on 101 Strings albums prove most effective as props for a secondhand sightseeing tour where, again, the postcard is the looking glass. For instance, in *The Emotion of the 101 Strings at Gypsy Camp Fires*, "Dark Eyes" starts with the Hungarian violin buttressed by a vocal chorus, cascading strings, brass, and accordion. Before we know it, the "lights on dimmers and gypsy violins offstage" cliché touted by the cynical theater critic in the movie *All About Eve* has materialized in our stereo-friendly living rooms.

Though the orchestra dominates, *Gypsy Camp Fires* uses just enough local color to evoke "Olive-skinned girls, with flashing dark eyes." Old Hungary is paired down to simulations of already simulated source material. "Brahms' Hungarian Dance No. 6" is followed by Victor Young's "Golden Earrings" from the movie of the same name, whose gypsy is played by a dyed-brunette Marlene Dietrich. As in all 101 Strings recordings, the festive liner notes (deployed with Cook's Tour fervency) complement the music: "The lovely rich tones of a violin fill the heart as it speaks of love that is old, new, lost, or yet to be discovered; for the music of the gypsy speaks of a spirit that is restless, free and beautiful."

East of Suez captures an Arabian Desert expanse more congenial to the duets of Kathryn Grayson and Gordon MacRae in the musical *Desert Song* than to the arena of violent Biblical prophecy it represents today. *I Love Paris (The Sounds and Moods of the City of Light)* includes "Frère Jacques," "Under Paris Skies," and other metaphor-melodies about things quintessentially "French." Here, bearing "all the charm and flirtatious caprice of La Vie de Paris," the ensemble "paints a picture of your unforgettable impressions of the city of light. From *Sacré-Coeur* atop *Montmartre* to a stroll down the *Champs Élysée*—this is *Paris*, home of painter, dreamer and everyone who has ever been in love."

Hawaiian Paradise includes sea sounds and "The Beachcomber Chorus" vaporizing in and out of exuberant Polynesian ditties such as "Little Grass Shack," "Sweet Leilani," and "Lovely Hula Hands." *Caribbean Cruise* (wherein the 101 Strings masquerade as "The Rio Carnival Orchestra") offers "A High Fidelity Travel Panorama" in "Spectra-Sound," featuring "Shipboard Romance," "Jamaica Jamboree," and "Club Tropicana," to name but a few. Each track captures the lure of this hot, moist, mysterious land "with its moon drenched nights filled with thoughts of love and strange voodoo secrets."

Not long ago, a school of anthropologists propounded a "village theory" based on the results of a widely distributed questionnaire.

It revealed that most people in the well-traveled Western hemisphere share the same limited range of significant experiences as those in small, hut-bound African villages. The average person in each setting is allotted two important lovers, two teachers, a memorable doctor during childhood and another during adulthood, an impressive religious figure, two best friends, perhaps one special family member, and one or two outstanding puberty rites. From there, we must each rely on our imaginative impressions of the outside world to define ourselves as individuals. In this sense, the 101 Strings are right on target when a "village" treatment such as *Italia con Amore (From Italy with Love)* contains musical strains and rhythms interchangeable with those found on *Caribbean Nights, Mood Vienna, Songs of the Seasons in Japan, African Safari,* and *Americana.*

Even the more miserable pages of world history have Strings attached. Their remarkable adaptation of Edmond De Luca's *Conquerors of the Ages* arranges violins and woodwinds to accompany Alexander the Great's invasion of Thrace; oboe solos as Rome forges her Byzantine Empire; ear-splitting percussion to attend Attila the Hun's sweep through Central Europe; a gong for Genghis Khan; a brass crescendo for Cortez; the "Marseillaise" to honor Napoleon; and the "Sieg Heil" operettas of Hitler's beer-hall putsch.

When they began in the early 1950s, the 101 Strings recorded at the Musikhalle in Hamburg, Germany, under director Dick L. Miller, arranger Joseph Kuhn, and conductor Wilhelm Stephan. They were billed as "The World's First Stereo Scored Orchestra," brandishing the latest in binaural technology with their Stereo-Fidelity sound spectrum.

The cover of *101 Strings Play the World's Great Standards,* arguably the first 101 Strings entry, shows a photo taken in Germany during a 1957 recording session. It shows approximately 121 musicians, including "eleven concertmeisters in the first chairs," and a conductor. The men are wearing tuxedos, tails, and white bowties; the two female harp players are garbed in long black gowns.

Three years after their inception, the 101 Strings were marketing their product to at least twenty-eight countries, selling over 10 million albums. Their contribution to stereo-mania came second only to their wanderlust. Like Mantovani, they modernized the classics by exposing them to new acoustic technology, by experimenting with the "stereo depth" of microphones, and by practicing the art of layering to generate sounds rarely heard at live concerts. The liner notes to their albums came with cryptic graphs of a sound spectrum ("all the human ear can sense and hear") ranging from 30 to 16,000 cycles of vibration per second.

The fundamental 101 Strings arrangement depended on a meticulous procedure. According to Robert Lowden, a Strings conductor and arranger from 1957 until 1967: "We would try to make a Chopin piece contemporary and more danceable. We did the classics in a more modern style, making the music less dense. The melody was important. Low strings played a melody, and high strings played a counter-melody. That was the shtick of the 101 Strings; then it would alternate."

In 1964, Al Sherman and Alshire International bought the 101 Strings and moved the recording sessions from Germany to London. Thenceforth, the Strings were made up principally of British session musicians from the London Philharmonic and the London Symphony Orchestra, and were never a "set" ensemble. After Joseph Kuhn died at the age of 34 from a spinal tumor, composer Monty Kelly took over the arrangements and masterminded a new packaging scheme, with the "Stereo Fidelity" tag.

Kelly also had a flair for embedding the "inimitable style" of his own compositions between famous cover songs whose lyrics he reworked into titles. His "When the Trees That Are Green Turn to Brown" and "Trav'lin Again" had enough of a "Sounds of Silence" style to fit on *101 Strings Play Million Seller Hits of Today Composed by Simon and Garfunkel.* Another Lowden original called "Orange Grove Avenue," besides being a gloss on Simon and Garfunkel, was the address of Budget Sound, Inc., the Burbank location where all of the Alshire records were pressed.

On *The 101 Strings Play the Hits of the Beatles,* songs like "Sixpence and You" and "Tropic of Chelsea" made great strides to fit in unobtrusively among the actual Beatles melodies. The

Strings could play funny games with unwary listeners who might believe that such songs as "Freeway Fantasy," "Pandora's Smile," and "Torna Sundra" were real screen themes on *Hit Sounds from Hit Movies*. *The Sounds of Today* attempted to bridge the generation gap by incorporating electric guitars, sitars, and psychedelic organs into lush versions of "California Dreamin'," "Never My Love," and one priceless original called "Blues for the Guru."

Lowden looks back on the 101 Strings of the 1960s and early 1970s as a cultural panacea: "I think it was a market for a certain people. During the Viet Nam war, it helped to cool things down a bit. An awful lot of records sold, around 50 million. Alshire put albums out for everybody: big-band aficionados, mood music people, rock people."

To prove that our own backyards are just as committed to cine-memory, the 101 Strings' interpretation of the *Grand Canyon Suite* continues Ferde Grofé's attempt to miniaturize one of America's vast tourist treasures into snippets of theme songs that were subsequently played over and over on television shows and commercials.

The 101 Strings managed to reproduce America as it might be seen through the eyes of touring foreigners. Their music elicits a feeling akin to the one we experience when watching German tourists visiting the micro-Bavaria at Busch Gardens. The world America thought it had conquered and flattered through imitation flatters it back with French intellectuals deconstructing the cowboy, Japanese entertainers impersonating Vegas lounge singers, or Saudi Arabian and Indian adventure movies that ape American culture but never get it quite right, since they lack the precise intricacies of dress, gesture, and language to which we cling for identity.

Inside-out Americana abounded in the 101 Strings' releases of doppelgänger easy-listening versions of almost every conceivable genre and composer: Broadway shows; film scores; pop classics; country and western; covers of compositions by Victor Herbert, Nelson Riddle, Burt Bacharach, Hank Williams, Jimmy Webb, and Carole King; wedding songs; soul; marches; hymns and prayers;

music of the Catholic church; big-band Swing; outer-space themes; and countless tributes to such stars as John Wayne, Elvis Presley, Richard Rodgers, Dolly Parton, the Dorseys, Otis Redding, Glenn Miller, the Beach Boys, the Carpenters, and of course the eponymous honorees of *Hits Made Famous by Gladys Knight and Stevie Wonder.*

By the early 1970s, the 101 Strings responded to the "Je T'Aime" trend by following the by now well-rutted trail into the regions of eros. They pressed a couple of X-rated singles on Alshire's A/S label; then they released *The Sounds of Love* under the name "101 Strings Orchestra." It included Bebe Bardon's all-breath-no-words interpretations of various sexy pop hits, including a version of "Je T'Aime . . . Moi Non Plus" reworked into "Love at First Sight." *The Sounds of Love* alternated Bardon's sigh-a-longs with Joe Adams, a Peter Lawford sound-alike, poeticizing about wistful, unrequited love over instrumentals of "This Guy's in Love with You" and "Yesterday."

The Strings followed with *The "Exotic" Sounds of Love,* a much more flagrant and kinky affront to their wholesome-music-missionary position in the mood music cosmos. Embellished with an "Adults Only" warning, the jacket cover shows an eager young woman's head being held by an out-of-frame male; the inside cover gal is a leather-clad dominatrix wearing an eye-patch. Each track gets the *Emmanuelle*-in-Hell treatment with the sound of martinets and masochists on "Whiplash" or the Oriental porno-mystique of "Karma Sitar" and "Instant Nirvana."

Despite their assembly-line zeal, the 101 Strings were seldom predictable. Each album encompassed specialized styles and musical instruments to go with each theme. *Astro Sounds* proceeded to colonize the cosmos with an aggregation of noises inspired by budget science-fiction movies. With liner notes billing it as "the far out sounds of tomorrow's uncharted trip beyond the now generation," *Astro Sounds* combines "The Astro-Sounds of Magnificence" with guitar distortion. But tracks like "Astral Freakout," "A Disappointing Love with a Desensitized Robot," "Trippin' on Lunar 07," and "Bad Trip Back to '69" did not strike a homey chord with the typical 101 Strings crowd. According to Al Sherman: "We had many weird albums like *Astro Sounds,* but got so many letters from the midwest objecting to the zany formats that we stopped."

In contrast to the 101 Strings' macrocosm, The Mystic Moods Orchestra appropriated the microcosm. Using the most advanced audio equipment, it treated music as a backdrop to everyday life's "authentic" sounds—thunderstorms, ocean waves, trains, auto races, horses, cattle, footsteps, and the minutiae of insects. Instead of using music to mask noise, the Mystic Moods Orchestra tricked the ear by putting the noise right into the music.

The Mystic Moods Orchestra is significant for many reasons. It was among the very first ensembles to use on-location sound effects for musical purposes, although it was predated by Snuff Garrett's *Lonely Harpsichord on a Rainy Night.* The Mystic Moods' audio technology anticipated many of the four-channel sound environments currently being developed by HDS (High Definition Surround), IMAX, and other businesses specializing in home theaters and theme park simulators.

Mystic Moods inspiration comes from sound technician and producer Leo Kulka. In 1961, while in Burbank, California, Kulka used two stereo mikes and an Ampex tape machine to record a violent storm outside his bedroom window. He subsequently played the tape whenever he needed to relax.

Moving from Los Angeles to San Francisco in 1964, Kulka opened a studio and started experimenting with storms and other sound-effects combined with his favorite music. He converted the results through a four-channel recorder. Music and effects accounted for three of the channels, while the fourth contained wind-chimes and subtle percussion. Kulka timed the songs and the storm so that thundercracks and musical crescendos coincided.

These sessions formed the Mystic Moods prototype. Kulka claims to have previously done arrangements for Muzak and contributed recordings and mix-downs for Chicago's background music company Seeburg between 1960 and 1961. With the help of arranger Larry Fotine, Kulka arrived at a folk remedy for the proper background music formula: "I take a popular tune and turn it upside down and inside out. The result: you're sure you've heard the song before, but cannot identify it because it doesn't sound the same."

In 1959, Kulka indulged in a naughty little experiment that involved recording the piston pops of oil wells on Long Beach, exploiting their coital associations, and marketing an X-rated gem sold under the bar at Nick O'Dell's restaurant in Hollywood. A somewhat prurient gentleman by nature, Kulka later made a record of romantic Wurlitzer tracks called *Organasm* that the Postmaster of Illinois confiscated as "obscene." It therefore comes as no surprise that the Mystic Moods Orchestra packs such a psychosexual punch.

Not until he teamed up with sound-effects wizard Brad Miller, however, did Kulka's concept really come to life. In 1965, Kulka and Miller mastered a series of similar four-channel tapes and installed them at the San Francisco Airport's Hilton Inn.

The Hilton had a large, circular cocktail lounge on the top floor called "The Tiger Room," which Kulka and Miller proceeded to divide into four sections, subdividing each section into ten windows and equipping each window with an equalizer filter connected to different-colored lights that were, in turn, analyzed into ten frequency octaves. The bass descended to deep red, and the higher frequencies grew lighter up to white. With some of their tapes connected to the equalizer, they attempted to make a prehippie light show for the scotch-and-soda crowd. To add to the illusion, they applied perfumes and the smell of new-mown hay throughout the room, turning up the air-conditioner not only to make the room cooler but to complement the sound of rain.

Kulka says that he and Miller had hoped to market this as a "synaesthesia": "When the brain gets so confused, you don't know whether you're seeing lights or seeing sounds. When designing the Hilton program, we stayed away from pulsation and stuck to melodic sounds that kept the lights mostly in the red. We used big orchestras and string basses. The ear delights in variety; so does the eye. I always saw music in color."

At first, Kulka and Miller saw their ideal venue as being Las Vegas night clubs. Some Vegas club representatives sat through a demonstration and loved it, but they declined to install it in their own establishments because they noticed that the Tiger Room patrons were spending too much time watching and listening, instead of drinking. Moreover, the Tiger Room management began to tinker with the system design. "They decided the music we provided wasn't sufficient," Kulka claims. "Against my wishes, they used a rock band. But it did not work. If you confuse the mind too much, you can evoke a *petit mal* seizure."

Someone at the Tiger Room did have such an attack one day, forcing the Hilton management to throw the entire system out. Another petit mal incubus occurred when Kulka demonstrated his synaesthesia system to the Audio Engineering Society. Someone in the audience rapped his cane on the table and complained of a near epileptic seizure, due to the constant, pulsating rhythm of a jazz tune. Kulka recalls the incident with bemused embarrassment: "A doctor friend, a psychiatrist, later told me that kind of pulsation might create problems. I've gone into markets, telling them they are killing their business with high-speed rock."

With their Las Vegas ambitions shattered, Kulka and Miller decided to repackage the product for the retail record market as a kind of "total home theater." Their big break came when deejay Ernie McDaniel, a good friend of theirs at San Francisco's KFOG radio station, agreed to play some of their tapes for a lark.

Brad Miller, who would go on to produce, engineer, and record subsequent Mystic Moods ventures, remembers how lucky they were: "In the mid-'60s, FM stereo was the new toy on the block. McDaniel was at KFOG and had a free-for-all show in the evening. We took a copy of the master tape to the radio show one night, and the phones went nuts!"

People called in to tell about the memories the music inspired, the delightful romantic evenings it spawned, and their conviction that it was the safest form of an artificially altered state. To show appreciation for the community's zeal, Kulka and Miller left it up to the listeners to determine the ensemble's name. "Mystic Moods Orchestra" was the winner from a pile of over 100 entries.

Kulka and Miller took the Mystic Moods concept to Chicago and approached Mercury Records, which listened to the music and laughed. Undaunted, they approached Mercury's Philips subsidiary, which was more receptive. Weeks went by, until one evening when the Philips A&R man, accompanied by his wife, telephoned Kulka from San Francisco's Fisherman's Wharf. Kulka recalls: "The man came to see me, dripping with water from a big rain storm. He started railing because he couldn't get a cab and that the tape I sent him started out with rain and thunder. He kept complaining, but his wife said to him, 'Shut up and listen!' "

The first Mystic Moods release was the album *One Stormy Night*, recorded at Gold Star, the studio Phil Spector made famous. The ensemble consisted mostly of freelancing Los Angeles musicians playing standards like "Autumn Leaves" and "Sayonara," along with a library of backlog songs not used for their intended movies. Miller clarifies that: "The orchestra was a nondescript group of players which I assembled. It was really built around arrangements, not a fixed orchestra."

One Stormy Night promised among many things "a time of soft and glowing sentimentality when the drops tapped out their special message on the window pane." What could easily have been a fluky experiment with very little commercial potential drew many more adherents than ever expected. Although *One Stormy Night* (the most successful of the series) only inched its way to about 63 on the charts, the Mystic Moods had already become legendary.

Both Kulka and Miller insist that the orchestra, while important, was always subordinate to the sounds. According to Miller:

> *Many radio people in that era thought the sound effects were annoying. The Philips people always said that, if I took the sound effects off, people would like them more. But I took them off, and they didn't play them any more or less. I'm not really Mancini or competing with Percy Faith. This is very unique with a special niche. I'm not suggesting it was original. On AM radio, we didn't work at all because the rain sounded like frying bacon. This whole concept was really directed at hi-fi and FM stereo. My forte has always been realism and quality.*

Recalling the listening public's reaction to *One Stormy Night,* Kulka told a special anecdote: "I'm sitting at the Bohemian Club. One man sits beside me with his drink and comments on *One Stormy Night.* He bought it, took it home, brought a girl to his house. He complained about the sound of a freight train during his seduction and the girlfriend bursting out laughing. He told me he'd like to get his hands on the guy who made it. And there I was."

Miller took full control of engineering in time for the recording sessions of *Nighttide,* the second Mystic Moods Orchestra album. *Nighttide* was, in some respects, a more ambitious effort, with great songs from the cinema such as "Theme from *A Summer Place,*" "Days of Wine and Roses," "Nevada Smith," and "Lara's Theme" (from *Dr. Zhivago*) paired with appropriate sounds ranging from pounding surf to horses. Miller had gone to specific locations for each effect. All beach settings were recorded at Carmel's Monterey Bay. The crickets chirping on "Strangers in the Night" were recorded on an autumn evening in a setting overlooking Hollywood Hills; the horses neighing and galloping into the opening bars of "Shane" were miked at Southern California's Santa Susana Pass–Chatsworth section, a former Chumash Indian gathering site turned movie ranch for westerns.

The cinematic theme continued into the third album, *More Than Music.* A trademark Moods thundercrack introduces John Barry's tune "Wednesday's Child" from *The Quiller Memorandum.* The theme song from Cinerama's *Grand Prix* includes a sense-submersion effect of race cars roaring from right to left. A marching band accompanies "Paris Smiles" from *Is Paris Burning?,* until crashing waves introduce the "Theme from *The Sand Pebbles.*"

The Mystic Moods of Love —re-released as *Moods for a Stormy Night*—came with a specially scented cloth to enhance the listeners' pheromones in case the amorous audio was not enough. It climaxes with Wagner's "Tristan and Isolde" played over cricket mating chirps. *Love Token* fuses heavy orchestrals with trippy electric guitar to cover "Both Sides Now," "Hurt So Bad," and a "Jimmy Webb Collage."

Arriving contemporaneously with the poetry-and-music collaboration between Rod McKuen and Anita Kerr on their album trilogy of *The Sea, The Sky,* and *The Earth* was the Mystic Mood Orchestra's *Highway One,* which offered brief interludes of mood music blending with the sounds of midways and seaside resorts. The narrator, Rosko (a New York deejay, the voice on many Busch beer commercials, and a recent CBS announcer for the Winter Olympics), speaks to what seems an imaginary woman, his words suggesting the ravings of a desperately kitsch Casanova or a psychopathic voyeur. Location sounds on a beach and at a carnival boardwalk in Britain taunt us in the background as we try to decipher some coded meaning in such poetaster brainstorms as "My fingers as I wandered into your private love affair. . . . "

The Mystic Moods Orchestra always managed to employ expert studio musicians for a sound-and-sense feast that gave pleasure to the young and the middle-aged alike—just in time for San Francisco's "Summer of Love." "A young, hip crowd was interested," Miller recalls when asked to explain how acid rockers could slide with such ease into mystic easy-listening:

> *I was in downtown San Francisco in 1966.* One Stormy Night *was released in March of that year. It was already top ten in the Bay Area. I was in an elevator, and here was this young lady about 20 years old who had a copy under her arm. Part of the pop culture at that time was going through experimentation. All music has classical origins. So, the pop culture at that time was trying to provide more texture as opposed to the usual electric rock bands.*

If the electronic experiments of Perrey & Kingsley constituted space-age bachelor pad music, the specialized sound explorations of the Mystic Moods Orchestra were psychedelic crash pad symphonies that used the stereo sensorium instead of drugs for mind expansion. The Mystic Moods philosophy was very similar to Timothy Leary's dictum that "set and setting" were essential for the right psychochemical excursion. Before the appearance of the

Beatles' *Sergeant Pepper's Lonely Hearts Club Band* and of the Moody Blues' *Days of Future Passed* (which used the London Festival Orchestra), the Mystic Moods Orchestra encouraged young people to leave the dance floor and float in an acoustically carpeted hole where the rain never gets in but can be heard all the same. The Mystic Moods may well have been an indirect impetus for Pink Floyd's *Dark Side of the Moon,* a musical story interwoven with constant background noise and dialogue.

The ambiance of lovemaking was always a crucial part of Mystic Moods recordings. Their erotic adventures graduated in the 1970s to soft-core pornography when a later distributor called Soundbird added a pull-out jacket sleeve to a reissued collection called *Touch,* to reveal two naked lovers about to embrace (perhaps in tribute to John and Yoko's *Two Virgins*).

The Mystic Moods Orchestra, in various incarnations, released close to twenty albums. Ironically, as the albums strove to become more "hip" (adding funk bands, combos, and so on), their popularity declined. In 1990, Brad Miller unveiled the first Mystic Moods album in fifteen years, with the orchestra reincarnated as a single grand piano played by Renée Hamaty against a turbulent seashore. The original intent—to make the sound effects just as important as the music returned. *Stormy Memories* shows that the Mystic Moods live on.

Music producer Don Graham stood before a *Billboard* new-age conference in the early eighties and proclaimed that the Mystic Moods Orchestra was the original new-age music concept. Today, amidst experiments in SurroundSound, wide-screen atmospherics, and other theme-park attractions, the Mystic Moods have once again proved to be ahead of their time.

When the world is seen through the anthropology of the 101 Strings and the psychoacoustics of the Mystic Moods, the words of Peter Crane, an IMAX publicist, make all the more sense: "With wide-screen simulators, you can see the Grand Canyon without worrying about the weather conditions, the 3 million other annual tourists or whether you'll fall off the edge. Besides just looking, you can get the history and geology of the place, all in three minutes for around five dollars. It's a different way of seeing reality."

The 101 Strings, the Mystic Moods Orchestra and the myriad technologies executed in their spirit do not duplicate the world so much as replace it.

10 / Walls Talk!

I'm not in the least musical; I don't own a record player or a single cassette. In fact, I used to be the despair of my girlfriend when we traveled because I so clearly enjoyed canned music and used to turn it on in hotel rooms. But the subject is fascinating—all part of mood-control. For me the intentions of background music are openly political, and an example of how political power is constantly shifting from the ballot box into areas where the voter has nowhere to mark his ballot paper. The most important political choices in the future will probably never be consciously exercised. I'm intrigued by the way some background music is surprisingly aggressive, especially that played on consumer complaint phone lines and banks, airlines and phone companies themselves, with strident, non-rhythmic and arms-length sequences that are definitely not user-friendly . . .

—J. G. Ballard

As Saigon fell in April of 1975, U.S. envoys and Vietnamese refugees scrambled to the American Embassy rooftop as U.S. helicopters hovered down to rescue them from the approaching Viet Cong. The Embassy was deserted—an epitaph to Western ambitions—its corridors carpeted with broken window glass as paper money, bureaucratic documents, and personal ledgers rustled in the wind. But amid the chaos and desolation, the Embassy's Muzak® system remained undisturbed, playing on like a tree falling in an abandoned forest, heard by none but making its global impact just the same.

Once again, Muzak had proved itself to be a beacon of order

in a world gone mad. These days from the late 1960s to the early 1970s were, in fact, among Muzak's finest hours. LBJ (nostalgic for his Austin franchise) had Muzak installed at his ranch. With the passing of the Presidential torch at the 1969 Inauguration, the Nixon Administration had Muzak broadcast from loudspeakers into Capitol Hill's open air. The Polaris submarines played Muzak to ease the pressures on crew members during their hair-trigger missile watch; and the U.S. Armed Forces listed Muzak among its "Optional Equipment."

Muzak served forty-three of the world's fifty biggest industrial companies. Germany, France, Great Britain, Spain, Norway, Finland, and Denmark shared the European market; Argentina, Uruguay, and Peru covered South America; and then there were the United States, Canada, and Israel. Total Muzak earnings exceeded $400 million per year. And as if the world were not big enough, Buzz Aldrin and Neil Armstrong listened to it on their Apollo lunar cruise.

How did Muzak do it? What special, secret, and magical formula has enabled the music that everyone supposedly hates to please so many? One Muzak programmer suggests an answer: "When musicians are left to themselves to make art for the sake of art, not considering public taste, demographics or psychology, they will put together something that won't please everyone. My task is to amalgamate tastes. Imagine trying to please 80 or 90 million different viewpoints of the way things should be."

In his autobiography *Altered States*, British film director Ken Russell hit upon this very delicate balance. He discussed an "unmade script" called *Music, Music, Music* in which a young composer desperate to make a living "resorts to writing Muzak for TV commercials, resulting in a crackup with all the products associated with his jingles, including baked beans, detergent and chocolate, all erupting through the TV screen and engulfing him in goo."

When a company must take such elaborate steps to make music that enables denizens of the workaday world to feel relaxed and invigorated at the same time, the "normal" can become downright hair-raising. Muzak has to pick and choose modes and selections stimulating enough to keep people engaged but sufficiently un-obtrusive to prevent emotional or psychological paroxysms. A Mu-zak programmer could therefore regard the mood music revolution of the 1950s and 1960s as both energizing and irritating.

Muzak has always been at the forefront in producing music that directly addresses our role in modern life. Its efforts to use tempo and timbre to reflect parts of day and to adjust them to the human "fatigue cycle" reveal how walls, corridors, lighting, and the con-tours of man-made enclosures alter our perceptions and bio-rhythms.

This interest in environmental and ergonomic research was ev-ident in 1967 when Dr. James Keenan (an industrial psychologist from Stanford University) spoke before Muzak's newly assembled Scientific Board of Advisers on the subject of the company's global importance. His address, "The Eco-Logic of Muzak," character-ized Muzak as being "synomorphic" with the modern world and interrelated with all matters of time and place: "Muzak helps hu-man communities because it is a nonverbal symbolism for the common stuff of everyday living in the global village. . . . Muzak promotes the sharing of meaning because it massifies symbolism in which not few, but all, can participate."

Throughout the 1960s, Muzak conducted several experiments through the U.S. Army Human Engineering Laboratories that were beneficial for many companies interested in using music to influence group behavior. These were masterminded by Dr. Wil-liam Wokoun, a thin, bespectacled, taciturn behaviorist with a crew-cut—the perfect stereotype of the kind of professor preparing calculations and other paperwork for a trip to Mars. He was such a classic Army scientist that he would have driven some Muzak officials crazy had they been tempted to buy or sway him. His scrupulousness only paid off for them when his findings turned out in Muzak's favor.

In 1963, Bill Wokoun had set up the first Army test measuring Muzak's effects on personnel at a cordon of U.S. nuclear missile sites in Alaska, along the DEW (Distant Early Warning) line. The job of each observer (judged to be the Army's most boring post) was to watch for radar blips that might signal intruding Russian planes. Wokoun had noted that the effectiveness of observers assigned to search for radar scope targets slackened after half an hour.

According to former Muzak vice president Bill Boyd: "They were doing things to make it a better job. They played with the furniture, lighting. Bill Wokoun started looking at music and quickly became aware that Muzak increased alertness in reaction time." As the study concluded, reaction time proved more steady when the subjects were reminded that their "buddy's life was in their hands."

Wokoun conducted his second and more elaborate missile test in 1968. This time subjects tackled a one-hour vigilance task. One group heard music with a wide frequency range while the other heard music with the high frequencies screened out. To observers watching through one-way mirrors, the subjects exposed to the wide frequency range were more alert and less inclined to press buttons when there was no proper stimulus. Wokoun also found that soporific strings posed the danger of letting minds wander and that Army brass worked much better to *brass* instruments.

These findings presage the results in another of Wokoun's Army tests: one that attempted to demonstrate how background music works as a better stimulus than other noise masks. This one involved 14 subjects (1 female and 13 males). They were assigned to work on a machine that measured reaction time to the nearest one one-hundredth of a second. The experiment's results: the subjects hearing a Muzak program proved to have a .27 of a second faster reaction time than those exposed to nothing but the white noise of a small fan.

Keeping soldiers vigilant even when nothing is happening has been a "persistent problem" in the military. Having proved music's worth, Wokoun went on to find out the types of music that did the best job. At Maryland's Aberdeen Proving Ground, he used a sample of 63 enlisted males, whom he assigned at random to three groups. They were placed in a soundproof room to perform vigilance tasks while 23 songs played. All three groups were exposed to the same Muzak selections but in varying orders. While the music played, subjects had to observe a series of "magic-eye" tubes that flashed intermittently and had to press a button whenever a stimulus had altered.

The results once again vindicated Stimulus Progression's Ascending Curve. The *increasingly variable* program, which mixed the tempo of the 23 songs for mood contrast, rendered the subjects' vigilance task performance less predictable. The *descending* program (beginning with most stimulating and working down to the least) resulted in response times that grew longer and more variable. But the *ascending* program (Muzak's usual functional service regimen, starting from the least stimulating and working up) yielded the best results.

Military vigilance workers may have performed better with Muzak's standard format, but workers employed in the world's oldest profession at a brothel in Stuttgart, Germany, grew concerned because their uptempo Muzak "Light Industrial" selections were not getting clients in and out fast enough to secure a profitable turnover. The proprietors had to make a special request for livelier music on their second and fourth quarter-hours.

From whorehouses to Baptist grammar schools, from mortuaries to pet cemeteries, Muzak's trials were never more intriguing than in one situation in which it was challenged to quell the beast. Tom Evans, a Muzak representative in St. Louis, Missouri, corroborates a story that appeared in the January 18, 1973, issue of *Rolling Stone*: "There was a situation when the National Stockyards in Illinois had too many 'dark cutters,' which happens when the release of adrenalin makes the blood congeal and the meat turn. They put the Muzak in and it calmed the cattle as they went to the hereafter."

Entering the 1970s, Muzak had an awe-inspiring roster of responsibilities (and matching clout) for defining our social ecology. Slogans as "The 'New Muzak'—A System of Security for the '70s" and "Muzak Is a Total Communications System" did little to allay the paranoia of Orwell obsessives below management's upper tier. In a time when big corporations were subject to bomb scares from leftist terrorists, Muzak offered its circuitry for music as well as emergency instructions. Former Muzak researcher Bill Wokoun once told a *Rolling Stone* interviewer that plans in one municipality to install Muzak in a police station interrogation area were nixed following the appointment of a new police chief.

Around 1972, Muzak engineer Paul Warner concocted Muzak-Controlled-Time, a plan intended to synchronize the world's clocks so that not a second would go to waste. With the help of Bulova, Warner had built a model of the clock on Long Island. The idea was that subscribers to the music service could hook into a signal that would send a cycle-pulse from a satellite network through a Muzak radio network that was tied to Greenwich Mean Time. "We actually sold the concept to the Sears Tower in Chicago when they were building it," Bill Boyd recalls. "But the clock couldn't get UL approval fast enough, and the plan fell through."

Warner is the same man who, when confronted with the constant question of whether Muzak ever used subliminals, retorted: "We're lucky to get music on it!"

The specter of another civil liberties versus background music bout had lurked again in October of 1969 when UNESCO's International Music Council convened on the "Right to Silence" question. Violinist Yehudi Menuhin, who served on the Executive Committee, vocally rebelled against having to be a "captive audience" as background music played on an airplane. After a vehement discussion, the Committee (with support from the International Council of Women) passed a resolution that denounced "unanimously the intolerable infringement of individual freedom and the right of everyone to silence, because of the abusive use, in private and public places, of recorded or broadcast music." The resolution also called for a "study from all angles—medical, scientific and judicial—without overlooking its artistic and educational aspects and with a view to proposing to UNESCO in the first place, and to the proper authorities everywhere, measures calculated to put an end to this abuse."

Years later, when Westinghouse took control of the company in 1981, Muzak seemed to have found the ideal owner. After all, Westinghouse was among the very first corporations to sponsor market research probing the idiosyncrasies of workers and consumers. This made it all the more puzzling when Westinghouse sent a steering committee to tour the Muzak studio, interview the personnel, and assure themselves that Muzak *wasn't* manipulating minds.

Elfi Mehan, a Muzak engineer who had been with the company for over twenty years, recalls the initial encounters with the new owner: "Westinghouse gave us a hard time. They asked questions about us brainwashing people. I was absolutely furious and told them no. I told them not anywhere as much as television. I made reference to all the nukes that Westinghouse produces and that they are not interested in brainwashing but in brain destroying."

Former Muzak custom-programming coordinator Amy Denio recalls one of few incidents when Muzak was approached by subliminal scientists: "We would get subliminal tapes. I remember getting these weird flyers and circulars. The closest to subliminals was a request for white noise from a think-tank in D.C. The idea was that white noise inspired creative thought, and that problem solving worked better."

As a business and music center, Muzak has always operated (like any other music company) on the basis of a remarkably effective system of ad hoc barter between a mercurial upper management and a (by comparison) artistically committed group of underlings in the programming department. The company's need to "stay in touch" with the needs of its corporate clients and its listeners gets all the more complicated each time a new president takes control and tries to institute changes that may simply reflect idiosyncratic tastes.

Among the more flamboyant and influential Muzak heads was Umberto V. Muscio, who took the company's helm in 1966 and immediately proclaimed: "This is the new Muzak, the contemporary environment! The age of Mantovani and strings is behind us."

Muscio's previous job as an executive at Fedder's air-conditioning disposed him to apply principles from the science of temperature control to the field of mood control. In the 1950s, Vance Packard, in his famous book *The Hidden Persuaders,* discussed how the advertising agency Weiss and Geller probed the psychology of people who preferred air-conditioning to fan ventilation and concluded that the product had a "hidden security value" since people "need to feel protected and enclosed and to keep the windows closed at night while they sleep so that nothing 'threatening' can enter. These people, it seems, are subconsciously yearning for a return to the security of the womb."

Muzak distinguished itself as an emotional buffer in otherwise intimidating environments by combining motivational psychology with the aesthetics of "cash flow." Instead of making music with the science of notation, scale, and time signatures in mind, Muscio used marketing terms that measured bottom-line impact over everything else. In 1967, he told the *Christian Science Monitor:* "Muzak no longer thinks of itself as just nice, bland background music with no commercials. Today, we think of music as our raw material. Our service actually lies in its sequential arrangement to gain certain effects and to serve a functional purpose."

Besides lending a distinct character to the company, Muscio doled out considerable money and time for various studies on ergonomics to determine how places of work could be optimized to take workers' psychological and biological rhythms fully into account. Muscio did all he could to plug Muzak into the "jet age," with a "mod" Jackson Pollack–style painting hanging behind his desk (supposedly Muzak portrayed on canvas) and a phalanx of secretaries with beehive hairdos responding to his every command.

Muscio was among the very first Muzak executives to insist on the term *functional music*, emphasizing Muzak as a management tool. But in the process, Muscio made statements and set priorities that would eventually backfire on the company's image when it finally contended that "Music by Muzak" has aesthetic worth. Two examples: Muscio's absurd contention that Muzak was meant to be heard but not listened to and the nasty (and since abandoned) Muzak koan: *Boring work is made less boring by boring music.*

Through the years, a few prescient people in the company have acknowledged Muzak's unwitting role in creating a style that many artists in the mainstream music world have inadvertently imitated. The more Muzak distanced itself from "art," the closer it came to being a distinct art form. Muzak programmer Elfi Mehan recognized and welcomed this paradox: "We have to make the music low-key enough not to intrude but good enough for people to keep the service. No matter who took over the company, there was always a spirit."

According to former Muzak composer Jane Jarvis: "You can program music to make it sound differently. If you put two slow numbers together, you cannot really apprehend the difference. The stimulus comes from the changing tempos and the tonality."

Jarvis, who joined Muzak in 1963, almost single-handedly computerized the company's music library, putting thousands of titles into memory banks that conformed to the Ascending Curve, while preventing any repetition of songs within a 24-hour period. Jarvis also wrote a few of her own tunes for Muzak that would play about 200 times per year, mostly short tunes to fill up empty space at the back of the quarter-hour sets. Many of her song titles bore the names of Muzak franchisees.

When not working at Muzak's labs, Jarvis had jobs as an organist at Milwaukee County Stadium and Shea Stadium, counterpointing her background music to the pirouettes and pivots of the Braves and the Mets. During her sixteen years at Muzak, she not only heard it while performing her nine-to-five duties but listened to it at home while she dressed, made breakfast, relaxed in the evening, and entertained guests. She remembers: "A lot of musicians thought I was selling out. But what a dreary world it would be if we could only listen to Bach. That is why tribute should be paid to the top-grade musicians that contributed to our station and understood what we were doing." These included Dick Hyman, Grady Tate, Nick Perito (conductor for Perry Como and Ferrante & Teicher), Frank Hunter, Richard Hayman, Elliott Lawrence, Arthur Greenslade, and Tony Mottola.

In a 1965 article for *Horizon*, journalist Alan Levy related an experience he had. He was listening to a compilation of songs that Muzak was then distributing as its "Anti-Competitive Tape"— fashioned to outmaneuver its background music rivals. The tape began with one example of a musical arrangement that Muzak would avoid using, as being too "dreamy" and soporific: "How High the Moon" by the Jackie Gleason Orchestra. It followed this with a Dave Brubeck arrangement of the same song that was too bouncy. Next came a too-distracting Stan Kenton version. And last, Muzak's approved "office version" of the song played—a rendition Levy described as "Sprightly, cool, and as invigorating as a mentholated cigarette commercial."

In late 1971, the congenial Jack Wrather sold Muzak to the New York–based Teleprompter Corporation, which had made its fortune by supplying visual prompts—idiot cues—for talking heads on TV shows. Once his $25 million bid won out, Teleprompter CEO Irving Kahn envisioned Muzak being piped through Teleprompter's existing cable TV lines, available to households the way it was originally intended. Unfortunately, one detail thwarted Kahn's ambitions: he was on trial in federal court on extortion and bribery charges in connection with a Johnstown, Pennsylvania, cable television franchise. Ultimately he was convicted and sentenced to a two-year jail term. Although Teleprompter paid for Muzak with its then plummeting stocks, other Muzak franchises got panicky about Teleprompter's notoriety and decided that they had a vested interest in keeping Umberto Muscio at the Muzak helm.

Teleprompter was owned by Canadian-born Jack Kent Cooke, a self-made tycoon who also owned the Washington Redskins and a house designed by Frank Lloyd Wright. According to Muzak lore, Cooke went to dinner one night at a nice Las Vegas restaurant beneath a starlight roof. As he sat there trying to digest his meal, he suddenly gazed up at the ceiling, called the headwaiter over, and started railing against the "disgusting" sounds. The headwaiter identified it as Muzak, the company Cooke had just bought. Now that he owned it, Cooke was determined to "fix" it.

After instituting some draconian personnel shake-ups, Cooke finally enlisted the services of Rod Baum, who had previously programmed selections for Bonneville's easy-listening radio syndications. Cooke handed Baum a book by Alec Wilder called *The American Popular Song*, which analyzes all of the major composers and explains what they did to make a song popular, both musically and narratively. Cooke indicated that he wanted all of the songs listed in the book's index to be recorded for Muzak consumption.

Faced with such a tall order, Baum hired all of the string orchestras he could find and retained such noted composers and arrangers as Frank Chacksfield.

The Teleprompter days form a fascinating chapter in Muzak's history, taking place as they did during that baffling social transition from the revolutionary 1960s to the disco 1970s. Teleprompter's overweening ambitions reflected its musical appetite. At one point, Muzak boasted a six-week lag time between a hit song's topping the charts and metastasizing on their channel, with more than one thousand new songs added each year. Nick Perito's arrangements of the *Last Tango In Paris* theme and Helen Reddy's "I Am Woman" even smuggled in such previous instrumental contraband as electric guitar, while producer Phil Bodner plied his trademark style of playfully regimented horns on such pop songs as "Amy's Theme." Bodner was especially tuned to the right Muzak formula. He had previously formed an ensemble called The Brass Ring, which had two Top 40 instrumental hits in the 1960s: "The Phoenix Love Theme," taken from the film score to Robert Aldrich's *The Flight of the Phoenix* (released the same year) in 1966 and "The Disadvantages of You" (originally the theme to a Benson & Hedges 100's cigarette commercial) in 1967, which included hypnotic Latin rhythms paired with a caressing female chorus of *la la las*.

For all the talk about Muzak's being too mechanical and antihuman, the company did not have a single synthesizer tune on its channel until the late 1970s. Some of the personnel at Muzak (who also happened to be musicians and composers themselves) would put their original works onto the channel for filler and collected royalties from their own employers—a situation that, Baum claims, got so far out of hand that he endeavored to license an unprecedented amount of new (and cheaper) music to increase the library. One of his solutions was to employ songs recorded by an inexpensive but efficient foreign orchestra.

In 1979, Baum was so impressed by a Czechoslovakian ensemble called the Brno Radio Orchestra that he purchased a library of their more recent scores for the company's use. For a few years at least, their alternately sanguine and brooding hybrid of classical, jazz, and spacey synth-pop served as the company standard. Baum recalls:

> Around 1948, when the Cold War was just starting, the Soviet government wanted to discourage the Czechs from tuning in on the German bands. It started the Brno Radio Orchestra to attract audiences and to sell the Stalinist party-line. Brno became one of the finest light music orchestras in Europe, rivalling the BBC groups. Since Muzak merely replaced Red propaganda with propaganda from the Ford Motor Company or Budweiser, I figured they were ideal.

Other Communist bloc ensembles like the Opus Strings also joined Muzak's library, exuding an eerie enchantment precisely because they were so foreign.

Among the many reasons Baum became Muzak programmer was "to *elevate* the musical tastes of the American public": "When I joined Muzak, the president wanted to know if I could put some music to tape that he could sell to trucking companies to keep drivers awake. I said no, they had No-Doz already."

In 1976, the first salon for background music was held at the Meridien Hotel in Nice, France. The background music business had grown far beyond the confines of Muzak, with splinter organizations offering on-site tape systems and music broadcast at special FM frequencies. Seeburg had grown to offer three main libraries of slow-, fast-, and medium-tempo songs available either on a forty-hour-long automatic record system or on eight-hour reel-to-reel tapes. Background music's "aesthetic law" also reigned for Muzak's two main competitors: AEI (Audio Environments, Inc.) and Minnesota Mining and Manufacturing Company's Sound Products.

In 1968, Yesco emerged to provide one of the very first "foreground" music services. Founded by Mark Torrance and Michael J. Malone, Yesco replaced background instrumentals with original artist songs. Torrance later briefly served as Muzak's president in 1987 after Marshall Field V bought Muzak and merged it with

YESCO. In 1971, Malone started AEI (Audio Environments, Inc.) which later became AEI Music Network, Inc. Oddly enough, AEI used its foreground "business music" in a similar manner that Muzak treats background music, stressing "elements" over "musical style" and using melody as a dramatic device for the retail and hospitality stage.

Though priding itself on its "alternative" to the standard background music format, AEI certainly had not abandoned it. Two channels, *Lifestyle* and *Interiors*, were purely instrumental and unobtrusive in their execution. "*Lifestyle*" was programmed with tempo-controlled songs and careful attention to creating a progression through textural changes. Living up to its motto, "Wire the world," AEI had made several corporate acquisitions, including Britain's Rediffusion Music Limited.

3M Sound Products started in 1964 as an on-premise tape system that, like Muzak, focused on sound environments for business settings and optimum spending. Today 3M uses only a DBS system that runs via custom-built, random-access playbacks. It offers several categories including foreground music, but its ever-popular background instrumental channel includes renditions ranging from "Stardust" to "Theme from *Entertainment Tonight*."

Besides paying attention to tempo and volume, 3M's system takes into account such problems as how well the sound bounces off tables. One 3M Sound Products dealer remembers an embarrassing incident at a restaurant chain outlet in which the company installed speakers designed for a particular floor plan. When the restaurant subsequently moved its counter, one of the speakers ended up transmitting music directly over the cash registers so that the microphone for announcing orders picked up nothing but music, and the business transactions were chaotic.

Another striking feature of Muzak, 3M, and other background music services is their monaural transmission system. Although the songs are now recorded using the best digital stereo technology money can buy, the companies broadcast the selections through a single channel. The result is a series of ceiling sound-vents emitting exactly the same depth-of-sound and frequency.

This may initially appear to be a miserly and inferior solution, but it has its justifications. In a modest-size McDonald's in Connecticut, I witnessed the splendidly homogenizing effects of this process. At the time, the establishment was packed with groups of customers, each carrying on its own conversation in one or another language. This intolerable mishmash was somehow alleviated by the carefully assembled speakers piping in the near-subliminal music. The reconstituted version of a song like "Both Sides Now" neutralizes nature's multichannel distractions into a single, benevolent source. The mono effect provides the paradoxical service of standardizing noise, enhancing private conversation, and even making the food taste better. The net result is a triumph for both acoustics and social order—at least until you leave McDonald's.

Muzak has more than once created a unique listening experience from what began as a response to technical and economic limitations. In keeping with this tradition, Muzak found that its unidirectional speakers and limited range had advantages in business environments not found in the more advanced stereophonic and quadraphonic wonders that were touted throughout the 1970s. Much as General Squier used electronic wires to standardize geography for military interception, Muzak (perhaps by accident) demonstrated that monophonic music piped through a public address system could facilitate order over otherwise unmanageable surroundings.

Another example of good use of monaural sound involves the series of long corridors at Newark International Airport that radiate from the main terminal to the various departure gates. A person walking through might notice at this and other airports the seemingly endless succession of ceiling apertures broadcasting light instrumental versions of such songs as Olivia Newton-John's "Magic" at uniform volume.

A few years ago, Britain's Rediffusion Music, Ltd. (formerly RediTune), attempted to make a stereo machine. According to the company's Managing Director Chris Ring: "We did introduce a two-hour version of our usual four-hour mono cartridge system, but it was never popular and I finally withdrew it from the few remaining customers in 1991." According to Muzak's Rod Baum: "When you play stereo music in a restaurant, you can't get people to sit in the right spot to enjoy it."

The style of background music is related to the consumer context. A fast-food outlet like McDonald's, with its large turnover of patrons, may tend to pipe in up-tempo music to encourage fast eating and fast exit; while a supermarket may play a lower-tempo selection to encourage shoppers to linger over items that might otherwise be overlooked.

Several studies probed this tempo-to-eating correlation. In one, sponsored by Muzak in the late 1980s, the subjects were drawn from Fairfield University's faculty and staff cafeteria. The sample group consisted of eleven people (ten men and one woman) between 25 and 60 years old, none of whom were aware of being monitored. The music was broken into two sixty-minute instrumental (nonclassical) tapes played at a constant volume. The music on one tape was performed at slow tempo (56 beats per minute); the music on the other tape was performed at fast tempo (122 beats per minute). Music was played on weekdays between noon and 1:30 P.M., in a sequence going from fast to slow to no music at all during the 16-day trial. Two experimenters pretending to be cafeteria patrons observed each subject under different conditions, activating timers the moment subjects took their first bite of food. They concluded that the fast-tempo music increased eating speed, although the converse hypothesis that slow music made slower eaters did not apply. But if the sequence increased from no music to slow-tempo music to fast-tempo music, the number of bites increased with each newly introduced condition.

A Muzak Research Study conducted by researchers from Eastern Kentucky University explored "Utilizing Music as a Tool for Healing." *Environmental Music by Muzak* was installed in such places as the preoperative area, operating rooms, and recovery rooms at Union Hospital in the Bronx, New York, with favorable results in common patients, visitors, physicians, and staff. Muzak's programming for the ICU unit at St. Joseph's Hospital in Yonkers led researchers to conclude that special music preferences included:

an emphasis upon major modes, rather than minor modes; tunes that were melodious, but not sad or somber; music that would not evoke wistful reminiscences about the "good old days"; and music that would be bright and melodious, yet not exciting. Their rhythm had to be regular, although not predominant, with enough variation to avoid monotony. Variations in loudness were controlled in the music programs to insure that no sudden loud musical peaks would precipitate a fatal cardiac arrhythmia.

Muzak's Stimulus Progression format seems to work best in reverse order for other patients. For them, starting with overly stimulating music and working down to softer, more soothing sounds—"entrainment"—functions as a kind of biofeedback.

Regardless of the empirical research on the subject, the final verdict on background music's effects and aesthetics lies with daily listener encounters. Complaints about background music song content prove that people *do* listen, although its presence in these instances has an impact that companies like Muzak do not encourage. When Frank Chacksfield arranged a version of Judy Collins' version of "Amazing Grace," clients in the South were offended and threatened to cancel subscriptions. A religious school in Tulsa, Oklahoma, played Muzak in its administrative office, but the school dropped the service, contending that it feared that the lyrics of popular songs might have a bad effect on kids.

Muzak executive Barry Freedman recalls working for another background music company in Chicago that got frequent calls from employees in a high-tech engineering firm. They complained that an old Russian Army song kept cropping up on the tape and was offending the majority of their workers, who were recent Eastern European immigrants.

Rod Baum, ever the raconteur, loves relating an anecdote that demonstrates Muzak's primary social benefit:

In an office for a garment factory outside of Atlanta, the workers got tired of the Muzak and used a radio

for their background music. If they turned on rock, 25
percent of the people in the workplace didn't like it. So
they got a committee together and took a vote. They
played the classical station, and only 10 percent of the
people ended up liking it. So they tried a country sta-
tion, and 60 percent didn't like it. They had another
meeting. They decided on one day for each format:
country one day, classical the next, disco for maybe half
a day. But the 10 percent who liked whatever was play-
ing got tired of people glaring at them. Finally the office
manager called us and asked if they could have the
Muzak back. It proved what I was doing was working.
Muzak proved the least of all possible evils.

In 1979, when Muzak made its first attempt to launch a satellite,
the craft had reentered the atmosphere and burned. Ironically,
among the songs included in the launch was a version of the Fifth
Dimension hit "Up, Up and Away." But after several tries, Muzak's Direct Broadcast Satellite system at last transmitted its music
from Raleigh, North Carolina, to its satellite orbiting the earth at
a distance of 22,300 miles.

Muzak, which always avoided vocals, transmitted the human
voice on its instrumental channel for the first time in quite a while
when it agreed to include the now legendary "We Are the World"
broadcast in 1985, simultaneously with radio stations across the
country. According to Rod Baum: "We had read about the broadcast in *Billboard*, so we thought we'd join in. They could have
called it 'Hands Across the Muzak World.' "

By 1985, before it merged with Yesco, Muzak was operating its
own original artist channel called FM (Foreground Music) One.
When Chicago department store heir and magnate Marshall Field
V took over in 1986, Muzak concentrated on its domestic product
with the goal of replacing 20 to 25 percent of its library per year.
The company had then changed hands again, this time becoming
the property of Centre Capital Investors, L.P., which was pushing
for Muzak's entry into more high-tech markets. Muzak had a custom-made tape service called TONES and several "foreground"

Muzak channels of classical, contemporary instrumental, and Adult Contemporary vocal. "Hitline," which featured current AM rock favorites, was especially popular with clothing stores. The company also started ZTV in 1992, a video program of music and special shows. Yet despite the wide assortment of alternatives, the Environmental channel (in the "elevator music" tradition) stayed Muzak's top seller for a while.

On the surface, the sonic adventures of an Itzak Perlman seem much loftier and more exciting than the productions of the typical Muzak composer/programmer. Without the artistic license to experiment with "tone colors," Muzak appears doomed to reconstitute ditties like "Danke Schoen" to make them sound more blithe than the originals, but the process is more complex.

Today, Muzak is increasingly sensitive about its philistine image and is taking great pains to have its instrumental covers remain as faithful to the originals as possible. The motivation for this rests on practical business considerations far more than on aesthetics. According to Elfi Mehan: "People will complain if they recognize a song they like has been revamped too much."

Muzak keeps fine-tuning. Saxophones are often used to substitute for vocals, although guitar also suffices. Songs are still computer-encoded by their rhythm, tempo, instrumentation, and original recording artists. You will never hear two Beatles songs in succession or one piano melody followed by another.

Former Muzak designer Christopher Case always stressed the need for careful modulation of obstreperous saxes, plodding guitars, and gawky drums into a "mellow groove." An ex–disk jockey, King Crimson fan, and former employee at Muzak's one-time competitor Seeburg, Case was described by one man who worked with him as an obsessed and haunted man who would usually sit at his desk with his jacket fully buttoned. But during his brief tenure, he helped Muzak revamp its public and self-image.

In an interview, he claimed: "There was an old Muzak philosophy. But now it's not cut and dry, whether you listen or don't. It is just something that doesn't interfere. To think that people don't listen is stupid. People are listening." He defined Muzak as "music artfully performed in a manner to uplift, not intrude":

Some of the things I listen for are present in Pythagorean number theory. It has to do with harmonies. Pythagoras states that there's a certain harmony in nature. You see it in the circumference of the earth, angles and positions between planets, seeds in a particular flower. Nature expresses number and mathematics; music is mathematics, with time signatures, chord structures, vibration rates. You take it another step, and conclude that, if music does not reflect what occurs in nature, it is disruptive. If it's harmonious, it is a benefit. One of the things I considered before taking the job is that Muzak touches everyone. It was an opportunity for me to benefit the world."

11 / "Beautiful Music"

THE RISE OF EASY-LISTENING FM

Wouldn't it be great if you could turn down the world?
—Ad for WDBN's "The Quiet Island"

Lite FM—home to such wistful voices as Karen Carpenter, Phil Collins, and Gloria Estefan—is just one of many mood-monitored soundscapes that radio has offered us through the years. In fact, the latest spate of Adult Contemporary formats stressing original-artist vocals and dispensing with light instrumentals has interloped upon a once-thriving format called "Beautiful Music."

Beautiful Music radio was an effort launched in the mid- to late 1960s that provided soft and unobtrusive instrumental selections on a very structured schedule with a minimum of commercial interruptions. Of all existing FM formats, Beautiful Music was the most carefully thought out and disciplined—almost to the point of functioning as a free background music service, with a day-parting regimen designed to please listeners on their way to work or while relaxing at home.

The history of these adventures in mood radio is intimately tied to the advance of FM technology. When Edwin Howard Armstrong discovered the FM (frequency modulation) signal in the 1930s, technicians were already aware of subsidiary communications authorizations (SCAs)—FM signals that can only be accessed with a special receiver. During World War II, the U.S. Army used SCAs, with some success, to send top-secret messages to troops. Once the military stopped using them after the war, Congress passed the Subsidiary Communications Authorizations Act of 1956, directing the FCC to permit radio stations to lease SCAs for commercial purposes. Seeking to replace relatively expensive and inefficient phone lines, companies such as Muzak® also leased SCAs from radio stations to get better sound with fewer technical interruptions.

The FCC ruled in 1964 that FM stations catering to cities with populations in excess of 100,000 could no longer use FM just to simulcast their AM shows; instead, they had to provide original programming during at least 50 percent of their broadcast day. In the 1940s, the FCC had supported the opposite approach: authorizing parallel broadcasting so that listeners could make the transition from AM to FM with less confusion. At a time when many broadcasters (and listeners) still considered FM to be simply an auxiliary medium, simulcasters were furious with the ruling, since they normally used their FM franchises as SCA reserves. That soon changed, however, when FM radio began developing its own character and became immersed in two main musical styles: classical (which catered to a more finicky audience) and light instrumentals (which had the larger following).

While mood music companies were using radio waves for private gain, mainstream commercial stations were gradually adopting Muzak-type formats of relaxing orchestrals, light classics, and showtunes at no charge and with a minimum of on-air chatter.

Christopher Case had worked at such a station for seven years before becoming a Muzak programmer. He recalls: "FM bands had a much better signal-to-noise ratio than AM. They were more conducive to serious and quiet music. Back then, all commercial formats were already covered on AM with jazz, rock, and country. Light music offered a relatively untapped market and generated big profits."

The advent of FM mood-waves is due largely to the efforts of Jim Schulke, the "Godfather of 'Beautiful Music' Radio." Schulke, a lean and somewhat reclusive man, was the kind of analytical genius who could dissect a ratings book as if it were a lab animal. While working as a director of advertising for Magnavox, he devised a method of buying airtime on FM stations in bulk and then reselling the blocks to interested advertisers. He perceived the FM band as a lucrative frontier and made a deal with NAFMB (the National Association of FM Broadcasters) for FM usage after agreeing to pay annual dues. Upon hiring a ratings service to conduct a ten-market study on FM listening, he not only discovered that the band had a substantial following but confirmed his suspicion that light instrumental was the most popular mode.

Schulke noticed that a few stations had their own way of juxtaposing songs so that they were mood-consistent or formed a "matched flow." According to Schulke, whose ear-opening study eventually led to his becoming NAFMB's president: "These weren't very scientific methods, but they worked."

The art of "seamless segues" was also practiced by Philadelphia's WDVR (now WEAZ), where station manager Jerry Lee used an album-rotation system to produce similar fare. A flamboyant and crafty promoter, Lee managed to make his the first FM station to rake in million-dollar profits. In the mid-1970s, Lee maintained his high business profile by driving around in the original "super-car" from James Bond movies, which he had purchased.

Schulke eventually started a firm called QMI (Quality Media, Inc.) to sign up sponsors for FM independents. To help his stations get better ratings and to pull in more agencies, he later formed SRP (Stereo Radio Productions), bringing in Phil Stout as his vice president of operations. Schulke was, in effect, FM's first bona-fide *mood-musicologist*—so precise in his philosophy that he concocted a list of "do's and don'ts" commonly referred to in the industry as "Schulkeisms."

Schulke forbade the playing of any songs that contrasted with one another or varied too much in tempo or tone. There were no overbearing voices to draw attention; only the less fevered singing of such performers as Andy Williams and of choruses such as the Anita Kerr Singers and the Johnny Mann Singers were permitted. He likened his science of "matched flow" to the ebb and flow of tides, in an era when the average radio listener still had an attention span of longer than seven minutes.

Ironically, his stations, designed to attract advertisers, had to limit the number of commercials for fear of compromising the aural atmosphere and detracting from the impact of each advertiser's message. He also saw rock music as occupying the highest level, and light instrumental music the lowest, on a scale of "intrusion levels."

Schulke measured his success through direct listener response. Disk jockeys were told not to announce the songs' artists, in order to prevent excess chatter and to avoid alerting listeners to the repetitions in programming necessitated by the small pool of artists in the station's library. His most conclusive finding was that soft strings were the surest guarantor of listener approval in a focus group consisting mostly of women between the ages of 18 and 49. According to Schulke, "Females have the ability to hear higher frequencies than men. They are better gauges for good fidelity. The gender demarcation was so important that we concluded, if we lost our dynamic range, we lost our females."

Thanks to Schulke and Stout, the breezy and at times hypnotic tunes of such light greats as Ray Conniff soothed women in their kitchens when not serenading them in supermarket aisles. Schulke became so adept at determining his program's direction that a colleague once credited him with being "the only guy who can dust off three or four Mantovanis and five or six Percy Faiths and make a million dollars."

Schulke remembers how good he became at ad-libbing a pitch for potential clients: "I would experiment by switching on a Xerox

machine during business consultations. After surreptitiously turning it off, I noticed that the voice levels dropped and everyone
seemed so much more relaxed. I'd then tell them that is exactly
what my music does. Turning on my stations was like turning off
the machines."

Beautiful Music's other distinction from competing radio formats was the syndicator's centralized control—an arrangement
that squelched the whims or quirks in taste of local deejays and
general managers.

According to Phil Stout, co-pioneer of Beautiful Music with
Schulke and a mood music programmer since 1960: "It wasn't like
there were hundreds of people involved in Beautiful Music. It was
a rather incestuous little group that not only knew one another
but branched off into other companies." Stout always made Schulke's programming work best, as he commandeered the backroom
studio of SRP's New York headquarters. His trial-and-error approach to music selections called for up to two days' work to put
together a one-hour tape.

SRP did have genre competitors, however. One of these was
Marlin Taylor who, in September of 1967, started WJIB, the Boston area's first mood music FM station. After just two months on
the air, the station was overwhelmed by letters and phone calls
from advertising agencies and newspaper editors lauding the
concoction of Percy Faith, Ronnie Aldrich, Andre Kostelanetz,
Roger Williams, and various selections from the London Phase 4
series.

In 1969, Taylor convinced the president of a company called
Bonneville to bring a similar format to New York City's WRFM,
which wanted to outdo a successful mood music Gaslight Revue
emanating from WPAT in Paterson, New Jersey. "They let me be
my own program director," Taylor recalls. "In seven months, the
station jumped [from] #23 to #5 in the Arbitron ratings."

Bonneville, a corporation run by the Mormon Church in Utah,
asked Taylor to put his program into a salable package for more
of its FM clients. Out of this endeavor came Bonneville Broadcasting System, a syndication firm that listed Taylor as its founder
and president from 1971 until 1983. Bonneville spread its FM

tentacles from coast-to-coast, relying on its own version of Schulke's "matched flow" with four quarter-hours of music recorded on reel-to-reel tapes.

The "Schulke format," which Schulke and Stout soon christened "Beautiful Music," became very successful. The "Beautiful Music" label stuck, and the format reigned at such stations as Atlanta's WPCH and Miami's WLYF (the first FM channel to make #1 in a major market).

Smaller syndicators attempted similar experiments. Al Ham, a former A&R man for Columbia Records, came up with *Music of Your Life*, an AM nostalgia format that commingled instrumentalists like Frank Chacksfield with vocalists like Bing Crosby. Ham's knack for putting together the proper balance of singing and music came from his intense involvement with much of Columbia's early mood music fare. He—as both producer and bass player—had worked with Ray Conniff, Percy Faith, Johnny Mathis, the Four Lads, and Mitch Miller.

Avoiding the direct competition it would have faced on the FM dial, *Music of Your Life* proved to be a successful cottage industry. Radio stations would sign a contract, pay Ham a flat fee per month, and rent reel-to-reel or vinyl recordings all segued with Ham finesse. The only remotely similar AM animal was WAIT, a Chicago AM station that started in 1962 and claimed to be the first format of its kind; but its style was much more like today's Adult Contemporary, with a 1:1 ratio of vocals to instrumentals and announcements every quarter-hour.

Medina, Ohio, was home to WDBN, a Beautiful Music forerunner and one of Schulke's first inspirations. The station styled itself as "the Quiet Island" ("in radio's sea of noise"). It signed onto the air in October of 1960 and was already broadcasting in stereo by November of 1961.

The Quiet Island seemed destined for good fortune. When the FCC imposed a maximum FM power ceiling of 50,000 watts on stations in the Ohio region, the Island, being an older station, enjoyed "Grandfather" rights that allowed it to retain its ERP (Effected Radiated Power) of 118,000 watts. The Pulse, Inc., an audience-rating company for national broadcasts, published a study in 1964 showing that almost 30 percent of all American homes enjoyed FM reception. The following year, the Mediastat Research Company cited FM penetration of up to 50 percent of all homes.

By January of 1970, when an American Research Bureau study of FM listening showed that WDBN commanded the nation's sixth largest FM audience, the Quiet Island tightened its iron-clad music policy. The plan centered on three basic elements. The first of these, *Orchestration and Instrumentation,* specified the use of pianos, guitars, heavy strings, horns, and even vocals, with no "improvisational bridges and saxophones" to jar the audience. The second rule involved *Tempo,* which varied according to the time of day: the wake-up hours between 6:00 and 9:00 A.M. required "Orchestra-Up" consisting of bright and exciting music to enhance that first cup of coffee; from 9:00 A.M. to 8:00 P.M., Jack Jones–style "love tunes" were the main course; and from 8:00 P.M. to midnight, basic string orchestras with "only sentimental vocal chorus" were allowed. The third and final rule related to *Memory or Familiarity,* with each quarter-hour containing "a musical appeal to an age group between 25 and 49 years of age." Former station owner Bob Miller admits that the quarter-hour division might have been influenced by Muzak's "Stimulus Progression."

WDBN ran such ads as this: "People seem to like each other better when they're on The Quiet Island. One of these days around dinner time, take your family on a vacation away from it all. From your husband's bad day at the office. From your children's hard day at play. From the little aggravations you had to put up with from seven to six."

Thriving until 1988, The Quiet Island not only entertained; it offered punchy manifestos against what it considered rock-contamination:

> *Isn't the rattle of your neighbor's garbage can lids enough without having to listen to freaked-out music? Pull yourself out of your old radio routine and get into something nice and sweet.*
>
> *They say many young people today will be deaf by*

*the time they're 30. Their own music is doing them in.
Life has gotten louder for the rest of us, too. The song
bird, the cricket, the soft crunch of snow underfoot are
all becoming lost in the roar of the Seventies. . . . Fortunately, there's still one place where you can hear
something beautiful. WDBN-FM.*

The mid-1970s marked a change that had far greater impact on
everyday musical perceptions than most people could ever realize:
"Beautiful Music" evolved into "easy-listening"—a label that
caught on and still sticks, but has been misinterpreted and misused
ever since. "Easy-listening" is not a copyrighted term or a registered trademark, and it has uncertain origins. By the late 1960s,
"Easy-Listening" was already being used as a Top 40 chart hit
category in *Billboard* magazine to designate light instrumentals
and vocals—anything from Paul Mauriat's "Love Is Blue" to the
Lettermen's "Our Winter Love."

SRP's other major change was its graduation from strictly playing commercial records and other preexisting music to using custom-made instrumental covers. Schulke and Stout made a deal
with the British Broadcasting Company to purchase music recorded by some of Britain's best composers, arrangers, and conductors on both sides of the Atlantic.

SRP's first custom recordings were made in London in 1973,
under the direction of Leroy Holmes, who sold 1 million records
of the "Theme from *The High and the Mighty.*" According to
Stout:

*The idea behind custom music was to record the very
popular or familiar pieces unavailable in string format.
The bottom line of my easy-listening programming was
familiarity, I would scatter original material by people
like John Sbarra with the "down-homers"—those very
familiar pieces.*

*While supervising the 1973 London sessions with
Leroy, I heard some fantastic instrumental string music
on the BBC. So I called them and discovered they had
a number of string orchestras on staff. They used ma-*

*terial on the air twice and then erased it so they could
continue to give work to these musicians. I asked about
a deal to sell some of the stuff to us for exclusive use in
the U.S. They agreed and provided us in excess of 200
cuts per year, and we gave them lists of what we
wanted them to record. This arrangement went on for
seven or eight years.*

Ronnie Aldrich, John Fox, Nick Ingman, Ron Goodwin, Norrie
Paramor, Geoff Love, Syd Dale, the BBC Midland Orchestra, the
Cascading Strings (arranged and conducted by John Gregory), and
a cadre of other talents launched their careers in this venue; some,
including Ingman and Dale, moonlighted for Muzak and various
background music production libraries.

Ron Goodwin, most noted for "633 Squadron" (a toe-tapping
march that prodded London tube riders on workday mornings),
had a facility for bouncy yet understated tunes fit for any civic
occasion. He got one job replacing Henry Mancini to score Alfred
Hitchcock's *Frenzy* when the mercurial director suddenly decided
that he wanted a lighter score in place of the macabre one he had
initially requested.

Syd Dale was another composer who offered valuable stylistic
innovations for both SRP and Muzak. He invented "The Double
Dozen," a simulated big band that dispensed with gangly saxo-
phones, trombones, and trumpets but kept the bass clarinets,
oboes, and other woodwinds to create a kind of "burnished brass"
with a far less blaring texture.

John Sbarra belongs to a new generation of composers committed to the "Beautiful Music" sound—replete with string
arrangements, subtle background choruses, and low-profile synthesizers. As Phil Stout claims in his liner notes to Sbarra's CD
compilation *Movie Themes of Tomorrow,* the music of John Sbarra
goes "right next to a perfect martini and gorgeous sunsets."

Of course, other musicians, arrangers, and conductors, including
James Last and Franck Pourcel, gained considerable easy-listening
radio exposure even though they did not make custom recordings.
Stout remembers:

> *At one point in the seventies, Roger Williams came by
> the SRP studio. He told me: "As an artist I understand
> why you play the material of mine you do, but I want
> to know why you don't play the rest of it." I explained
> to him that we were not interested in overarranged,
> intrusive cuts, and I think at that point he walked away
> more comfortable and understood the slot we found for
> him.*

Compared to most other radio formats, Bonneville and SRP
stations followed a strict regimen. Their diligent plan to stroke the
public's heart and soul sometimes paid off with fevered responses
from overzealous, sometimes loopy listeners. Stout reminisces: "I
got a letter in the late sixties from a psychiatrist. The doctor was
treating a woman who was a huge listener to one our stations. A
particular piece of music we had in rotation was a favorite of hers,
and when we took it out she went bananas. It prompted her psychiatrist to drop SRP a line, asking why we weren't playing it, and
if we could put it back in."

Stout also received another letter, this time a two-pager, from
a woman who accused SRP's programmer of wallowing in lost
love. Although just about all of the music was instrumental, the
woman could not help perceiving that the titles tended to allude
to failed romances.

Marlin Taylor encountered an even more unsettling situation:

> *One horny woman in New York claimed a song we
> played pushed her "hot" button. She complained that
> WRFM was using it and other songs to send her sub-
> liminal messages. She'd leave gifts for me as a bribe to
> stop playing them. After I had long since departed from
> the station, she took me to court in lower Manhattan
> because I didn't return her gift. The judge threw it out.
> He discovered she was loony, but I still had to hire an
> attorney!*

There were also censorship problems with some SRP subscribers in the Bible Belt. For example, if the program included a vocal

version of "What Kind of Fool Am I?" Stout would have to cut the song out because of the line "I don't give a damn."

Among their other cultural contributions, Beautiful Music stations have more than once brought a particular deserving song or artist out of obscurity. Stout, while sifting through old records, retrieved Johnny Pearson's "Sleepy Shores," a song previously unappreciated by many despite its frequent appearance in television commercials. The public got to enjoy it all over again thanks to SRP's faithful airplay. Another Beautiful Music hit attributed to SRP was Caravelli's instrumental recording of Bob Dylan's "Wigwam." Dylan's original version was also listed in *Billboard*'s "Easy-Listening" Top 40 in the latter part of 1970.

Taylor recalls other instances of uncovering obscure gems:

> I played a song called "Dolannes Melody" by Jean Claude Borelly that had a pan-pipe. People started calling in asking what the instrument was. Nobody ever heard it before. I later picked out "The Lonely Shepherd" performed by Zamfir with the James Last Orchestra. It was an unfamiliar melody which drove the listeners crazy. We generated as many as 15 to 20 calls a day for a single play. Nobody else was playing it. My peers told me it was nuts, but the listeners loved it. After that, Zamfir sold over 500,000 albums in television promotions alone.

The advent of Beautiful Music coincided with a historically sensitive period in America's demographics: a time when the generation gap was much more apparent than it is today. The music catered to an adult audience that had spending power and tended to shut itself off from the blaring counterculture.

As hippie-oriented underground radio experiments died and the promotion of product (versus art) reasserted its dominion over the airwaves, mainstream FM rock stations resorted more and more to Beautiful Music's entrepreneurial system. AM was also feeling the draft. When the Carpenters segued into the 1970s with "Close to You" and Neil Diamond went from his gritty "Cherry Cherry" to the legato "Song Sung Blue," the music industry was already sneaking Beautiful Music motifs into the pop charts to accommodate the baby boomers' metabolic meltdown.

SRP's influence became so pervasive in the following years that *Billboard* magazine, in the fall of 1979, issued a front page encomium, citing Beautiful Music as the #1 format in the United States. About 80 percent of that audience was listening to SRP.

Yet Bonneville, under the aggressive entrepreneurship of its head John Patton, had encroached on Schulke's territory to become the biggest Beautiful Music syndicator. Bonneville greatly expanded its music library, launched a satellite transmission system, and hired Lex de Azevedo and his Million Dollar Custom Orchestra to record more music. By the spring of 1980, many of Schulke's customers had been coaxed onto Bonneville's ledger.

Despite selling his SRP to Cox Broadcasting in 1981 for $6 million, Schulke continued to concentrate on the music. But something was happening: Despite the optimistic 1979 findings in *Billboard,* Schulke began to realize that the older adults who listened to his stations got older, their spending power weakened, and their incomes became fixed. Schulke describes the unmistakable signs of easy-listening's impending demise:

> *Beautiful Music started to slide by 1980, then slipped as its audience got older. Before Lite FM as we know it caught on, I created a format that highlighted original artist vocals. I sold SRP to Cox Broadcasting just before the* Billboard *article proclaimed Beautiful Music as Number One. I was accused of selling the oil well before the oil leaked. But I needed something that satisfied a new demand. After a lot of research, I came up with soft vocal programming called* Schulke II.

Before Schulke II was implemented, Schulke took the first step in luring clients away from Bonneville by making a phone call to Bill Moyes of the Research Group. He convinced Moyes to finance a $400,000 Comprehensive Music Testing study that would span four years. Schulke's research involved conducting tests in an auditorium where prescreened subjects listened to about fifteen seconds of a particular cut and then wrote down what they liked about it. He found that vocals were their cutting edge. From there *Schulke II* started broadcasting a nearly all-vocal program, interspersed with occasional instrumentals—the opposite of Beautiful Music and the forerunner of today's Lite FM or Adult Contemporary.

"Lite FM had driven the nail into the Beautiful Music coffin," according to former Muzak programmer Rod Baum. "Beautiful Music didn't contemporize enough and started sounding schmaltzy. People started preferring songs sung."

Consequently, few industry observers were surprised when the May 26, 1990, issue of *Billboard* read: "Fallen on Hard Times, Easy Moves Toward Soft AC." Even though easy-listening's defenders continued to hope for an imminent comeback, the vocal strains that enticed listeners between ages 25 and 54 were the fashion.

Desperate stalwarts kept suggesting alternatives. Ed Winton, an easy-listening veteran, launched a "Mello" program for WEZI in Memphis and WMLO in Tallahassee, Florida. Bob Carson, another syndicator, conjured up "The Renaissance" as an adult-alternative hybrid.

But other FM classical and jazz stations started upstaging easy-listening by adapting Beautiful Music's principles. They opted for lighter and more contoured concertos while retaining the figleaf of high-brow integrity. James B. Oestreich, in *The New York Times*, lamented that "classical music is to be treated not as art, but as entertainment or background." For example, WNCN in New York reportedly reduced the number of vocals, choral music, and atonal and aleatory compositions it played in favor of works by more feathery composers such as Vivaldi, Telemann, and Boccherini—easy-listening for Bonwit-Teller patrons.

With easy-listening moribund, critics redirected their bile toward Lite FM. Stephen Holden, in another *New York Times* piece, grudgingly admitted that "lite radio embraces a larger segment of modern pop history than any other current radio format." But he went on to call the format "an innocuous musical purée." Notwithstanding its "original artists" pretense, Lite FM manages to appropriate Muzak's knack for placing ambiance above discrete musical identity, mixing genres and historical contexts with such aplomb that John Lennon's "Imagine" plays right alongside Perry Como's "It's Impossible."

But even as easy-listening withered away on the public airwaves, it found a new niche on private cable radio lines. To re-create Muzak founder General Squier's dream of music-wired homes, companies like DCR (Digital Cable Radio) had replaced Squier's wires with the wonders of today's satellite down-link. DCR (located in Hatboro, Pennsylvania) sent digital sound to subscriber stereo systems via their existing cable television service. ("It's cable for your stereo!")

Phil Stout had overseen six of DCR's easy-listening adult-oriented channels. An ensemble to which Stout currently gives considerable air time is the London Studio Orchestra, alternately titled the Starlight Orchestra. Its intricate, varied, and, at times, impressively eccentric output—Beautiful Music blended with folk, new age, pan-pipes, some hints of techno, and an intermittent chorus—is the culmination of several recording sessions conducted in Holland during the mid-to-late eighties. A single London Studio Orchestra compact disc can contain tracks that fluctuate from a relatively serene cover of "My Way" to an innovative and haunting rendition of Erik Satie's "Gnossiennes"— all done in the elevator music tradition of amalgamating arrangements, instruments and styles previously assumed to be incompatible.

Looking back, Stout concludes:

> Beautiful Music generated a hardcore loyalty. The listeners had a private relationship. When the stations started discontinuing it, there was a groundswell of resentment. You ended up with a disenfranchised audience. We are getting a good response from our easy-listening channel. People are saying they're glad to have this music again because they're not getting it on radio.

Japan is considered a nation of background music junkies, and digital radio serves a teeming market there, as well. Since 1961, businessman Mototada Uno has been piping background music into homes, offices, and train stations. For him, ordinary TV, radio, and stereo did not provide enough ear candy for the average Japanese household and workplace; something more "ambient" was in order. Over the past decade, as profits in his country's service sector multiplied, Uno eventually controlled 70 percent of Japan's cable radio outlets, serving more than 1 million homes and businesses—mostly upscale people. His Osaka Yusen Broadcasting Corporation provides Japanese zither and koto music, pop confections, and the sounds of bells, insects, animals and even synthesized street noises (in case an employee wakes up late and needs to give the illusion of being stuck in traffic when phoning the boss). Osaka Yusen sees the private home as a modern ganglion of the workplace and a perfect outlet for aural seductions once reserved for business establishments.

Until the fall of 1992, WPAT of Paterson, New Jersey, retained easy-listening traces, with livelier music during the day, more subdued sounds at dinner time, and a much softer after-midnight program containing fewer interruptions than usual; then it, too, succumbed to the AC virus. According to Ralph Sanabria, who once worked with Schulke and later became WPAT's program director: "Karen Carpenter is a big part of this new format, but Gloria Estefan has captured another generation in the same spirit. Now, the battle lines between rock and easy-listening are less clear than they were twenty years ago."

But as Adult Contemporary mollifies a generation of aging former hipsters, the growing popularity of various contemporary instrumental categories threatens to spawn a new breed of programs that blend the old and new. Today, such meditative formats as KTWV's "The Wave" in Los Angeles and Stephen Hill's syndicated *Music from the Hearts of Space* come closest to filling easy-listening's void. The fact that new-age music blossomed just as Beautiful Music started to wilt is no coincidence.

TOP TEN "BEAUTIFUL MUSIC" INSTRUMENTALS:

[as listed in the April 1983 issue of *Radio Only*]

1. Percy Faith: "Theme from *A Summer Place*"
2. Henry Mancini: "You Don't Know Me""
3. Peter Knight: "Tonight"
4. BBC, Johnny Douglas Midland Orchestra, exclusive SRP Custom-recording: "Words"
5. Roger Williams: "Theme from *New York, New York*"
6. Vangelis: "Chariots of Fire"
7. Hollyridge Strings: "Theme from *Love Story*"
8. Henry Mancini: "Evergreen"
9. Living Strings: "If I Were a Rich Man"
10. Hagood Hardy: "As Time Goes By"

12 / Violins from Space

Dateline: Peoria, Illinois. November 12, 1981. On a freezing midnight, Connie Cook, a divorced middle-American housewife, is awakened by the white light of a spacecraft hovering outside her bedroom window. After being transfixed by its glare for close to ninety minutes, she returns to bed and proceeds to dream of four aliens "sort of standing in the sky." The aliens reappear several dreams later at her bedside, combining tactile affection with predictions of "good will for the earth's peoples." Ms. Cook (who previously had trouble with "Chopsticks") begins to compose several pieces of music a month later that she claims to receive via telepathic dictation: a fusion of soft, dreamy jazz and rock with lyrical translations from "the Pleiades," a star cluster whose messages include:

> By and by we learn to fly
> Within each other's heart.
> Space and time, the ancient rhyme,
> Is overcome in our heart.°

Connie Cook's "encounter" touches the heart of an elusive category many still prefer to call "new-age" or "space music." With its slow, diaphanous, wistful, and often droning style, space music builds on musical textures and precedents that are as much a mystery to the recording artists as they are to the listener. To quote Stephen Hill, a leading space music connoisseur, who heads the Hearts of Space label: "Our supermediated techno-culture has undergone an extraordinary increase in its rate of change, with dynamic and unpredictable psychological reactions. One of these, I believe, has been the need for a healing, deepening, slow-paced sound food to balance out the overwhelming forces of banality and hyperstimulation."

To sate these needs, space music evokes vague images of regal landscapes perhaps encountered in past lives or the tones of a harmonic convergence between earth and other celestial bodies. Harpist Andreas Vollenweider had expressed to *Newsweek* in 1985 the desire to "build a bridge between the conscious and the subconscious." Some practitioners boast of their music's mysterious healing properties, capable of curing body ailments, relieving tension, inducing better plant growth, or simply making the average workday seem less hellish.

Space music is just as important for its ability to confound our spoon-fed sense of time and place. Its mercurial stirrings create openings between worlds: inner and outer space; ancestral rhythms and ultra-civilized electronics; the clock on the wall and the hallucinatory "psychonaut" time that drifts in and out of waking life. Most of all, space music negotiates the margin between

---

°From "You and I" by Connie Cook. © 1990 Cook 'n Mark Productions, Box 405, Canton, IL 61520. Reprinted by permission.

a composer's imagination and the complex digital technologies at his or her disposal that seem ready at any moment to assume a life of their own.

Listening to Constance Demby, Andreas Vollenweider, Richard Burmer, or Yanni, we cannot help suspecting that their compositions modeled on "half-formed dreams" are subject by their very nature to alien intrusion. The mystique of communing with some larger, transpersonal, extraterrestrial Gaia is commonly included as part of space music's packaging. Explaining compositions such as "The Galactic Chalice" and "Celestial Communion," Constance Demby refers to "the transformative journey" with "sounds to awaken and activate soul memory of our true origin." One Chicago musicologist was so intrigued by Connie Cook's "other-worldly" sounds that he claimed that some of her notes had no terrestrial musical precedent and could not even be put on paper.

While claims of extraterrestrial inspiration or tampering are difficult to refute and impossible to prove, one earthly influence can illuminate at least some of space music's stylistic origins. In classic Oedipal fashion, many new-age artists have overlooked the most obvious and least loved aliens of all—their parents' Mantovani and other mood music records.

New-age music differs in obvious ways from its "Beautiful Music" predecessors. Its insistence on unfamiliar and fluid "sonic landscapes" avoids Beautiful Music's familiar melodies, its full (unsynthesized) orchestras, and its up-front appeals to nostalgia. Pianist David Lanz once professed to *Musician* magazine that he rarely uses "thirds," the intervals that usually determine whether a chord will be major or minor. He claims: "So rather than voicing a chord with a major third, we'd use the root, two, and five. Or root, five, dominant seventh. It implies both major and minor, which is nice. Kind of a Zen thing."

Regardless of the studied ambivalence, the press's repeated comparisons of new-age music to elevator music reflect something more than smug critical dismissal. Space music is, in fact, easy-listening with amnesia, sounding like the future but retaining unconscious ties to elevator music of the past.

In effect, space music currently faces an identity challenge similar to Muzak's. Some baby-boomer Muzak® personnel (previously enthralled by rock music) are tempted to wipe their library clean of anything suggesting the "schmaltz" their elders imposed on them long ago. Now, however, their bread and butter depends on their cranking out background music that retains precisely those elevator aria shades.

New-age music miraculously attained glory just as the Beautiful Music generation was being nudged aside by a younger, but equally upwardly mobile generation. While the *Chicago Tribune* described new age as "the soundtrack to the Brave New World," *Business Journal* characterized the average new-age connoisseur as being "predominantly white, college-educated, mostly 25 to 40, professional—some campus age, but not with discretionary income." Josef Woodard in *Musician* magazine designated new age as "music for Yuppie mating rituals." Young adults no longer energized by rock and alienated from the classics may latch onto this kind of music with the same élan their post–World War II parents displayed in discarding Swing in favor of mood music.

The first new-age formula was a mixture of Pink Floyd's trippy art-rock, the Mahavishnu Orchestra's jazz–rock fusions, and Tangerine Dream's synthesized brainscapes transformed into a softer, floating style performed with synthesizers, harps, electric pianos, and other hypnotic effects.

New-age musicians valiantly tried to pass their craft off as purely artistic but inevitably encountered the same pall of condescension and scorn that their Muzak and easy-listening predecessors endured. From its beginnings, new-age music was doomed to controversy and censure from a musical establishment still wedged into nineteenth-century prejudices that equated good music with direct listening.

The initial foreshadowing of the new-age sound occurred in 1964 when Tony Scott unofficially kicked off the movement with his album *Music for Zen Meditation.* He proudly described it as a passive product in a "twisted" world of competition and sensationalism.

These criticisms of Western culture and of the tensions inherent in its musical structure played on years later when new-age pianist

George Winston (the star of the Windham Hill label) recorded self-described "sound incense" that was so trance-friendly that Keith Jarrett (himself an improvisational creator of jazz sound-scapes) felt obliged to distance himself from it with this critique:

> The implications of his [Winston's] music are interest-
> ing, because it's used for meditating, for relaxing, for
> falling asleep, for having conversations—the exact op-
> posite of my reasons for playing. If someone can fall
> asleep or meditate while the music is going on, to me
> that's spiritually not right.*

Many new-age musicians and record producers tried to change their sound by adding jazz riffs and acoustic guitars. They also altered their press releases to make their enterprise sound more musical and less mystagogic. Some eschewed the "new-age" label altogether. For instance, once Andreas Vollenweider won a Grammy for "Down to the Moon," his press shunned "new-age" in favor of "instrumental pop music."

Nevertheless, new-age/space/adult alternative music proponents keep reviving the debate over background music's aesthetic value. New age, like Muzak, claims to be "more than music," but its packaging (from the sounds to the album art to the liner notes) aims at something loftier than simply animating the business world.

Connie Cook is a walking testimonial to the space music pan-acea. If her alien arias sound too logically discordant to cynics, her fellow new-age practitioners' promises of music to realign the spine, help rediscover past lives, strengthen the human immune system, and promote general peace of mind are hardly more ten-able. Soviet educators, during the Union's final days, used Cook's music to teach Ukrainian students to speak and read English. Igor Shpak taught the lyrics to Cook's "White Light" and had advised her to visit Russia as a gesture of positive communication, espe-cially since the Soviet Union had hundreds UFO witnesses of its own.

*Judie Eremo, ed., *New Age Musicians* (Milwaukee: Hal Leonard, 1989), p. vii.

In 1985, new-age musician Steven Halpern came out with his book *Sound Health* to advocate music as an aid to meditation and healing. Speaking in the October 1988 issue of *Keyboard*, synthesizer player William Aura described his experiment with a fusion of new-age and dance music by performing several biofeedback tests on the effects of polyrhythms:

> *I'd put a rhythmic zither strum in the right ear of a person hooked up to biofeedback gear, and they'd start pacing to that strum. When we introduced an arrhythmic strum in the left ear, and their consciousness attempted to follow both, they lapsed into a hypnotic state in about two minutes. We had discovered something that people knew eons ago—that polyrhythms can be used for hypnotic induction, for altered states of consciousness, even for soul travelling.*

Robert Rich, another soundscape specialist with a psychology degree from Stanford University, is fascinated with REM sleep and "hypnagogic" states, which fuel his "all-night concerts for sleeping audiences." He once set up a "Rainforest" exhibit in San Francisco to serve as an environmental forum—an eco-friendly mixture of technology and nature intended to fill spectators with awe and concern for the endangered earth.

For all the attendant talk of cosmic cures, new-age music raises a nagging question: Is the supernal sound that heals souls and aligns spines any different from the easy-listening music that soothed martini drinkers after a day at the office decades ago?

The first noticeable similarity between Beautiful Music and new-age music relates to the functional role of lush strings in the former and synthesizers in the latter. Vangelis, for one, stunned the world with his opalescent *Chariots of Fire* film score, which re-created the timbre of a full orchestra merely through the pressing of a few sequencer buttons. What is most remarkable is how well much of new-age music blends in with that of the Percy Faiths of the world. If David Lanz were to do a rendition of "I'll Never Smile Again" or if Raphael applied his arpeggios to "Softly, as I Leave You," the two genres would be more apparently inter-changeable.

New-age and easy-listening music also share an affinity for a sound that surrounds listeners with aural gauze and coaxes them into forgetting their troubles. The two space music artists with the most obvious parallels to Mantovani are Constance Demby and Raphael.

For her album *Novus Magnificat,* Demby used an Emulator II Synthesizer to create digital samples of real symphonic instruments. She then compressed them on magnetic disks in order to re-create them on a keyboard. The effects of violas, harps, piano, organ, French horn, tympani, cello, and a chorus recall Mantovani's intricate weaving. It is also significant that both Mantovani and Demby use the metaphor of the cathedral to describe their music's inclinations toward the sacred.

Like Demby's *Novus Magnificat,* Raphael's *Music to Disappear In* suggests a "sound bath." Raised by Benedictine nuns when his family got ill, Raphael spent his solitary childhood becoming well versed in Gregorian chant and classical music. In 1967, he participated in the San Francisco Summer of Love, masquerading as a velvet-caped European count who serenaded passersby with his gypsy violin. He studied piano and composition at the San Francisco Conservatory and soon moved to Big Sur's Esalen Institute, where he worked as a staff musician. He was so impressed by a contemporary shaman during his Esalen stay that he started pursuing music as therapy, mixing world rhythms with Western melodies to heal and relax.

Space music can then be best regarded as an outgrowth of easy-listening that is even further removed from the musical foreground. Beautiful Music supplies ghost tunes of originals, whereas space music distills the ghost tune's mood, its sound, and a smidgen of its style and reprocesses it into an "original" composition once again, this time unanchored to any distinct emotional or historical context. It avoids nostalgia mainly because its uncertainties force us to look back and ahead simultaneously. It derives power from the clash between the musician's emotions and the space-station grandeur of high-tech gadgets and computer wizardry.

Some of its best examples suggest science-fiction fantasies rooted in comic books and optimistic space tales. Space music thus celebrates a nostalgia for the future as it paradoxically looks ahead toward unsolved childhood mysteries.

Space music is, however, entering another phase. Some artists have grown less unconscious about their easy-listening predecessors and are actively reaching out to these forgotten ancestors to absorb their influences directly and intentionally. Richard Burmer (from the American Gramaphone label) describes himself as a "composer of lush sonic tapestries" influenced by dreams: "I love Percy Faith, especially the 'Theme from *A Summer Place.*' I want to do my own version of it. It makes me feel so good, looking back on growing up at that time period." This interest in sentimental themes shows up in titles like "The Rain Will Bless the Love" and "Shining by the River."

Seeing no inherent conflict between the terras firma and incognita, Burmer uses mellotron, autoharp, and an Emulator II synthesizer equipped with a library of digital samples to reinterpret hand-me-down melodies inspired by preexisting cinema icons:

> *Walt Disney was a big influence on me. I think about some of his animated things.* Fantasia, Sleeping Beauty *. . . they are surreal landscapes. All heightened, with Tinkerbells and stars. That is sort of what I feel in my music, a lot of these sprays and cascades here and there, mainly making a person feel good. Though there are some percussive, aggressive moments, my album* Bhakti Point *is about a journey to an imaginary paradise.*

Burmer is among many artists appearing on American Gramaphone's "Day Parts" CD series, which was conceived by Chip Davis, founder of Mannheim Steamroller and *Fresh Aire*. Designed to capture what Davis calls "the four major mood groups," they reflect the predominant emotions and thoughts of people at various times of day, with styles ranging from quasi-Baroque to new age to solo acoustic, and a smattering of soft rock.

Davis, a former radio disk jockey who claims to have written jingles and over 2,000 pieces of original music for Levis, Lee

Jeans, Black & Decker, McDonald's, and AT&T, has no compunction about directing elevator music principles into the private lives of those who live among high-tech condos and nouvelle cuisine. Another reason for his easy-listening congeniality may be his first post-college job: singing with the Norman Luboff Choir.

His four mood groups—*Sunday Morning Coffee, Dinner, Party*, and *Romance*—are also marketed with special gift packs that include coffee with mugs, recipe books with napkins, barbecue sauce, or a Japanese bubble-bath with scented candle. Except for the Afro-Caribbean themed *Party*, all titles mix Baroque stylings, classical piano, and predominant synthesizers. The effect not only encourages meditation but suggests well-defined and cozy situations in which to exist.

The best of the mood groups, *Romance,* combines the works of several American Gramaphone instrumentalists with cameos by Debussy's "Clair de Lune" and Beethoven's "Moonlight Sonata." The result is a pleasant blend of classical, romantic, Beautiful Music and space music. Davis claims:

> *Romance is about man's need for companionship—not necessarily sexual, but friendship or giving time to yourself as well. Romance, by the dictionary definition, is more involved around adventure than love. So this music is geared not only to enjoy those times, but out of a deeper reason to point them out. The mood is there although you don't notice it. But if you put a frame around the picture, you tend to notice the picture more.*

The relatively new term "transcendental romantic" is used to describe a sound that combines grand piano, wordless choruses, and strings (both real and synthesized). Mychael Danna specializes in melodic textures with intended emotional effects. Born in Winnipeg, Manitoba, Danna owes much of his musical inspiration to Canada's gray, monochromatic winter skies. He bought his first synthesizer the same day a hand injury dimmed his future as a piano player. Armed with a University of Toronto degree in music composition, he became composer-in-residence at Toronto's

McLaughlin Planetarium and also scored many of Atom Egoyan's independent films.

Danna's album *Skys* adapts music to a series of photographs he took during a 1986 spring trip. In his liner notes, he writes: "The relentless rain and fog over wet sand dunes made for poor sunbathing, but left a strong and distinctively moody impression in my mind of these skies which dominated the landscape." Besides working with his digital sampling keyboard, Danna uses "monochromatic arpeggios" on real pianos, and a "murky string sound" along with "long legato oboe and trumpet calls." Danna is representative of a number of younger instrumental artists who are willing to appreciate the more nostalgic, sentimental music of their elders, albeit with a slightly darker edge.

Windham Hill's Liz Story, who usually plays the piano with a bass player providing accompaniment, has converted to more recognizable, traditional melodies. David Darling takes the cello into the twenty-first century by blending acoustic cello with eight-string electric cello to give the illusion of a full string orchestra. But in the tradition of Mantovani before him, Darling relies on the unique sonic delights of the recording studio for his effects, putting the cello into a digital delay pattern that evokes atavistic memories of caverns and other undefined places where primordial time and space linger.

By adapting to the dictates of commerce, space music has found some emotional footing. Since the early 1980s, new-age cover art alone has assumed what some in the business call "a corporate identity," with the emphasis on high-tech pastorals and interstellar sanctuaries. A study in the Fall 1990 *Journal of Popular Culture* identified five stylistic trends in new-age covers: stark designs, natural landscapes, impressionistic fantasies, abstract art, and the common practice of retaining mystery by omitting the recording artist's photo.

In the study Windham Hill's Anne Robinson expressed a desire for album jackets to "create an atmosphere for the listener.... We are really seeking to describe a mood with our records." Consistent with its delightful contradictions, space music intrigues because it resorts to high-tech manipulations extolling "nature" in a manner perversely similar to the 101 Strings' evocation of foreign lands through color-treated photos.

New-age music ("Parade of the Tall Ships") provided the appropriate background sound for the 1986 Centennial celebrating the refurbished Statue of Liberty. Human-interest stories on network news broadcasts and commercials for everything from investment firms to breakfast cereals have also used the supernal strains of space music. For example, synthesizer specialist Yanni wrote the theme music for ABC's *World News Now*. A commercial for the Acura Legend uses space music to evoke the drama of near-death experiences while a narrator explains how a state-of-the-art air-bag can save lives. The music also shows up in hospital maternity rooms and surgery rooms and on airlines to help allay pain and worry.

New-age or space music may ultimately succeed better in getting us in touch with "artificial" chrome malls than with "natural" deserts; better yet, they may help our imaginations amalgamate both. Using space music to explore ourselves, many of us get so tangled in its consumer technology that every attempt to escape the wires and to groove to the quasar beat merely pulls us into another gorgeous "pseudo-dimension."

13 / Metarock

Heavy metalist Ted Nugent hates Muzak® so much that he once made a $10 million bid to buy the company—just for the pleasure of erasing the tapes. An avid hunter who took rock and roll to its carnivorous extremes, Nugent reinforced his rowdy image by using Muzak as a scapegoat for all things uncool, unrebellious, and, worst of all, unloud. This was, of course, another in many quixotic efforts to preserve the ever-fraying battle lines between the "hip" and the "square" at a time when Bob Dylan, the man who said "Never trust anyone over thirty," was already becoming a golden oldie.

In 1989, Muzak calculated an appropriate response when its program manager, Christopher Case, recorded an elevator-style cover of "Journey to the Center of the Mind," a song Nugent had made popular with the Amboy Dukes in the late sixties. Refurbished by the Jim Devlin Orchestra with a mellow wash of horns, piano, violins, and moderate tempo percussion, this once fulminating paean to psychotropia took on a brave new meaning—a much gentler companion piece to its Mr. Hyde prototype.

Nugent's comeuppance continued when the makers of the British television documentary *"Beautiful Music"* commissioned mood maestro John Fox to arrange an easy-listening version of "Cat Scratch Fever." One could simultaneously laugh and cry while watching Nugent listen to a tape playback of his feral frenzy whipped into submission by Fox's dainty piano arpeggios. Though dumbfounded, Nugent was also forthright in his response: "I gotta tell you. The guy grasped the emotion of the song. I mean, he was playing on the keyboard really articulately the vocal pattern that I sang. And I have to hand it to the guy—the guy knows what he's doing."

Suddenly, Nugent and John Fox were not really enemies at all, more like doppelgangers staring at each other through funhouse mirrors. But long before the Muzak-Nugent match, there was always an underappreciated correspondence between rock's counterculture and elevator music's counterpunch.

By the early sixties, when the 101 Strings went from globetrotting to exploring domestic themes, they plowed through rock and roll's dense jungle at a time when cadres as diverse as religious fundamentalists and jazz purists still complained about its baleful influence. The 101 Strings' answer to the Elvis Presley revolution was an album called *Backbeat Symphony* (subtitled *Rock and Roll in the Sound of Magnificence*), which boasted "the majesty of the symphony—with a beat."

Selections included "Rigoletto Rock," Verdi's theme set to bopping drums and sentimental strings, which could easily have been an instrumental backing for the Platters. "Sherabop" consisted of variations on a theme from Rimsky-Korsakov's *Scheherazade,* refurbished with a full doo-wop vocal section. "Swingin' at Igor's" adapted a Borodin melody (already modernized as "Stranger In Paradise"), sending the rocking brass, chorus, and rhythm section through a Phil Spectorish reverberation process. "Twangy Serenade" (Schubert paired with electric surf guitars) sounded something like the Ventures at the Philharmonic. The album's title track included plunking piano chords and up-tempo violins similar to Percy Faith's "Theme from *A Summer Place.*"

The *Backbeat Symphony* album was in essence a prototype of many subsequent easy-listening endeavors that would fuse "longhair" music with "mop-top" pop. Blazing the trail with caution, the album's liner notes assumed a high school instructor's tone.

> *As a group, the teen-ager has the highest musical appetite in the world today. And too often this appetite for music (predominated by rhythmic, danceable tunes) must be satisfied with badly written songs with borderline obscene lyrics. For teen-age audiences, the beat is here. The longhair and parent alike should accept this fact. It is not wrong. It is wrong only when satisfied by material of inferior content. If the teen-ager is to develop musical tastes along with other maturities it can be readily appreciated that an exposure to good music in some form is a prerequisite to this development.*

Although the sixties' "generation gap" was among the most publicized and packaged controversies, many overlooked the more subtle and important similarities between the two age groups. Music of the Beach Boys, the Beatles, and even some of the Stones retained traditional melodic structures and instead of posing a threat ultimately supplied a cache of fresh material for easy-listening artists seeking to stay on the blunt end of the cutting edge.

This explains the barrage of metarock albums such as Percy Faith's *Themes for Young Lovers, Morton Gould Makes the Scene,* Don Costa's *Instrumental Versions of Simon and Garfunkel, Floyd Cramer Plays the Monkees, Danny Davis and the Nashville Strings Play Instrumental Versions of the Herman's Hermits Songbook,* the Johnny Arthey Orchestra's *The Golden Songs of Donovan,* Liberace's *A Brand New Me,* the Living Voices' *Positively 4th Street and Other Message Folk Songs,* and the 101 Strings' *Million Seller Hits Written by the Beatles and Other "Now" Writers.*

Underground filmmaker Todd Rutt claims to have had a revelatory moment in Colorado while listening to a background music ver-

sion of Iron Butterfly's "In A Gadda Da Vida." This led him to conclude that understanding metarock requires a different and rarefied
aesthetic law: "Strip away something original with orchestral strings
and what you have is something so far removed from the real thing
it assumes a new reality."

French easy-listening arrangers were among metarock's most creative avatars with their variations on *musique d'élévateur*. Franck
Pourcel could even be considered a metarock pioneer in 1959 when
he and his "French Fiddles" had a *Billboard* Top 10 hit with a light
instrumental version of the Platters' rock-a-ballad "Only You."
Pourcel followed pop and rock into its manic phases through the
sixties with enchanting and intricate renditions of songs such as "San
Francisco (Be Sure To Wear Flowers In Your Hair)" and "Nights In
White Satin." In the mid-seventies, he plied his orchestral gloss on
an instrumental salute to ABBA and was soon setting some of his
arrangements to the disco throb. Pourcel even gave a nod to eighties synth-pop, particularly with the electronically enhanced keyboards
on his highly elevated adaptation of Kim Carnes's 1981 hit "Bette
Davis Eyes."

At about this time, a well-established French-Italian composer-
arranger, born Claude Vasori, was also tinkering with ways to combine the time-honored art of massed strings with new sounds and
"current" tempos. Vasori became Caravelli in 1959, shortly after he
composed the music for the Gina Lollabrigida movie *Where the Wind
Blows*. He accepted producer Ray Ventura's invitation to record albums with a large string-filled orchestra and was billed initially as
Caravelli and His Magical Violins.

By the time Columbia Records marketed him as Caravelli and
His Magnificent Strings, he had perfected a way for his strings to
enjoy a "Je T'Aime"–style badinage between hysterically high and
lusciously low registers. In 1977, he released one of his most daring
and acclaimed records—a version of Bob Dylan's 1970 instrumental hit "Wigwam." Here his audacious use of strings to approximate
Dylan's wordless hum became a prized addition to many of America's
easy-listening radio stations.

Raymond Lefevre forged another French link between easy-listening radio and the American Top 40. Having shown a predilection

for the "now" beat years with his 1958 instrumental cover of "The Day the Rains Came," he blasted away with a fusion of lush strings and rock pulsation on the 1968 hit "Ame Caline (Soul Coaxing)." This mad masterpiece opens with a frisky piano rhythm but soon floats with shimmering violins that almost screech as his choir lets out a joyous cry. This, like Paul Mauriat's recording of "Love Is Blue" (which charted at around the same time), appealed to conflicting generational tastes.

Paul Mauriat is the best remembered of France's pop orchestral instrumentalists. He, like many of his peers, built on the groundwork laid by such light music compatriots as Paul Bonneau and Roger Roger. As a composer, he had left his mark on the early sixties when, under the pseudonym Del Roma, he wrote the melody to "Chariot," which Petula Clark popularized in Europe. By 1963, with English lyrics added, Little Peggy March turned it into the #1 smash "I Will Follow Him."

Arguably among the boldest of the lot, Mauriat took inventive measures to incorporate rock into his repertoire, creating a psychedelic soundscape replete with electronic guitars and keyboards, vibrant horns, tickling percussion, and a volley of stereophonically enhanced strings. Mauriat could morph a wailing counterculture anthem such as "Let the Sunshine In" into an orderly yet brilliantly loopy blend of electric guitars, violins, and a sitar—all climaxing in a brassy finale more fitting for a tribal-love-rock Vegas revue.

Metarock was also evolving stateside. Percy Faith, as previously mentioned, helped ignite the fever with his 1963 release *Themes for Young Lovers.* But with the exception of a rocking drumbeat Faith rarely if ever used rock instruments. On the Mauriat tune "I Will Follow Him," he maintained the rhythm by relying mostly on the string pizzicato and horn sections. Andre Kostelanetz, in contrast, applied bolder strokes to the song on his 1964 album *I Wish You Love,* combining horns and strings but also setting up a double date between a harpsichord and a Duane Eddy–style guitar.

Eddy himself brought out a great hybrid of sweet orchestral and surf rock on his 1960 hit "Because They're Young" and the 1962 album *Twangy Guitar/Silky Strings*—both arranged and conducted by Bob Thompson. And long before they released several easy instrumental albums in the seventies and eighties, England's Shadows occasionally allowed their producer Norrie Paramor's strings to mate with their Stratocasters. Permutations on this splendid strings-and-surf combination could have gone on and on, but unfortunately such ideal projects as *Percy Faith Meets the Ventures* were never conceived.

Despite his stature with the ballroom baton, Lawrence Welk also took some intrepid steps to appropriate the teen beat. When the West Coast band the Chantays appeared on his television show to perform the 1963 hit "Pipeline," Welk's Champagne Music players sat with patronizing smirks, immobilized in the background. But that same year Welk and his orchestra took out their strings, horns, and harpsichord for a champagne cover version with a rock accompaniment that sounded suspiciously like the stylings of the teenage surf rockers they were covering. The Chantays and the king of the bubbly beat were, after all, Dot Records label mates. A year before, on his album *Young World,* Welk had gone toe-to-toe with both the Ricky Nelson title song and Elvis Presley's "Heartbreak Hotel." And into the late sixties he plied a psychedelic harpsichord to his cover of the Lemon Pipers' "Green Tambourine" while bolstering the melody with a sugarcoated feminine chorus.

No easy-listening mastermind had better metarock skills than Stu Phillips. A graduate of the Eastman School of Music in Rochester, New York, Phillips quickly transposed his learned background into mercenary endeavors after Milton Berle hired him as a copyist for the *Texaco Hour.* Besides writing commercial jingles for Yuban coffee, Q-Tips and Tarreyton cigarettes, he scored incidental music for the *Donna Reed Show* and the *Monkees,* arranged for the Doodletown Pipers, and wrote music for the cult biker film *Run Angel Run* and Russ Meyer's *Beyond the Valley of the Dolls.*

Phillips is best known, however, for his years as resident arranger at Capitol Records. There he arranged, produced, conducted, and wrote for the Hollyridge Strings, the ensemble that recorded the first Beatles instrumental cover songs. Albums such as *The Hollyridge Strings Play the Beatles Song Book* gave this orchestra its rightful status as the ectoplasmic Beatles, supplying brilliant pizzicato, piccolos and studio reverb on what the album notes describe as "tuneful, gorgeously listenable versions" of Lennon-McCartney songs.

Phillips went on to do *The Hollyridge Strings Play Instrumental Hits Made Famous by Elvis Presley*, *The Hollyridge Strings Play Instrumental Versions of Hits Made Famous by the Four Seasons*, and *The Beach Boys Song Book*. His mood music excursion entitled *Feels Like Lovin'* is so phantasmagoric that it must be heard to be believed. Selections such as "Stop! In the Name of Love," "Goin' Out of My Head," "Goldfinger," "Tired of Waiting for You," and "Ooo Baby Baby" get not only a string section but "a lonely trumpet, a haunting trombone, and, of course, the ever-present rhythm, throbbing like a heartbeat, playing the tempos of love." The ambiance throughout is as soporific as it is taunting, with an "oohing" chorus carefully embedded to sing only the "mood words."

"Nancy Sinatra and Paul Petersen loved *Feels Like Lovin'*," Stu Phillips recalled during a recent telephone interview. "Petersen said it was his make out album. I got a response about ten years ago, when my brother Lee, an attorney, represented Lamont Dozier, one of the writers of 'Stop! In The Name Of Love.' I asked him if he ever heard my version of 'Stop'?" I sent him a tape. He called me and said, 'I can't believe I wrote that song! I can't tell you how much I like it.' He said he never believed his song could sound like that, so sensuous. During my contract dispute with Capitol, Perry Botkin, Jr. and Mort Garson did several Hollyridge albums. But I continued that eerie vocal effect on a Hollyridge Strings album called *Hits of the '70s.*" Phillips also recounts some technical finery:

> *The strings had that great echo because of tape delay, which offered almost a repetition of a note. This was especially effective with the pizzicato. Those string players' fingers almost bled from plucking so hard. But their bravery helped to produce that distinctive sound. Much of this also had to do with frequency, the high end of the spectrum. The high-end violin sound also depended on the amount of violins. The more the better! Most of the time I didn't use violas. I found that cellos playing in the viola register had a better, less muddy, recording sound. There were about 14 violins and six celli. But I was also trying to get more of a rock sound. Once I replicated the*

rhythm sections of the rock beat, I would then throw the
strings over instead of voices. I love the Hollyridge Strings.
I'm very proud of doing those records.

Easy-listening arranger-conductors often popped up as background artists on other notable rock-pop recordings. Dick Jacobs made a positive impact on early rock 'n roll by adding a vanilla coating of pizzicato strings to Buddy Holly's 1959 hit "It Doesn't Matter Anymore." Perry Botkin Jr. sprinkled his celestial powders over "Rhythm of the Rain" and other ballads by the Cascades. John Barry's strings complemented Chad and Jeremy's "Yesterday's Gone" while Geoff Love and His Orchestra accompanied "A World Without Love" and many other Peter and Gordon tracks.

Britain's composer, arranger, and producer Mike Leander also deserves special honors. He supplied the stately, melancholy backdrop on Marianne Faithfull's debut hit "As Tears Go By"—a glistening assortment of strings, harpsichord, and oboe that he would modestly call (in Mark Hodkinson's Faithfull biography *As Tears Go By*) a "plinky-plunky orchestral" sound. When George Martin could not make a recording date during the Beatles' *Sgt. Pepper's Lonely Hearts Club Band* sessions, Leander arrived to provide those poignant layers of lush on "She's Leaving Home."

In 1965, the Mike Leander Orchestra released *The Folk Hits,* a timely collection of such favorites as "Mr. Tambourine Man," "It Ain't Me Babe," and of course "As Tears Go By." Here, however, the lush string orchestra is absent. The songs are executed instead with the "jingle jangle" of a small ensemble: harpsichord, flutes, woodwinds, drums, and a wraithlike chorus looming to chime in a lyrical line or two at unpredictable moments. (Leander would continue with his orchestra into the seventies, but he also acquired a second career as Gary Glitter's manager.)

Johnny Arthey is another Merseyside arranger, composer, and conductor who made metarock forays. A broadcaster for BBC Radio, he was best known for plying strings behind singers such as Sacha Distel, Mary Hopkin, and Peggy March. Arthey also made easy-listening versions of what would seem to have been unlikely songs, his bank of violins forging a very peaceful coexistence with such stomping extremes as the Dave Clark Five's "Bits and Pieces." Covering Manfred Mann's "Do Wah Diddy Diddy," he matched strings with an electric guitar that sounded somewhat comical trying to simulate Paul Jones's vocal. Years later, Arthey even applied his Anglicized coating to the Jamaican beat when he formed the Johnny Arthey Orchestra and Reggae Strings.

Britain's Ronnie Aldrich transmitted his alternately high and low "twin piano" notes through Decca's "Phase 4 Stereo" on late sixties and early seventies albums such as *It's Happening Now* and *This Way "In."* Buttressed by the London Festival Orchestra and instruments ranging from electric guitars to Chinese tree bells, he offered sparkly arrangements of the Archies' "Sugar, Sugar," Crosby, Stills, Nash, and Young's "Woodstock," and the Moody Blues' "Ride My See-Saw." "I'm trying to keep to the feeling of unsung words," he once claimed when explaining why he kept the melody simple but the arrangements ornate. On a version of White Plains' 1970 hit "My Baby Loves Lovin'" for instance, he shifted from a quaint Baroque chamber-style opening to the simple Roger Cook–Roger Greenaway tune without jazzing it down. After an ethereal harp and acoustic rhythm guitar introduction, Aldrich's crystal clear Steinway tackled Shocking Blue's "Venus" while staying ever faithful to the original's bubble gum beat.

Some wonderful metarock also appeared on the "Beautiful Music" stations, particularly those custom-made tracks recorded by leading pop orchestral names and licensed to various radio syndicators. Under his Starborne Productions label, Jim Schlichting commissioned Frank Chacksfield to record arrangements that included a remarkable and hypnotically subdued version of the early sixties Bobby Vee hit "The Night Has a Thousand Eyes." Bonneville, another leading provider of FM dream themes, included such exclusive gems as John Fox's sweetly orchestral "Lucy in the Sky with Diamonds," Lex De Azevedo's reflective revision of the Beach Boys' "God Only Knows," and the Pat Valentino Orchestra's sultry interpretation of Tears for Fears' "Everybody Wants to Rule the World."

Since the sixties, Muzak's rock acquisition has been stunning. Many songs from Bob Dylan, the Doors, the Beatles, the Rolling Stones, the Mamas and the Papas, R.E.M., the B-52s, U2, and Van Morrison have been sonically recoded into tasteful, airy, and mystical confections. "I feel a little weird when I hear it in an elevator," John Densmore (the Doors' drummer) told an interviewer when asked if he ever got sick of hearing "Light My Fire." But several Doors songs held up well as Muzak permutations. "Riders on the Storm" already had the electronic cocktail piano that had enraged Paul Rothchild to the point of quitting as the band's producer. So it did not have to undergo any major surgery when it was converted to a Muzak instrumental: a low-register guitar replaced Jim Morrison's croon, while the rest of the composition remained almost identical to the original.

Muzak was already adept at mirroring the times in 1968 when it piped out lyric-free versions of songs from *Hair,* just a week before the "tribal-love-rock" musical opened on Broadway. Better yet, the same orchestra that had recorded the original soundtrack album played Muzak's selections, the sessions supervised by none other than *Hair*'s cocomposer Galt McDermott. This was primarily because Muzak's music director, Andrew Wiswell, also worked at RCA and had produced the *Hair* album.

If there existed a metarock equivalent to the Purple Heart, it would have to go to Rupert Parker, who duplicated such rock complications as Led Zeppelin's "Stairway to Heaven" and Queen's "Bohemian Rhapsody" on a harp. By the early 1990s, he had proved so adept at separating the melody from the mania that Muzak was using him on what it by then called its all-instrumental "Environmental Channel."

By the mid-1980s, Devo was among the very first bands to manufacture its own metarock, regurgitating its songs into pseudo-elevator versions on the *E-Z Listening Disc.* The meta-"Mongoloid" suggests the theme song from *Jeopardy,* while the band's interpretation of its previous interpretation of "I Can't Get No Satisfaction" got one more face lift, transforming the Stones' ill-tempered evergreen into a computerized anthem.

Mothersbaugh, Devo's resident philosopher and himself a devout elevator music fan, explains how what he calls his "inframusic" came about.

Muzak helped me shape my musical politics. When I heard Muzak versions of the Beatles, the Byrds and Bob Dylan, my goal was to do the same to my own music before anyone else did. Our E-Z Listening Disc has an interesting history. We were writing Muzak-style versions of our songs before we even had our first album out. We did a movie called In The Beginning Was The End: The Truth About Devolution *in about 1976. It won first place in the Ann Arbor Film Festival. We re-recorded a Beatles song by running it through a frequency analyzer. I ripped a couple of things right off an easy-listening channel and put them through this instrument. It became this bizarre robotic version of Muzak-type songs. WE WERE MUTATING MUZAK! . . . The first E-Z Disc sold out so fast that we did a second volume a couple of years later. Rock and Roll is so bankrupt that, out of desperation, they'll be mining those territories.*

Shortly before his death, John Lennon shocked his fans by disclosing to *Rolling Stone* magazine that he enjoyed easy-listening at home throughout the day while Yoko Ono was out on business. A decade later, Morgan Fisher released *Echoes of Lennon,* an instrumental collection of "the Intellectual Beatle"'s more melodic songs set to synthesizers and subtle percussion—a soft, slow, and haunting style that sometimes makes them barely recognizable. Yoko, enthused about Fisher's project from its inception, christened it with Onoisms: "By slowing down the music to its extreme limit, Morgan Fisher has allowed the musical notes to float in a space the size of the universe."

Fisher, whose previous musical background was far from easy-listening, was once a Mott the Hoople member and played keyboards for such raucous acts as Queen and Dead Kennedys. But he also demonstrated his knack for a lilting, easy style by collaborating on an "ambient" album called *Slow Music.* He also worked with elevator chanteuse Julee Cruise. Fisher sees his mood music interests as a logical progression from his rock roots.

There is a tradition in Japanese art called "Ma" in which the goal of the drawing or painting is to lead the viewer to a state of emptiness and relaxation. I have tried to incorporate those ideas into my music. The notes lead to pauses. If the notes weren't there, the listener couldn't appreciate the pauses. Just as, if I hadn't played so much hard rock, I wouldn't be able to play really tranquil music, which perhaps can create more space and relaxation than music made by people who haven't traveled to the extremes.

Fisher's use of Japanese precedents to explain his mood music philosophy harkens back to some observations that the late composer and theorist Glenn Gould made in an essay entitled "The Prospects of Recording" (published in the April 1966 issue of *High Fidelity*). Here, he speculated on future moodsong:

Background music has been attacked from many quarters—by Europeans as a symptom of the decadence of North American society, by North Americans as a product of megalopolitan conformity. Indeed, it is perhaps accepted at face value only in those societies where no continuing tradition of Occidental music is to be found.

In the heart of the "swinging sixties," when ossified jazz buffs and hormonally agitated hard rock fans whined in unison about elevator music's "horrors," Gould was among the precious few musical highbrows to stick out his neck in defense of what he called "restaurant Muzak" and all of its connotations. "The stylistic range of most background music at present," Gould also observed, "offers an appreciably greater variety of idiomatic citation than can be found among all the disparate ideologues to which 'serious' musicians of recent times have subscribed."

In truth, rock and roll—and especially such pop offshoots as folk rock—forged an unacknowledged bond with—and even reenergized—the art of the easy-listening instrumental. One form corresponded in a parallel world with the other. Among the highlights of such heavenly musical marriages are the electric guitar, harpsichord, horns, swinging drums, and swirling strings on David Rose's interpretation of Donovan's "Wear Your Love Like Heaven"; Martin Denny's raga-mated "Incense and Peppermints," which nearly duplicated the Strawberry Alarm Clock's every vocal nuance with flutes and electronic keys; and the impish appearance of a fuzz guitar against a bank of violins when 101 Strings' reworked Simon and Garfunkel's "The Boxer." Such examples show how mood maestros faced and met all the challenges of the "Now Sound"—without compromising that *elevated* spirit.

Choice Metarock (20 Titles Listed Alphabetically)

1. **California Dreamin'** (Hugo Winterhalter)
   16 BEAUTIFUL HITS (CD Deluxe DCD-7901) 1994
2. **Green Tambourine** (Lawrence Welk)
   LOVE IS BLUE (Ranwood RLP-8003) 1968
3. **Happy Together** (Percy Faith and Chorus)
   TODAY'S THEMES FOR YOUNG LOVERS (CS-9504) 1967
4. **Incense and Peppermints** (Martin Denny)
   A TASTE OF INDIA (Liberty LST-7550) 1968
5. **Karma Chameleon** (Fantasy Strings)
   DAY BY DAY (Kem Disc KD-10182) 1993
6. **Lay Lady Lay** (Ferrante and Teicher)
   GETTING TOGETHER (UAS-5501) 1970
7. **Leaving on a Jet Plane** (Andre Kostelanetz)
   I'LL NEVER FALL IN LOVE AGAIN (Columbia CS-9998) 1970
8. **Let the Sunshine In** (Paul Mauriat)
   LET THE SUNSHINE IN/MIDNIGHT COWBOY/AND OTHER GOODIES (Philips PHS-600-337) 1969
9. **Logical Song** (Franck Pourcel)
   DIGITAL AROUND THE WORLD (EMI-Odeon 064-073-551T) 1981

10. **Mrs. Brown, You've Got a Lovely Daughter** (Danny Davis and the Nashville Strings)
PLAY INSTRUMENTAL VERSIONS OF THE HERMAN'S HERMITS SONG BOOK (MGM SE-4309) 1965

11. **The Night Has a Thousand Eyes** (Frank Chacksfield)
SOUNDS OF ROMANCE (CD Good Music Company 199927) 1998

12. **98.6** (David McCallum)
McCALLUM (Capitol ST-2748) 1969

13. **Pipeline** (Lawrence Welk)
SCARLETT O'HARA (Dot DLP-25528) 1963

14. **San Francisco (Be Sure to Wear Flowers in Your Hair)** (Franck Pourcel)
LOVE IS BLUE (Imperial LP-12383) 1968

15. **Strawberry Fields Forever** (Hollyridge Strings)
THE BEATLES SONG BOOK, VOL. 4 (ST-2656) 1967

16. **Telstar** (James Last)
INSTRUMENTALS FOREVER (Polydor 184059) 1966

17. **Things We Said Today** (Hollyridge Strings)
THE BEATLES SONG BOOK, VOL. 2 (ST-2202) 1965

18. **Venus** (Ronnie Aldrich)
HERE COME THE HITS! (SP-44143) 1970

19. **Wear Your Love Like Heaven** (David Rose)
HAPPY HEART (Capitol ST-393) 1969

20. **Wigwam** (Caravelli)
BY REQUEST: FEATURING THE HIT "WIGWAM" (Peters International PLD-1000) 1977

14 / Elevator Noir

The world is so different in the daylight. In the dark your fantasies get so out of hand. But in the daylight everything falls back into place again. Let's have no more nights.
—**Mary Henry from *Carnival of Souls***

Sometime in the late seventies, a background music company was broadcasting an instrumental collection it had licensed from Italy. Amid "O Sole Mio," "Santa Lucia," and other Mediterranean delights, a version of Nini Rosso's "Il Silenzio" played in its proper sequence. The song's uncanny similarity to the military dirge "Taps" induced a woman to have a nervous breakdown in a hospital waiting room when she interpreted it as a *memento mori* intended solely for her terminally ill husband.

Another woman, this time hearing Music by Muzak® on a flight, began screaming as the plane went down the runway. It was the thirties tune "For All We Know," and even without the lyrics its second phrase, "We may never meet again," played at the wrong place and time. Such stories prove that background music, with the slightest disagreeable song content, altered tempo, or stray key can make the "comfort zone" slip into the "Twilight Zone."

Muzak programmers and engineers, who once used only major chords, were always aware that the simplest audio nuance could set off a lachrymose tone. Among the songs Muzak had to delete from its in-flight service were "Stormy Weather," "I've Got a Feeling I'm Falling," and "I Don't Stand a Ghost of a Chance". Muzak put "The Yellow Rose of Texas" into the deep freeze after President Kennedy's assassination in Dallas. For several days following the tragedy, Muzak worried that other popular songs might spur unpleasant associations and switched temporarily to an all classical repertoire. Sure enough, one of the previously scheduled songs turned out to be an instrumental version of another popular thirties tune: "I'll Be Glad When You're Dead, You Rascal You!" Even Muzak's Christmas music elicited complaints from a hospital after some of the patients found the sound of Yuletide tunes on the Monday after Thanksgiving too depressing.

While most people take background music's melodic buffer for granted, more creative and morbidly disposed listeners may imagine the sounds of *elevator noir*—darker melodies and antimelodies that creep into the environment to make the world an even scarier place. After all, elevator music has traditionally been played during life's most tenuous moments: a pivotal office engagement, another stay of execution in the dentist's waiting room, or the nail-biting anticipation of a late plane arrival.

Some background music has been known to induce "musicogenic" epilepsy, triggering a chemical brain reaction that elicits thoughts of suicide or murder. One 39-year-old epileptic woman in Britain complained that, when particular background tunes played at her neighborhood supermarket her eyes, fingers, and lips twitched; her thinking clouded; and she got sweaty and anxious before losing consciousness. Neurologists Peter Newman and Michael Saunders examined her to determine whether they could induce a similar seizure. Nothing happened when they played Gilbert and Sullivan selections, Beethoven's *Choral Symphony,* or Handel's *Messiah.* But when a song by the Dooleys called "I Think I'm Gonna Fall in Love with You" came on, she had another fit. The woman's EEG readings showed abnormal brain waves in the temporal lobe where sound is registered and interpreted. Around the time of this incident, medical researchers had documented 76 similar cases.

If music designed to soothe can be altered to torment, the field is open for misanthropes to play havoc with the canons of harmony and melody in the service of bad vibes. Many consumers are sado-masochistic enough to spend money viewing movies that frighten or disturb them, so why should they hesitate to frequent establishments designed to set their nerves on edge or to kindle crying jags? But the elevator noir field has thus far been explored mostly on commercial records. Just playing Bernard Herrmann's *Psycho* soundtrack, for instance, is sufficient to turn any dwelling into the Bates Motel.

Not until the mid-1970s did elevator noir gain Brian Eno as its intellectual avatar. Although he is sometimes hailed as the reluctant father of "New Age" music, Eno scoffs at the title because New Age compositions lack the seeds of "evil and doubt" that seem to pervade his work. Behind all of Eno's cold, metallic engineering is a frightening and moody world that is anything but emotionally neutral. He champions a kind of sonic ambivalence that encourages grave meditation or feelings of impending doom.

Eric Tamm, in his book *Brian Eno: His Music and the Vertical Color of Sound,* chronicles Eno's progress from his early days as a rock musician to his current career as a creator of mystifying "ambient" compositions "that could be listened to and yet could be ignored." Eno created "ambient" music by chance while putting together some background effects for a planned improvisation with Robert Fripp. He stored what Tamm describes as "two mutually compatible melodic lines of different duration" on digital recall and replayed them through an echo-delay system. Leaving the machine on by mistake, he was impressed by the spell it cast on the surroundings, especially when subaudible. The result was "Discreet Music," a piece consisting of repeated chord progressions not rooted in any set key.

Music for Airports, however, confirmed Eno's talent for obscuring the deceptive divisions between Muzak and art. Although he insists that his version is artful and Music by Muzak is not, Eno's ambient projects betray a few similarities to traditional mood music. Interweaving lackadaisical piano phrases with an unearthly choir, he even borrowed a technique that Jackie Gleason perfected decades ago by structuring entire pieces around sensual utterances such as "oooh" and "aaah." While Muzak and commercial mood music re-create sing-songy melodies, Eno invokes Stockhausen, whose own experiments with treated vocals and electronic tones also claimed a closer affinity to "high art" than *Your Hit Parade*. Critic Ken Emerson, perhaps weary of Eno's ambient manifestos, described *Music for Airports* as simply "avant-garde Muzak."

The *Music for Airports* sound is unique and disquieting for several reasons, most of which are technical. The album's second piece consists solely of a female choir electronically modulated with limited pitch and a delay on the fade-in and fade-out of the voices. Eno recorded the long notes on separate sections of tape and then looped them. The loops ran at different lengths and sequences to unleash a mixture of extended silences and unannounced sound clusters that formed what Eno has called "a sequence of notes that makes a kind of melody."

Eno's subsequent mood projects include *Music for Films, The Pearl* (a series of eerie collaborations with pianist Harold Budd), and an intriguing album called *Apollo* that consists of a darkly romantic homage to the moonward Apollo XI astronauts (who had Music by Muzak piped into their spacecraft). Eno, along with his brother Roger and Daniel Lanois, had been commissioned to design music for Al Reinert's documentary film about NASA's lunar missions. The results were the usual drone and relay of magnetic tape, but at least two tracks on this album—"Deep Blue Day" and "Under Stars II"— flirt more with conventional, even happier, harmonies and betray a closer proximity to true elevator music.

In the background music tradition, Eno's recordings are tailored for public places and events and are often commissioned by major corporations. An Eno audio-video sanctuary once appeared in Toyota's 14-story Amlux Auto Salon in Tokyo. His other "multimedia" sculptures have surfaced in Venice, Milan, New York, and Los Angeles. In June of 1982, the Three Rivers Arts Festival in Pittsburgh played *Music for Airports* at the Greater Pittsburgh International Airport for a nine-day period from noon to 10 P.M. Many patrons reportedly complained to airport personnel about this *un*easy listening and asked that the regular background music be restored.

Eno describes his ideal installation as "a place poised between a club, a gallery, a church, a square and a park." *Thursday Afternoon* is probably his most chilling soundscape. Commissioned by Sony exclusively for compact disc, it consists of a low, unsteady 61-minute key modulation vitalized by soft cacophony and occasional chord changes. Here his music comes closer to his other avocation: painting. He likens each slow, recurring musical cluster to a hologram composed of identical layered images in varying resolutions.

Perhaps Eno came closest to elevator noir on his treatment of Pachelbel's Canon, from the album *Discreet Music,* where the harmonious chords at the beginning suddenly disintegrate into random, overlapping patterns. A similar melodic meltdown occurs on the pipe organ piece that Mary Henry (the lead character in the cult horror film *Carnival of Souls*) plays during one of her moments of unearthly possession. A terminally confused woman survives what should have been a fatal car accident, moves to a quaintly off-kilter community in Utah to become a church organist, and encounters an apparition that is bent on taking her to the land of the dead, where she belongs. One evening during practice she plays what sounds like a nice, concordant Christian hymn. Suddenly she stops, gazes at her bewitched hands, and proceeds to alter the composition, making it sound like a carnival calliope dripping into amorphous half-chords. The note sequences drift further apart and become so disconcerting that the head of the congregation accuses her of blasphemy.

In 1998, 20 years after the original album appeared, Eno had *Music for Airports* performed live by the Bang on a Can All-Stars—a show that toured airports and other public sites in the United States and Europe. When interviewed, Eno again complained that traditional background music is "old-fashioned" and insisted that his approach is a better alternative. He also declared that his music provides an ideal background for people coping with the odds that the plane they or their loved ones are in might succumb to a blazing crash.

Director David Lynch and composer Angelo Badalamenti collaborated on their own blend of easy-listening irony on the soundtrack to the now legendary television series *Twin Peaks*. This twisted homage to whitebread culture, which centered on the corruption and death of homecoming queen Laura Palmer, often chimed in with variations on a theme of elevator music gone mad: synthesized strings, regimented finger snaps, repetitive bass lines, somnolent snare drums, and the shadowy wails of singer Julee Cruise, whose style suggests an amalgam of Claudine Longet and the Doors.

In the winter of 1990, *New York Times* critic Stephen Holden attended a Julee Cruise–Badalamenti concert at New York's Symphony Space and probably did not realize he was being complimentary when he described the sound as "surrealistic elevator music with quasi-symphonic textures that border on kitsch." Just compare the echo chamber resonance of Cruise's "Rocking Back Inside My Heart" with the Ray Conniff Singers' rendition of "It's Dark on Observatory Hill" to hear how easy-listening's good vibes can be twisted into something much more witchy but no less catchy.

Badalamenti's best *Twin Peaks* offering was "The Laura Palmer Theme," which fused a spine-tingling dirge with a lavish, soap operatic crescendo for use in some of the show's more gruesome scenes. But this shadow music also acts as a chorus for most of the story's small town denizens who are vexed by electromagnetic spirits that loom in air vents, telephone wires, and television noise and even materialize as breezes blowing through sycamores.

"A good example is in the movie *Fire Walk with Me*," Badalamenti reflects. "Laura Palmer is walking by a tree-lined street; the birds are in the trees, singing happily; she's carrying her schoolbooks. There is a cut on the soundtrack, a montage, which starts out so nice and pretty, but then you have all this high-string dissonance against it. It reflects that whole internal thing that this young teenager has gone through in her world. It paints the various worlds. From up above, down below, and everything in between."

"I have heard psychologists and shrinks," Badalamenti continues, "lots of doctors who have picked up the *Twin Peaks* album. They play it while doing work with their patients. The doctors say the music gets to the people. They get caught up without getting overly emotional. I was shocked. . . . When I got to Barcelona for the Olympics, I got off the airplane, and there was the theme from *Twin Peaks* playing right in the Barcelona airport!"

The *Twin Peaks* elevator music connection goes deeper. Badalamenti (under the less exotic name Andy Badale) had previously done several Muzak arrangements from Nashville, mostly piano tracks and instrumental versions of country songs with tenor saxes replacing the whiskey baritone. Badalamenti also adorned the *Twin Peaks* score with the drums of Grady Tate and guitar of Vincent Bell, also two past Muzak contributors.

Meanwhile, Canada's Mychael Danna had wandered deeper into elevator noir territory on his score to the 1999 Atom Egoyan film *Felicia's Journey*. He blended his own melancholy compositions (which range from Celtic dirges to angst-ridden, Bartokish violins) with the sounds of the more customary easy-listening instrumental. Danna also used the kind of lush, echo-redolent strings associated with Mantovani, but these are sounds he did not create. He instead took them directly from archival library sources whose context he in turn distorted to suit the film's darker purposes in presenting the story of a psychopath who leads an outwardly regimented life. The "title" track begins with the first phrases from an uncredited (ca. 1950s) production music recording called "The Cascade Waltz," composed by Ray Davies (not to be confused with the singer/songwriter from the Kinks) as an apparent "Charmaine" sound-alike. The shimmering strings soon warp into Danna's forlorn textures.

"I used old stock music, things out of libraries," Danna recalls. "Then I twisted it around, bent it out of shape. . . . I wrote it for the character who is someone who has a very different view of himself than the world or viewer might have of him. He sees himself as a suave, gentlemanly, kind and caring man from another, gentler time period. A generation ago, basically. . . . He uses this music as a kind of reassuring, comforting cushion around his personality; around the ugly truth of his personality. But he also pierces through this cushion."

"Canadians tend to have a darker perspective," Danna admits when trying to explain his somewhat gloomy style. "Maybe it's the relative lack of sun." This climatic explanation also applies to the overcast skies of Finland, particularly the city of Helsinki, where the sunshine is even stingier. Here human souls are likely to take refuge in a more cerebral lifestyle: staying indoors, communicating primarily through cellular phones, and lapsing into moments of deep, sincere contemplation that only airheads blessed with more clement weather would mistake for mere brooding.

Helsinki is where the audio artist Anton Nikkilä crafts his hyperelectrified answer to mood music. Nikkilä, who also cowrote the script for the 1997 Finnish documentary *Thank You for the Music,* brings a highly verbal and philosophical subtext to his projects. His obsession with making dystopian soundtracks originates in part from his previous collaboration with a *perestroika* era rock group from Moscow. His 2002 album *White Nights* features tracks such as "100 Years of Soviet Cybernetics" and "How the Steel Was Tempered"— a mingling of horrific industrial noise, rhythms partly derived from scratchy vinyl, and samples from promotional "Stimulus Progression" albums that Muzak had released in the seventies and eighties.

Nikkilä once entertained the idea that Muzak is a "lubricant for the dark, satanic mills of the capital" but has since come around to seeing a more kindly side, especially the old *Music by Muzak*'s aesthetic pleasures. And Mr. Nikkilä is intriguing for his geographical advantage. Even more than America, Finland is the cornucopia of Western progress, a place with relative prosperity, where the classic ideals of the older Muzak philosophy would seem to foster ideal applications. Perhaps these cultural advantages give experimental souls from Finland a comfortable distance in which to indulge their escapist fatalism. They have the luxury to speculate more freely about worst-case scenarios in which the circuitry of the Western order is sabotaged.

As the sounds of elevator noir abound, and the once time-tested art of simple romantic melodies inevitably evolves from an object of parody to an elusive curiosity, one may find contradictory motives behind the tonal terrorist acts described in this chapter. On the surface, a leering, sadomasochistic face gloats over the bedlam. But beneath this is another, less confident, battered, and yearning face that mourns elevator music's passing.

15 / Who's Hearing Things?

I am the President of The Songwriters' Hall of Fame, and the V.P. of ASCAP! I am proud of the Credentials. One of my favorite "cahn-tributions" to my duties at ASCAP was to bring about a reception to honor the 50ᵗʰ Anniversary of Muzak®! All the so-called humor about Muzak has always been I think flattering— no one makes humor unless the subject is worthy of humor, and Muzak has earned all the humor for what it has done and keeps doing. I wish I could tell you how many times I have been in an elevator with a great big smile, all the passengers who wondered who the idiot with a smile was couldn't have guessed I was the writer of the song being played. (I actually was earning money during that elevator ride thanks to ASCAP!) Suffice it to say, I love Muzak!!!

—Sammy Cahn

In March of 1992, composer John Sbarra filed a copyright infringement suit in Federal District Court in Newark, New Jersey, against the now late John Addison, a renowned writer of film and television scores. Sbarra believed that Addison's theme song for the hit series *Murder, She Wrote* sounded too much like "Basketful of Wishes" (a tune he cowrote with his friend Joseph Di Buono in the early 1950s) to be just coincidental.

This plagiarism case was most intriguing because Muzak® became its unwitting catalyst. According to Sbarra, Addison could only have heard "Basketful of Wishes" as a background tune because the song's exclusive rights were sold to Muzak in 1981. The Brno Radio Or-

216

chestra did record an uptempo version for Muzak, which Addison might have inadvertently stored in his memory bank, even though he responded to the suit by retorting that he never listened to Muzak if he could help it.

But could Mr. Addison have recomposed the song unconsciously after absorbing it through the ceiling speakers of an airport, an office lobby, or a public restroom? Could the same tune that accompanied Angela Lansbury rattling away at her typewriter in *Murder, She Wrote*'s opening credits be a "substantially similar copy" of one that inspired thousands of clerk typists on their 9-to-5 shifts? If background music is as intrinsic to manmade environments as air-conditioning, can anyone be held responsible for assimilating it, humming it at home, hearing it in dreams, or (for the more inventive) transcribing it at a piano? Was the *Sbarra v. Addison* case one of pilferage or creative acclimation?

Long since relegated to legal limbo, Sbarra's case did not ignite an explosion of similar courtroom battles. If anything, background music companies such as Muzak continued to serve as a songwriter's alternate cash crop. Before the vogue for "sampling" threatened all conventional boundaries of musical custody, many recording artists and songwriters were aware that an instrumental imitation could be the highest form of financial flattery. Simon and Garfunkel's hit version of "The Sounds of Silence," therefore, maintained a peaceful (and profitable) coexistence with its Muzak incarnation. ASCAP has also held original artist versions of songs and their easy-listening counterparts to identical licensing standards when they are played in theme parks and other places of high consumption.

In the early 1990s, while I was conducting research for this book's first edition, I visited Muzak's headquarters when the company was still based in Seattle. I was amazed to find on the lobby wall the gold and platinum records of such people as Paula Abdul, Bobby Brown, Kenny G, and Steve Winwood, thanking Muzak for exposing their tunes to thousands of subscribers. Paul Simon once said that when he hears a song in an elevator he knows it is a hit. At one point, Gloria Estefan and the Miami Sound Machine liked Muzak covers of their songs so much that they piped them out to their waiting audiences before commencing with their live shows.

Whenever an elevator version of a song appeared, songwriters raked it in, while casual listeners had a chance to engage in creative barter with their aesthetically conditioned reflexes. One could take a favorite piece of music, try to find an easy-listening instrumental version of it, and, by contrasting the two, wander into an enticing and sometimes frightening gray area where a violin, a slackened piano, or a trumpet's imitation of a vocal inflection could liberate the mind from the lonely musical foreground.

Yesterday's supermarket ceiling serenades offered the musical equivalent of a parallel world, a temporary reprieve from the ordinary fare that people listened to in their cars or at home. While the originals were too specific, carried too much baggage, or made for a cluttered audio perspective, the elevator version provided audio depth of field, an appropriately vague contour for transient surroundings.

This situation began to change when Muzak and other piped-in music companies introduced terms such as *business music* to alter their public images. This change reflects a now widespread belief that *all* kinds of music can have comparable benefits in business establishments by reflecting a specific client's environmental aspirations.

This is especially true for those businesses that want to play music on their premises but would rather avoid contracting use fees directly with ASCAP or other music licensers. And the trend has spread internationally. By the late nineties, the promotional literature coming out of Muzak's U.K. offices brandished the motto "Music—with YOU in control." But the royal "you" to which it refers is likely to be the business owner more than the staff worker or the visiting customer.

The enthusiasm for "foregrounding" in the mid-1980s confirmed that, with the service and leisure industries becoming indistinguishable, any original artist recording could be put to Muzak purposes. Previously bloodcurdling equations such as art = commerce or leisure = retail have gained wide acceptance. *All* music has taken on a background role, or, even more likely, music has usurped the foreground of everyday life while people have grown content to fade ever more into the background of an all-encompassing mediascape.

From the mid-1990s on, Muzak's ownership has changed again and again. During these corporate permutations, the company has put the emphasis much less on its background music tradition than on the fact that *all* music has been commodified for use as an environmental enhancer—whether it be "smooth jazz" for bars seeking a "hip" image, classic rock for baby boomer mall shoppers, or the robotic throb of current dance music for chic boutiques.

Music with sung lyrics, once a Muzak no-no, is now acceptable. Foreground vocals, like car alarms and cell phone chatter, have become the norm in a sea of distractions. What used to be a carefully calculated program of Stimulus Progression has become a less scientific, more lifestyle conscious "Audio Architecture."

"Technology and the Internet are shrinking the globe," a more recent blurb on Muzak's Web site, declares. "Individuals have more choices and access to new products and services. Indeed, the world is becoming our superstore. Lines drawn by traditional demographic standards are being crossed. . . . Muzak acknowledges our need to intuitively understand people and their lifestyles."

This effort to add "prestige" and "personality" to the shopping routine suggests that elevator music's detractors do not really object to the idea of manipulating people through music—just as long as it is their kind of music and not what they uncharitably designate "schmaltz." As one of Muzak's major competitors in the foreground music biz dumbly proclaims: "It all started with a love of rock 'n roll and a realization that 'elevator music' just wasn't cool."

Anti-Muzak naysayers used to complain that background music was too "manipulative," but foreground music manipulation seems to be much more insidious. Walking into a Rite Aid and pelted with chart versions of country rock, smooth jazz, or hip-hop, one may feel subjected not only to the whims of the store manager but to a clutching fashion apparatus that never lets go. Whereas elevator music functioned as sonic air-conditioning, the newfangled alternative can be likened to designer scents pumped through a ventilation system.

One could also argue that the current use of original artist songs in supermarkets has the same distracting and demystifying effect that the compilation soundtrack has had on some of the newer movies. What better way to ruin a story than to slobber a bunch of pop or soul tracks over a film's narrative and closing credits—all to justify a CD release that can be called a soundtrack in only the loosest sense.

As foreground music crept into the public sphere, marketing niches became much more regimented. Music was tied ever more closely to decor, psycho-geography, and assumed client desires. Muzak developed specialized formats such as Hot FM, a selection of adult contemporary original artist vocals "ideal for lively restaurants, retain stores, manufacturing and assembly facilities—any place that energetic adults are living life to the fullest." The "breezy elegance" of light classical offers a "gentle and stylish atmosphere that appeals primarily to sophisticated, well educated employees and clients 21 years and older."

In contrast, the old Muzak—the type that inspired this book— functioned as a remote but benevolent overlord, undeterred by market-driven lifestyle "decisions." Foregrounding, and the various "tasteful" instrumental alternatives, are essentially ham-handed attempts to placate audiences that are poorly attuned to elevator music appreciation.

In the long run, Muzak and other piped-in music purveyors might do themselves and everyone else a service not by divorcing themselves from elevator music's "bad" image but by acknowledging that such music—as properly remembered by those who both heard *and* listened to it—became (perhaps by accident) an aesthetically valid musical category.

Even some who brag about hating elevator music can betray moments of Muzak inspiration. Author Douglas Adams, who otherwise sneered at elevator music, claimed that it was part of his inspiration for writing *The Hitchhiker's Guide to the Galaxy.* He told the June 1998 issue of *Fast Company* that, following his misbegotten Cambridge pursuits in English literature he landed a job as a royal Arab family's bodyguard. Standing watch outside their hotel room, he fixated on the elevator doors:

> *At night, when they're not in regular use, it's bad for them just to stop, so they're programmed to go up and down at*

*random. Every two or three minutes, an elevator would
arrive, open its doors, spit out some Muzak, and go away.
My job was to stay sane. This is why there is a lot in [my
book] about elevators.*

There is cause to wonder, and even doubt, whether Adams's science
fiction musings on art, business, and technology would have been
the same if the mystifying elevator tunes he heard had sounded more
like a glorified radio station.

Thomas Pynchon, in his sixties novel *The Crying of Lot 49*, presents a character who can sit in a restaurant, listen to the Muzak's
"all strings, reeds, muted brass" broadcast, and glean not only the
exact number of violins but the individual instrument, its frequency
cycles, and the musculature and personality of the musician playing
it. Pynchon's character would probably have been disinclined to do
the same once the din of consumer cattle cars squelched elevator
music's "Eco-Logic" and people were no longer able to escape from
their noisy selves.

16 / The New Sound of *1984*

Your environment is manipulating you regardless. Your whole life is based on environment and condition. TV, books, it's everywhere. To single out Muzak® as Big Brother is silly and not fair.
—**Christopher Case, a former Muzak programmer**

In many respects, Aldous Huxley's *Brave New World* is a utopian novel in disguise. Most of the "nightmare" auguries his book proscribes as dehumanizing and unnatural—bottled babies, ethnic amusement resorts, pharmacological bliss, multimedia "feelies," classroom lectures set to "hypnopaedic" jingles, and, of course, "synthetic music"—have since been embraced (to varying degrees) as signs of either good entertainment or hip social hygiene. But as the new themed order encroaches, elevator music fades to a much more aggressive program with no regard for morale or peace of mind.

Once someone interviewing me from an affiliate of National Public Radio countered my usual elevator music praise by reverting to that exhausted shibboleth about it all reminding him of Huxley's dystopia. "The 'Brave New World' is here," I responded, "but elevator music doesn't play in it!" I told him that people who flaunt their "sophisticated" musical tastes are manipulated all the more, confronted with a loud soundstage of conflicting styles that blare out from stores, car radios, and even dentist's offices. The Brave New World is here, but the synthetic music is not even pleasant.

There was always something snooty and sneering about Huxley's condemnations. Writing from the vantage point of a sealed world in another time and another empire, he could neither empathize with his story's postapocalyptic survivors of population overkill, social chaos, and anthrax bomb fallout nor be expected to appreciate the transitory comfort they derived from a "Super-Wurlitzer" that plays seductive "ether-music" and "the very very latest in slow Malthusian Blues."

Now that the once demure notion of background music has leaped into the flashy foreground, even the term *Muzak*® is not what it seems when it is erroneously designated as *muzak* or *musak*. The sound of what used to be called Music by Muzak is barely present anymore, but the Muzak trope has become so pervasive that people think they hear it even when it is not there. In England a book was published called *Muzak-Free London: A Guide to Eating, Drinking, and Shopping in Peace.* The catch is that, at least at the time, there was no Muzak in London—a misnomer that irked the Muzak marketing department enough to send the book's publisher an admonitory letter.

The British are especially prone to use "muzak" very loosely, flouting the Muzak company's trademark sensitivities by applying the term to any kind of music that happens to be piped in at an establishment. As an editorial on the BBC Web site offhandedly snorts:

> *anything played in a store—and chosen by that store to further its image—can be considered muzak. It is muzak, for example, when Hard Rock Café pipes oldies into its restaurants to help create a festive, nostalgic mood. It is muzak when Gap stores play popular rock or hip-hop to lure teenagers into the store to buy something. Muzak is*

any music appropriated by a business, and played on the premises of that business, to make itself more inviting to consumers.

Some prominent voices in the British press liken their "muzak" to all that is ominous in the world. Radio 4 announcer John Humphries, who believes piped-in music to be a "sinister evil," got downright militant in a Sheffield hotel by insisting that the proprietors turn the muzak off. Piped music is "a pollution from which there is no escape," claims Robert Key, a member of Parliament from Salisbury, who introduced a bill calling for an outright ban: "It can be heard in public places including doctors' surgeries, swimming pools and bus and railway stations. All music is devalued if treated as acoustic wallpaper. The public hate being trapped with someone else's choice of music, be it on a plane, a bus, or in a queue on the telephone."

Britain is also the home of Pipedown, a group devoted to wiping out piped-in music from as many public venues as possible. Pipedown was founded on the premise that people have a "right to silence" and claims to have been successful in a campaign to have "acoustic wallpaper" banned from Gatwick Airport. But the reason for focusing precisely on piped-in music begs the question as to why the same indignation is not directed toward live music—especially the live jazz combos (a common feature of many concourses and malls) that blast away on hot summer afternoons, forcing many pedestrians to flee at least a block away to escape the volume. Is Pipedown equally willing to pipe up with complaints when one cannot hear the ticket seller's directions in a railway station because some melody manglers are jerking around with another tired rendition of "Take The 'A' Train"?

In 1998, after commissioning a study to discern the negative impact of "muzak" on the hard of hearing, the Royal National Institute for Deaf People (RNID) announced its findings. "For the UK's 8.7 million deaf and hard of hearing people background muzak often causes pain, discomfort and unnecessary distress." The institute loosely defines *muzak* as "background music played in public places: shops, supermarkets, pubs, restaurants/cafes, hotels, on travel bulletins, TV programmes and piped down the telephone." But the study inevitably got cranky, stating that "muzak" is not just a problem in public places. For the hard of hearing, the frustrations are extending into their homes. The background music on television and radio apparently spoils their enjoyment of programmes and the ability to follow what is going on.

Another British Web site called "How to Complain about Muzak" gives the "muzak" impaired an opportunity to express their grievances. Here, at least, the definition of *piped-in music* gets a bit more precise and admits that background music is not what it used to be, a viewpoint with which many easy-listening enthusiasts can commiserate. "In recent years," the site's introduction declares, "the quality of piped music has changed, from relatively soft sounds to hard, thumping, aggressive, and louder sounds on any and all occasions. Restaurants have all of a sudden become noisy places operating on the assumption that the more background noise the better. Transmitting upsetting noise is an infringement of the rights of individuals."

There is some paradox to this chronically British anti-"muzak" mania. Besides being the home of Mantovani, Melachrino, and many other prominent easy-listening instrumentalists, England, just prior to and during World War II, hosted the background music studies that inspired Muzak's "Stimulus Progression" formula. Even with pro-"muzak" intentions, some Brits can still slip up. A fine example occurred sometime in the 1970s, when a magazine published by a British Muzak franchisee proudly sported the headline: "A Muzak transmission studio is a dream of 1984 automation."

Perhaps George Orwell had British programs such as *Music While You Work* in mind when he referred to Big Brother's "march" music broadcasts in his famous 1949 novel. But there is reason to suspect that he had a more sinister symphony in mind, one that sounded nowhere near as benign as John Philip Sousa.

British director Michael Anderson's 1956 movie adaptation of *1984* used background music a bit differently than in Orwell's story. The beleaguered protagonist Winston Smith hears pretty little waltz tunes piping out between Big Brother's browbeating broadcasts. Throughout the novel, Orwell does speak of some kind of music transmitted from the ever-present telescreens, but he makes no mention of it being soft and sweet. Hard-line march music and patriotic songs ("composed without any human intervention whatever on an instrument known as a versificator") were the vogue in Oceania. Orwell's vivid description of a "hate song" devised specifically to arouse the ire of the masses during Hate Week has the opposite properties of a piped-in waltz: "It had a savage, barking rhythm," he writes, "which could not exactly be called music, but resembled the beating of a drum. Roared out by hundreds of voices to the tramp of marching feet, it was terrifying."

Those seemingly independent connoisseurs, who either consider elevator music too manipulative or too bland, have themselves been duped into accepting one of Muzak's outdated corporate mythologies. Just because some misguided company executive decided several decades ago on doublethink slogans such as "music to be heard but not listened to" and "boring work seems less boring with boring music" does not mean that the world has to take them as gospel. Muzak itself abandoned those unfortunate quips long ago. It is as if the anti-Muzak mind-set is a ruse, a thought virus planted in order to distract people from the true (and far more virulent) mechanisms of music manipulation that abound. If anything, the act of actively listening to the old Music by Muzak and perceiving its artful qualities—after being instructed not to—is a supreme act of rebellion.

Attempts to replace elevator music with something more "edifying" have often met with comic results. A 1962 incident showed once again the art world's hostile Muzak hysteria. Sculptor Richard Lippold refused to exhibit his golden cobweb in Manhattan's Pan Am Building until the Muzak was removed. John Cage attempted to come to the rescue with a patchwork concerto that combined Lippold's web with Muzak and the electronic surveillance cameras, but the Pan Am Building authorities (leery of more "sensibility" eruptions) finally settled for getting rid of the background music altogether.

In a strange reversal, some stores have used Muzak's channels as a crowd repellent instead of an enhancer. The *Los Angeles Times* earned nationwide chuckles in 1992 when it reported that the Southland Corporation had installed a Muzak channel in its 7-11 chain stores in Southern California's Thousand Oaks district. The goal was to drive away gangs of loitering teenagers. The plan worked so well that Southland wanted to repeat the "Muzak Attack" in other parts of Los Angeles County. This story is all the more fascinating because the music played was not elevator music but Muzak's classical channel. The juvenile delinquents were wincing not at the Syd Dale Orchestra's rendition of "You Call It Madness" but at Bach's Brandenburg Concertos.

Author Steve Kahn, probably unintentionally, invited Muzak nostalgia in his early eighties science fiction novel *The Mall*. Here a cadre of drug runners and terrorists hold the patrons of a high-security mall hostage. As the PA system plays the tunes, the head kidnapper interrupts a rendition of "Moon River" to remind them:

> *That music, by the way, folks, is a good sign. The people who run The Mall wanted you to have it so I figure that if they're that concerned about you, then they'll probably be concerned enough to want to keep you alive. But, if not, I'll have to remind them that we can kill any one of you just as suddenly as we just killed the music.*

In a time when corporate moguls (like absentee landlords) exert control over everyday life while demanding more labor and cash, one can get downright misty-eyed for a time and place when companies such as Muzak made efforts to at least nurse its citizens. Oh, for the glory days of Muzak, when people such as the industrial psychologist Dr. James Keenan served on Muzak's Scientific Board of Advisors in the late 1960s. Dr. Keenan exemplified the kinds of theories that can evolve in those rare instances when corporate gain is congenial to social ecology:

> *While at Muzak, I liked to quote some Russian studies that showed the remarkable nature of some sounds. I was in Moscow, and they showed that high-intensity-pitched sounds really could do an interesting amount of stuff. High-pitched sounds can influence . . . your affect cells. I found that Muzak became the perception of how sounds affect metabolism. There are many sounds in the environment—mechanical energy, electromechanical, and*

electrochemical—that change the body. . . . There is a
certain rightness about some things; maybe it's cultural
or in the eye of the beholder. In the area of vision, a cer-
tain rectangle is judged to be more pleasing than squares.
The movie theater is generally a little more pleasing than
the TV screen. With music, there is also some kind of right-
ness. I think this is true across cultures. That's why
thoughts about Muzak always lead to mysticism.

There is something civically as well as aesthetically right about generic music complementing generic environments. This is one of the few examples in which a "one size fits all" policy makes sense. When entering a public space such as a supermarket or a mall, shoppers are entitled to an aural escape—a sound mark that delineates the safe retail environment from the more cacophonous and unwieldy world outside. If air-conditioning is therapeutic air for soot-infested cities, then supermarket music is therapeutic music for a world of conflicting musical attitudes.

All those who once complained about supermarkets full of "syrupy" strings can only declare a Pyrrhic victory. They must now contend with a soundscape that is much louder, more intrusive, more obstreperous, and much more cloying. When the elevator music is turned off, the hype really begins.

Oddly enough, the only dreamtime away from this chronically foregrounded waking life is in the recent spate of "retro" commercials that resurrect elevator music snippets for satirical purposes. The mild cha-cha that plays while shoppers browse for "Pork: The Other White Meat" or the sweet elevator strains drowned out when two slackers engage in a Doritos® crunching contest.

Elevator music, besides just being good music, is a distillation of the happiness that modern technology has promised. One can only hope that this truth may not be lost on a new generation of melody-starved adolescents, some of whom are already seeking out oldies by the Partridge Family and the Monkees to envision an idyllic past. They might have to settle for the original "Happy Together" by the Turtles (considered "muzak" by today's harsh standards anyway) when the ectoplasmic instrumental is not available. Or, through some strange hole in the sonic ozone (more likely the wonders of digital cable), they might hear elevated strains from another time and place wafting through the ceiling speakers in their neighborhood mall or even in an elevator. The sound that an old generation tried to forget and repress may make a second coming to soothe the hearts and stimulate the minds of those eager to hear a new world.

Afterword: Channeling the Phantom Band

"**W**hy would anyone want to write about Muzak®?"

Coming from Nick Perito, these were very discouraging words. This was one of orchestral pop's most accomplished arrangers, conductors, and composers, who had acted as one of Muzak's major maestros during the late sixties and early seventies. And now he was offhandedly writing off a source of his previous livelihood, not to mention a significant chunk of popular culture.

And there *I* was, on the telephone with what started out as a potentially depressing conversation. Mr. Perito, however, who may have sensed my sulk, immediately began to spout uplifting answers to his own question.

Perito had, after all, provided the dreamy orchestra for most of Perry Como's fifties and sixties output. For years, he was resident conductor for all of Ferrante and Teicher's best recordings (i.e., the ones that did not play prepared-piano pocket pool with the melody). The roster of artists for whom he has arranged also includes Andy Williams, the Carpenters, and Eydie Gorme.

Considering all the silly aspersions that media sound-byters and academic snobs cast upon Muzak's musical qualities, Perito had to warm up by explaining the intricate and sometimes frustrating relationship between Muzak's aesthetics and economics:

> *Muzak was incredibly tight with its recording schedules. Typically, a recording session outside of Muzak was about three hours long; and you were lucky if you got four songs in. Muzak insisted that we get as much product out as possible. We had to have it simple yet effective and would take only three hours to do 12 songs. The Musicians Union*

*agreed to this, since Muzak was a closed entity and did
not sell its records commercially. The Union gave Muzak
a break.*

Thus, Music by Muzak has only been available as a supermarket
symphonette and not as an item to add to the shopping cart.

"Each arranger had his own group," Perito continued. "Mine was
one of the biggest in terms of number of musicians. The people
performing on the dates were elegant top-notch studio players who
could quickly read anything at sight. We knew the nature of what
we had to do."

The corporate heads may have stressed a Philistine approach to
their product, but Perito and many of the other musicians who
worked on these sessions felt compelled to retain an inventively
melodious approach. If they enjoyed their work, they did not dote
on the final product, allowing a wide berth between performer and
listener that freed the songs from too much fixed meaning.

"We had the A-Team players in New York," Perito boasted.
"People like Doc Severinsen and Mel Davis on trumpets; Urbie
Green on trombone and Phil Bodner on woodwinds. We also used
great violinists like David Nadien, Joseph Malin, Eugene Orloff, and
many others. And also cellists like George Ricci and Allen Schulman.
Al Caiola, Bucky Pizzarelli, and Tony Mottola played guitars. The
recording engineers were also very talented. We all loved the challenges at each recording session. We did one run-down and then
made an album's worth of music."

Perito's knowledge comes from a time when Music by Muzak and
other types of background music were heard everywhere. By the
late sixties, Muzak's music had amalgamated the older light orchestral style with emerging pop and rock forms. A studio session's time
and tempo restrictions challenged arrangers and players to create
instrumental pairings and acoustical quirks that even escaped the
imaginations of arranger-conductors endowed with bigger record
labels and budgets.

Perito mixed grand string arrangements with electric guitars, organs, drums, and sometimes even psychedelic effects. A fine example
is the Perito treatment on "Sealed with a Kiss," a dreamy ballad

about frustrated love that could arguably be considered America's shadow anthem. Judging from Brian Hyland's original hit and subsequent versions by Bobby Vinton et al., the mystifyingly beautiful melody is also undeniably sad. Executed in its original form, "Sealed with a Kiss" potentially could have driven discouraged shoppers out of stores or sent office secretaries into misty-eyed tizzies.

Aware of both the song's beauty and its dire overtones, Perito faced a daunting task. He needed to retain the simple melody's integrity while, given Muzak's desire to be relaxing yet motivating, adding doses of levitation to counteract the sorrow.

The track begins with an acoustic guitar and strings paired on the opening melody. Soon a flute leads the procession on a moderately uptempo path, aided by the steady backbeat of drum brushes. The pace gets a bit quicker as muted horns and an organ introduce the second verse. After the organ slides into some bluesy but brief maneuvers, the flute, guitar, and strings take over once more to wind the song down. Even many of the song's devoted fans (this author included) can appreciate this version's additional mood swings. The kernel of a doleful love ditty is still there, but Perito weaves in a larger, less focused identity that floats along the listener's periphery.

On Muzak's 1973 demonstration album *Stimulus Progression No. 5*, Perito had arranged and conducted all twelve tracks. "Last Tango In Paris" includes a melancholy trumpet balanced with some of Vincent Bell's freak-out fuzz guitar. Perito had already integrated that fuzz factor when he conducted Ferrante and Teicher's "Midnight Cowboy" as well as conducting *and* arranging Bell's own hit single "Airport Love Theme." The album also includes Bell's trademark "water guitar" on the Perito-penned "C'mon Smile"—replete with a skip-happy beat, perky pop keyboards, a volley of folk-rock-inspired drums and tambourine, and, of course, the constant, at times nearly subliminal, string enticement.

Like many major record labels, Muzak took on a stereotypically corporate mantle, imposing strict engineering rules while always on guard against nosy outsiders who might steal its formula or play havoc with its patents. Muzak, in taking its scientific approach to music very seriously, could often use forbidding jargon. The promotional

LPs the company had released strictly for clients came with such disclaimers as: "This album cannot be purchased at any price. All selections were specially arranged, recorded and programmed by MUZAK for demonstration only." The notes to another album asserted: "MUZAK is a non-entertainment medium, employing rhythm, tempo, instrumentation, etc., to scientifically-determined specifications."

Many of Muzak's albums featured abstract cover designs by Ray Harrow, an artist commissioned to render in oils what Muzak attempted to convey in sound. Years before Brian Eno spoke of tone colors and "timbres," Muzak's Dr. William Wokoun specified on the back of the 1969 album *Reveille—The New Muzak* how "experiments have shown that people associate mood-tones with definite colors. Psychologist Lois B. Wexner found that exciting or stimulating moods remind many of us of red. On the other hand, calm, peaceful, serene, or soothing moods suggest green and blue."

At times, Music by Muzak and the movie soundtrack revealed an odd affinity in their methods of straddling the fence between "art" and "utility." By purposely underarranging songs, film composers and Muzak arrangers massaged hearts and minds through understatement, performing what merely *seems* to be a subservient role. Several film composers have responded to this self-imposed self-effacement with profound words about their art. Aaron Copland once claimed that film composers have an "ungrateful" task since their music is more like sonic wallpaper and not the center of attention.

In Tony Thomas's *Film Score: The Art and Craft of Movie Music*, Dimitri Tiomkin claimed that "The composer, by providing pleasant melodic music, can direct attention from what the make-up artist could not hide." Some cannot resist referring to their work in nonmusical terms, alluding to movie music as a form of interior design or sartorial craftsmanship. While Tiomkin invoked the beautician, Jerry Goldsmith likened his craft to that of a tailor who fashions melodies and rhythms to conform to each film's fabric.

Ten years after I interviewed her for *Elevator Music*'s first edition, former Muzak vice president and head of recording and producing Jane Jarvis (still active with a jazz combo) remains favorable in her recollections.

Muzak represented an aggregation of some of the greatest musicians of all time. The very musicians that recorded the music that so many people made fun of also played for movies, Broadway shows, symphonies, and for practically every big name in the music business. They were so skilled they could adapt themselves to any kind of music. Lots of people condemned Muzak but never really heard it.

Jarvis does have reservations, however, about what she regards as Muzak's bureaucratic shortcomings during her tenure.

Each new owner wanted to discharge himself of the company's history beforehand. They wanted to lay claim to new ideas. I believe that if the people there thought about economics instead of the ownership and how much they could get for it when they sold it, they could have perpetuated the Muzak tradition. Here I am a jazz musician. I put aside my own personal likes and dislikes. I even wrote songs with titles like "Music by Muzak."

Jarvis indeed wrote around 200 tunes for company use that often sported titles reflecting Muzak marketing slogans. There are her sprightly, string-laden airs "Muzak on the Move" and "The Song Heard Round the World," whose Bert Kaempfert–style arrangements feature a bouncy electric bass and strings in place of the vocal chorus. Playing part time in stadiums, Jarvis specialized in the organ and used it on Muzak frequently, often to bossa-nova-style beats with lead guitars and the obligatory tambourine on such familiar pop songs as the Monkees' "I'm a Believer." "We tried to keep a balance in what we recorded," Jarvis continued.

We recorded a lot of rock tunes but they weren't in heavy-duty rock. The way to validate using them was to keep some of the same instrumentation. Guitar players like Al Caiola and Tony Mottola were in great demand because the use of guitars in pop music was so widespread. Nick Perito and Frank Hunter were masters at retaining the identity of a rock tune but applying it to the given needs

*of Muzak. You never did think of certain rock tunes as
tunes with strings, but we did it that way. In many cases,
we made it a little more sedate and more musical in the
traditional sense. The emphasis was on the melody and
the validity of the tune, whereas very little of today's rock
music has a melodic line.*

Some songs that appeared on Music by Muzak veered into conventional instrumental territory. Lionel Hampton indulged in moments of what could best be summed up as "smooth jazz," and Dick Hyman could change from minimally improvised cocktail piano on versions of "My Special Angel" and "Oh, Lonesome Me" to an electric organ recital of "Meet Me in St. Louis." But these were usually the exceptions. Most of the Muzak library consisted of a much more specialized, sometimes rarefied, musical approach better mastered by arrangers and conductors whose careers were dedicated to large orchestras.

In the fifties, Lawrence Welk also made some Muzak recordings of standards such as "There's a Small Hotel," in which his interplay of organ, vibraphone, and pert horns still conformed to his Champagne Music specifications. Robert Farnon also entered Muzak's library at about this time, providing custom-made versions of "Manhattan Serenade" and "Eighteenth Variation from Rhapsody on a Theme of Paganini." And the brilliant string arranger Glenn Osser (who orchestrated albums by Johnny Mathis and Jerry Vale) treated Muzak listeners to violins, harps, and sweet horns on luxurious interpretations of songs such as "It's a Lovely Day Today" and "Moon of Manakoora."

Flashing forward to the early 1980s, Nelson Riddle had a Muzak engagement that consisted partly of re-recording "You and the Night and the Music" and other incandescent swing arrangements he had used on his late fifties albums *Hey . . . Let Yourself Go!* and *C'mon . . . Get Happy!* But Riddle also made Muzak arrangements of more "contemporary" numbers such as "Born Free," "Pieces of Dreams," and his "Route 66 Theme."

Like Perito, Frank Hunter is an exemplary elevator music avatar. "Exotica" hounds may know him specifically for his album *White*

Goddess, but Hunter had a behind-the-scenes finger in many pop music pies, assembling orchestras to accompany Pat Boone, songstress Jane Morgan, and an album of Italian songs by Frankie Avalon. Besides providing much of the romantic orchestration for Roger Williams's records, he did the lush string arrangements for some of Chad and Jeremy's Columbia material, including the duo's 1966 hit "Before and After."

Hunter's Muzak contributions occurred at a time when the company lived up to its image as a no-nonsense laboratory, when its scientists of sound were proudly pictured in white coats, jotting into their logbooks and looking intent on avoiding what Muzak literature called the "distracting or irritating musical devices of ordinary music." Hunter, like Perito, approached a typical Muzak session as a ceremonial combination of stylistic constraints on the one hand and imaginative opportunities on the other, particularly when it came to melding time-tested orchestral textures with more rock-rooted material.

"The newer songs posed the biggest problem," Hunter opines. "They were poor on melody. Without the voices, the songs had no structure. I can remember one time being told I had 40 titles to choose from. I had the material ahead of time, given the song, given a demo of a commercial record, and a lead sheet—from that you did an orchestration. And we had about three days to put together an arrangement."

Despite being skittish about some of the selections, Hunter was downright daring in his fusion of what some musical "purists" would regard as disparate musical elements. He, like several other Muzak arrangers, was also uncanny in his knack for setting sixties pop songs to even faster tempos and more aggressive percussion than the originals, all the while keeping that enigmatic distance that makes these recordings so fascinating many decades later.

Hunter's permutation of the Partridge Family's 1971 hit "I Woke Up in Love" begins with a harpsichord introduction and the counterpoint of marimbas. A flurry of reverberant strings soon plays the opening melody as drums keep to the teen beat. The trumpets proceed to blare while the marimbas chime each line's closing notes. During the bridge all the way to the finishing chorus, the strings, horns, drums, and marimbas coalesce. The result: a sound engineered to weave in and out of workplaces and crowded public spaces while preserving the melodic identity for all those even vaguely familiar with the song. All of the vocal inflections that David Cassidy may have performed with relatively little effort on the Top 40 record were here approximated in a much more methodical and thoughtful manner.

In what was certainly a more reflective moment on Muzak's mood scale (likely rated at the beginning of the Stimulus Progression quarter hour), Hunter's arrangement of "Summer Wine"—an acclaimed Lee Hazlewood and Nancy Sinatra duet—switches from the original's more languid allure to a somewhat bouncier Bert Kaempfert beat: an electric bass guitar skipping against pensive horns and violins. He would use the same Kaempfert sound when upping the tempo slightly on "There's a Kind of Hush," even allowing a few slightly improvisational trumpet digressions.

Like many of the people who performed in these sessions, however, Hunter unburdened himself by coming to terms with the folderol of finance.

> *Everything was guided by the budget. You looked at your material and picked the instrumentation. My first date for Muzak was for Andy Wiswell. Maynard Ferguson was on trumpet at that session. When doing an album, we did twelve songs in 2 1/2 hours. If you went over that you were in trouble.*

Great guitarists were among Muzak's finest treasures. Among them was the aforementioned Al Caiola, who played behind great easy-listening arrangers such as Percy Faith and Andre Kostelanetz. By the early sixties, he had recorded his own hit themes for *The Magnificent Seven* and *Bonanza*. While arranging and conducting many Muzak sessions, Caiola's fingers also finessed through such energetic yet unruffled versions of sixties pop fare as "Leaving on a Jet Plane" and "Music to Watch Girls By."

"I worked for Muzak quite a number of years," Tony Mottola recounts with a refreshing sympathy for the background music trade. "It was like a monthly occurrence. For the Muzak sessions, they would hire me as a solo guitarist or arranger guitarist. Sometimes I just did sessions with others. The solo guitar was very popular in the Muzak line because it is so easy to listen to."

Mottola has been a vital player in pop music sessions for decades. He worked with such Columbia mavens as Andre Kostelanetz and Mitch Miller and eventually helped to commandeer the fleet of instrumental Enoch Light albums on both the Command and Project 3 labels. As a session man, Mottola grew accustomed to fashioning his talents to meet producer demands but feels that Muzak allowed him relative control.

"The only time there was a problem," Mottola admits, "is if we departed from the melody too much. Muzak would be concerned with the melodic concept and not too much improvisation. Once in a while I will hear one of my things. It amazes me. I wonder if it's Muzak or another service. I also used to hear myself on WPAT in dentist and doctor's offices—years back when it was more an instrumental station."

By the mid-seventies, Muzak had added British arranger Arthur Greenslade, who was mostly noted for his iridescent strings. He was also a mover in the sixties "swinging London" scene and the international pop world, providing heavenly backgrounds for singers such as Shirley Bassey, François Hardy, and Dusty Springfield as well as the lush backings on "Je T'Aime . . . Moi non Plus" and several other Serge Gainsbourg recordings. He later arranged his strings for the early Genesis album *From Genesis to Revelation.* And when the Four Tops recorded a version of the Moody Blues' "A Simple Game" the mavens at Motown instinctively sought out Greenslade to provide the acoustical sheen.

By the mid- to late seventies, when he did most of his Muzak work, Greenslade was leaning more toward country pop, sometimes arranging songs that many would otherwise regard as unlikely string adaptations. In this capacity, he proved to be something of a maverick when he let the violins take on the potentially maddening "EEEOOOOAAAIIII!" part on "The Lion Sleeps Tonight." On "Convoy," the notorious novelty that cruised through the airwaves during the trucker CB radio craze, the eerie piano phrases and soft marchlike drumbeats make for a beguiling opening, but Greenslade again let the strings (not the horns) do the hard work of re-creating the unforgettably sing-songy chorus.

Into the 1980s, Muzak's menu could fluctuate from David Rose's simultaneously moody and upbeat take on "If You Could Read My Mind" to his delectably customed and more echo-filled version of the all-time favorite "Holiday for Strings." Britain's Frank Chacksfield could push the envelope by adding a wah-wah pedal guitar to his rendition of Bob Dylan's "If Not for You," while Kai Winding (of "More" fame) let a low, moaning electric guitar impersonate Bill Medley on an elevated translation of "You've Lost That Lovin' Feeling."

Way back in 1966, one Muzak executive had proclaimed: "The age of Mantovani and strings is behind us." More than two decades later, another Muzak rep said: "There are still a couple of companies out there doing that old-style 1,001 strings, ruin-your-favorite-song kind of thing, but we dropped all that in '87." Fortunately, both were wrong, at least for a while longer.

The intoxicating spell of massed strings for which Muzak is best remembered—the kind that David Letterman still pokes fun at and film composer Jack Nitzsche lovingly spoofed on soundtracks for movies such as *Performance* (the "Harry Flowers" track) and *One Flew over the Cuckoo's Nest*—remained on the company's roster well into the 1990s. Ceiling speakers across America and other parts of the world continued to emit the glorious mists of the Orchestron Symphony, the Opus Strings, the Silver Strings, the Sussex Strings, and especially the Brno Radio Orchestra.

Fortunate enough to come upon a Muzak daily program schedule from August of 1990, I noticed that its "Instrumental Channel" was beginning to program commercially available records from Ronnie Aldrich, Caravelli, Richard Clayderman, and Paul Mauriat as well as less ornate artists such as Kenny G and Acoustic Alchemy. But even then the Bill Loose Orchestra popped up with "Daydream Believer" and "You Won't See Me," the Jim Devlin Orchestra played "Philadelphia Freedom" and "Too Late to Turn Back Now," the Orchestron Symphony cooed out an "Indian Love Call," and Czechoslovakia's ever-prolific Brno Radio Orchestra fluttered along with "Now or Never" and "I Will Wait for You."

In all fairness, an individual Muzak tune does not provide the full audio picture of a typical broadcast from the period. The engineers also played a vital part in compressing the sound and refining away any excessive highs or lows that could jeopardize business, medical, or civic settings. There was also the sequencing—the quarter-hour clusters and music mood ratings—that allowed the music to ebb and flow like lab-generated circadian rhythms. "You cannot really understand music until you've listened to it for 24 hours," Jarvis emphasizes. "Then you truly could see the difference in Muzak programming."

Jarvis, looking back on a career that merged art and function, continues to entertain reservations about Muzak's old "hear but don't listen" marketing concept. "Muscio was a marketing genius," she admits. "When he explained what he felt Muzak should be, I had my misgivings because I'm a thoroughly trained musician. He told me to never analyze my recordings from a musician's point of view. His idea of 'music to be heard but not listened to' was a marketing ploy, but that wasn't on our minds when we did the music. We did this music with an artistic interest."

So why did the angelic melodies that alternately motivated and soothed so many drive a minority of "hearers" to unholy thoughts? There is ultimately neither a consistent nor a rational answer. Those who grew up in the shadow of bebop, rhythm and blues, and rock 'n roll (at the time when anti-Muzak sentiments came to prominence) saw elevator music as epitomizing the slow, safe, and sanitized culture of their elders. Many such elders, arguably less tenacious about their generation's music than the baby boomers (and boomer babies) were, seem to have just gone with the flow, content with their big band memories and direct-marketing "nostalgia" packages. Even some average record buyers, relatively unschooled in or otherwise disinclined to value classical music niceties, were prone to spontaneous snob attacks when a full string orchestra played "The Girl from Ipanema" instead of Samuel Barber's Adagio.

Muzak, in the span of time during which it pursued its art with every pretense of scientific artlessness, left a musical legacy that remains enigmatic to some and infuriating to others and always an affront to preconceived notions about musical "artfulness." Through a combination of corporate pressure and musicianly craftsmanship, Music by Muzak engineered its melodies, harmonies, and rhythms into a sonic code that was in turn transmitted across time and space to millions of listeners around the world.

By the end of my conversation with Nick Perito, I believe he had, for the first time in quite a while, sized up the philosophical dilemma that many former Muzak musicians have had to contend with sooner or later. Fortunately, he came out of the quandary unscathed and shared the big picture.

> *It's sad to think that this kind of background music is no longer around. Muzak was the blend that tried to fit everything. We liked to think that we were giving people pleasant memories. The music was a wonderful balm for the up and going, the frantic, the running, the hurried. Muzak was "making nice," putting a little shawl around you. It didn't attack or provoke. When we recorded Muzak music, I liked to think that we weren't going to war; we were going to the peace table.*

Revised, Expanded, Annotated, and Selective Discography

The following discography includes recording artists who (for the most part) could undoubtedly be regarded as easy-listening—listed by artist, title, label, catalog number, and chronologically by year of release (when available). Compact discs have "CD" before the label entry. In the spirit of thematic consistency (as well as available space), this is a *selective* discography containing music that one would reasonably expect to hear on an elevator or on what was once called the Beautiful Music radio format. The styles range from the standard lush orchestras to small group settings involving guitar, harp, and piano. The main criterion for these selections is the artists' adherence to a simple, sweet melody and fealty to "mood music" ideals and a minimum of prima donna distractions.

Special thanks go to Jack Fetterman, Jed Hacker, Jane Jarvis, Matthias Künnecke, and John Leon for their help with this compilation.

RONNIE ALDRICH (His Two Pianos with the London Festival Orchestra)

On London Phase 4 Stereo (except where otherwise indicated)
MELODY AND PERCUSSION FOR TWO PIANOS (SP-44007)
1962
THE MAGNIFICENT PIANOS OF RONNIE ALDRICH
(SP-44029) 1963
THE ROMANTIC PIANOS OF RONNIE ALDRICH (SP-44042)
1964
MAGIC MOODS OF RONNIE ALDRICH (SP-44062) 1965
THAT ALDRICH FEELING (SP-44070) 1965
TWO PIANOS IN HOLLYWOOD (SP-44092) 1967
TWO PIANOS TODAY! (SP-44100) 1967
THIS WAY "IN" (SP-44116) 1968

FOR YOUNG LOVERS (SP-44108) 1968
DESTINATION LOVE (SP-44135) 1969
IT'S HAPPENING NOW (SP-44127) 1969
HERE COME THE HITS! (SP-44143) 1970
CLOSE TO YOU (SP-44156) 1970
LOVE STORY (SP-44162) 1971
COME TO WHERE THE LOVE IS (SP-44190) 1972
INVITATION TO LOVE (SP-44176) 1972
SOFT AND WICKED (SP-44195) 1973
IN THE GENTLE HOURS (SP-44221) 1975
LOVE (SP-44253) 1975
REFLECTIONS (SP-44264) 1976
WEBB COUNTRY (SP-44278) 1977
EVERGREEN (SP-44286) 1977
EMOTIONS (SP-44310) 1978
ONE FINE DAY (Amberjack AJK-902) 1981
IMAGINE (Audio Fidelity AFE-1026) 1981
BEAUTIFUL MUSIC (Audio Fidelity AFE-6306) 1982
MUSIC FOR ALL SEASONS (CD Realm 1CD-8204) 1992
TWIN PIANO MAGIC (CD Rebound Records 314-520-234-2) 1994

JOHNNY ARTHEY ORCHESTRA

INSTRUMENTAL PERFORMANCES OF THE SAME
    EXCITING VOCAL VERSIONS (Mercury SR-60996) 1967
THE GOLDEN SONGS OF DONOVAN (RCA LSP-4106) 1969

JOHN BARRY

STRINGBEAT (U.K. Release: Columbia 3SCX 3401) 1961
ALL TIME HITS (Ascot AS 16002) 1964
GREAT MOVIE SOUNDS OF JOHN BARRY (Columbia
    CS-9293) 1966
JOHN BARRY CONDUCTS HIS GREATEST MOVIE HITS
    (Columbia CS-9508) 1967
READY WHEN YOU ARE, J. B. (Columbia CS-1003) 1969
PLAY IT AGAIN (U.K. Release: Polydor ACB 00204) 1974
THE MUSIC OF JOHN BARRY (U.K. Release: CBS 22014
    (S 81277/8) [2]) 1976

THE BIG SCREEN HITS OF JOHN BARRY (U.K. Release: CBS 31862) 1980

THE VERY BEST OF JOHN BARRY (CD Polydor 849 095-2) 1991

THE EMI YEARS, VOLUME TWO: 1961 (CD Caroline/Scamp SCP 9709-2) 1993

THE EMI YEARS, VOLUME THREE: 1962–1964 (CD Caroline/Scamp SCP 9710-2) 1995

LOUNGE LEGENDS: JOHN BARRY (CD Polydor 585 317-2) [German Import] 2001

LES BAXTER

RITUAL OF THE SAVAGE, LE SACRE DU SAUVAGE (Capitol H-288) 1951

CARIBBEAN MOONLIGHT (Capitol T-733) 1956

MIDNIGHT ON THE CLIFFS (Capitol T-843) 1957

'ROUND THE WORLD WITH LES BAXTER (Capitol T-780) 1958

SPACE ESCAPADE (Capitol ST-968) 1958

LOVE IS A FABULOUS THING (Capitol ST-1088) 1958

YOUNG POPS (Capitol ST-1399) 1960

BROADWAY '61 (Capitol ST-1480) 1961

JEWELS OF THE SEA (Capitol ST-1537) 1961

VOICES IN RHYTHM (Reprise RS 6036) 1962

THE ACADEMY AWARD WINNERS 1963 (Reprise R9-6067) 1963

LOVE IS BLUE (GNP Crescendo GNP-2042) 1968

MILLION SELLER HITS (with 101 Strings) (S-5188) 1970

QUE MANGO! (Alshire S-5204) 1970

BUGALOO IN BRAZIL (Keith Prowse Maurice Production Library KPM LP1070) 1970

MOVIE THEMES (with 101 Strings) (S-5324) 1975

THE LOST EPISODE OF LES BAXTER (CD Dionysus/Bacchus Records BA07-2) 1995 [Live]

LES BAXTER: BY POPULAR REQUEST (CD Dionysus/Bacchus Records BA 0014) 1996 [Live]

QUE MANGO! (with 101 Strings) (CD Caroline/Scamp Records SCP-9718-2) 1996

BAXTER'S BEST (CD Capitol CDP-7243-8-37028-2-4) 1996

THE POP SIDE (CD Collectors' Choice 161) 2000

TERRY BAXTER

THE BEST OF '68 (Columbia Musical Treasures P2S 5224) [2] 1968
THE BEST OF '69 (Columbia Musical Treasures P2S 5332) [2] 1969
THE BEST OF '70 (Columbia House P3S-5454) [3] 1970
THE BEST OF '72 (Columbia House P3S 5832) [3] 1972
SONG SUNG BLUE: The Best Songs of '72 (Columbia House DS 1010) 1972

VINCENT BELL

POP GOES THE ELECTRIC SITAR (Decca DL-74938) 1969
GOOD MORNING STARSHINE (Decca DL-75138) 1970
VINCENT BELL: AIRPORT LOVE THEME (Decca DL-75212) 1970

MR. ACKER BILK

STRANGER ON THE SHORE (LP: Atco SD-33129/CD: Philips 830779) 1962
PLAYS LENNON AND MC CARTNEY (GNP Crescendo LP: GNPS-2191/CD: GNPD-2191) 1988
ACKER BILK: THE COLLECTION (Castle CD: CCSCD-209) 1988
ACKER BILK AND STRINGS, with the Leon Young String Chorale (Castle CD: MBS403) 1994
IMAGINE (Castle CD: PLS511) 1994
STRANGER ON THE SHORE: ANTHOLOGY (CD BMG International 70912) 2001

STANLEY BLACK

On London/Richmond/London Phase 4
SOME ENCHANTED EVENING (London LL-1098)
MUSIC FOR ROMANCE (London LL-1149)
RED VELVET (London LL-1592)
MOONLIGHT COCKTAIL (London LL-1709) 1957
GREAT FILM THEMES (London PS-113)
THE CASH BOX INSTRUMENTAL HITS (London PS-158)

SOFT LIGHTS AND SWEET MUSIC (Richmond B-20031)
ACCENT ON ROMANCE (Richmond B-20024)
RED VELVET MUSIC FOR ROMANCE (CD Dutton Vocalion
    4127) 2002

MARTIN BÖTTCHER

German Imports
BLUE SOUND, HIGHLIFE, HONEYMOON (Telefunken
    Germany SLE 14445) 1966
NEW SOUND IN TOWN (Telefunken Germany SLE 14484)
    1968
WONDERFUL WORLD (Telefunken Germany SLE 14534)
    1969
MOONLIGHT GUITAR (Telefunken Germany SLE 14576) 1970
LOVE STORY (Telefunken Germany SLE 14609) 1971
SOUND KALEIDOSCOPE (CD Motor Music 539 107-2) 1997

BOTTICELLI ORCHESTRA

HITS UNLIMITED (Omega OM 555.0080) [Holland Import] 1972
DIE GROSSE EUROPA HITPARADE (Decca Phase 4 Stereo
    SLK 169100) [German Import] 1973
BOTTICELLI UNLIMITED (London Phase 4 SP 44214) 1974
THE SOUND OF TODAY (London Phase 4 SO 44273) 1974

BRASS RING (Featuring Phil Bodner)

LOVE THEME FROM "THE FLIGHT OF THE PHOENIX"
    (Dunhill 50008) 1966
SUNDAY NIGHT AT THE MOVIES (Dunhill DS-50015) 1967
THE DIS-ADVANTAGES OF YOU (Dunhill DS-50017) 1967
THE BEST OF THE BRASS RING (Dunhill DS-50051) 1968

BRIARCLIFF STRINGS (and Voices)

SOME ENCHANTED EVENING (Columbia Harmony 11165)
ACADEMY AWARD HITS: Briarcliff Strings and Voices
    (Columbia Harmony 11216)

GREAT HITS OF TODAY: Briarcliff Strings and Voices
(Columbia Harmony 11228)
GREAT THEMES FROM GREAT MOVIES (Columbia
Harmony 11278)
FUNNY GIRL (Columbia Harmony 11283)
MUSIC FROM THE MOVIES (Columbia Harmony 11315)
BRIARCLIFF ORCHESTRA (Columbia Harmony 11404)

AL CAIOLA

PARADISE VILLAGE (Al Caiola and His Islanders) (United
Artists UAS-6263) 1962
THE RETURN OF THE SEVEN (United Artists UAS-6560)
CAIOLA ROMANTICO (United Artists UAS-6527)
GUITAR FOR LOVERS (United Artists UAS-6403)
LET THE SUNSHINE IN (United Artists UAS-6712)
SOFT PICKS (Bainbridge CD: BCD-1031)
SOFT GUITARS (Bainbridge LP: BT-1010) 1980
GUITAR OF PLENTY (Bainbridge LP: BT-1030) 1987
ITALIAN GOLD: Treasured Collection (Alanna CD 5189) 2000

NORMAN CANDLER

Germany's Norman Candler (a.k.a. Gerhard Narholz) had a vital role in
easy-listening radio, stereo recordings, and production music. The
Intersound titles contain some Muzak tracks.

MAGIC STRINGS: Sentimental Journey (Telefunken 6.21102) 1972
LOVE ME WITH ALL YOUR HEART (with Harald Winkler on
guitar) (Telefunken 6.21173) 1974
A TRIBUTE TO JOHN LENNON (Norman Candler and Magic
Strings, Telefunken 6.24820) 1975
NORMAN CANDLER CANDIES, Vols. 1 and 2 (Telefunken
6.28306) 1975
CANDLER BY CANDLELIGHT (London SP-44251) 1976
MORE THAN EVER (Guitar by Francis Goya) (Intersound
ISST173)
MUSICALS AND OPERAS (CD Intersound ISCD001)
EVERGREENS (CD Intersound ISCD002)
MELODIEN DIESER WELT (CD Intersound ISCD004)

THE SOFT MAGIC (CD Intersound ISCD101)
DANCE AND DREAM (CD Intersound ISCD128)

CARAVELLI

PARISIAN STRINGS (S Time Records 72028)
MICHELLE (Columbia CS-9324) 1967
PORTRAIT OF PARIS (Columbia CS-9407) 1967
SAN REMO GREATEST HITS (Columbia CS-9613) 1967
LA, LA, LA (Columbia CS-9690) 1968
PLAYS SIMON AND GARFUNKEL'S GREATEST HITS (CBS
    KC-31467) 1972
A LA CARAVELLI (CBS Records CBS-68258) [French Import]
    [2] 1973
BY REQUEST: Featuring the Hit "Wigwam" (Peters International
    PLD-1000) 1977
COMME TOI (CBS 25518) 1983
BEST OF CARAVELLI (CD Tristar 80933) 1994

CASCADING STRINGS

THE CASCADING STRINGS CONDUCTED BY JOHNNY
    GREGORY (Wing 1028) 1960
THE CASCADING STRINGS PLAY (Fontana 6382 035) 1965
GOLDEN MEMORIES (Fontana 6308 061) 1967
THE CASCADING STRINGS (Fontana 6308 016) 1970
(as THE NEW CASCADING STRINGS)
AMAZING GRACE (Fontana 6308 082) 1971
CONTRASTS (Philips 6308 1070) 1972
GREGORY CONDUCTS THE SOUNDS OF TODAY (Philips
    6308 142) 1973
SPOTLIGHT ON THE CASCADING STRINGS (Philips 6625
    020) 1975

CASTAWAY STRINGS

PETER, PAUL AND MARY SONG BOOK (Vee-Jay VJ-1113)
ANDY WILLIAMS SONG BOOK (Vee-Jay VJ-1114)
BOBBY VINTON SONG BOOK (Vee-Jay VJ-1116)

OTTO CESANA (Cesana Strings)

ECSTASY (Columbia CL-631) 1956
BRIEF INTERLUDE (Capitol T-1032) 1957
VOICES OF VENUS (His Chorus and Sextet) (Columbia CL-971) 1958
SHEER ECSTASY (Warner Bros. 1390) 1960
SOUND OF ROME (RCA LSP-2600) 1962
DREAM, DREAM, DREAM (Audio Fidelity AFSD-6162) 1966
VELVET TOUCH (Audio Fidelity AFSD-6167) 1966
AUTUMN REVERIE (Audio Fidelity AFSD-6170) 1967
LUSH AND LOVELY (Audio Fidelity AFSD-6176) 1967
NIGHT MAGIC (Audio Fidelity AFSD-6179) 1967
DEVOTION (Audio Fidelity AFSD-6182) 1967
LEAVES IN THE WIND (Audio Fidelity AFSD-6188) 1968
ENCHANTMENT (Audio Fidelity AFSD-6191) 1968
DEVOTION (CD 3 V's TVR-2101) 2000

FRANK CHACKSFIELD

VELVET (London LL-1443)
SOUTH SEA ISLAND MAGIC (London LL-1538)
MEDITERRANEAN MOONLIGHT (London LL-1588)
ON THE BEACH (London LL-3158)
EVENING IN PARIS (London LL-4081)
IMMORTAL SERENADES (London PS-122)
LOVE LETTERS IN THE SAND (London PS-145)
THE MILLION SELLERS (Richmond S-30045) 1960
EBB TIDE (Richmond 30078) 1961
THE NEW EBB TIDE (London Phase 4 SP-44053) 1964
EBB TIDE AND OTHER MILLION SELLERS (London Phase 4 BSP-23) 1969
PLAYS THE BEATLES SONGBOOK (London Phase 4 SP-44142) 1970
PLAYS SIMON AND GARFUNKEL AND JIM WEBB (London Phase 4 SP-44151) 1970
RISE (Excelsior XRP-7000) 1980
AFTER THE LOVIN' (Excelsior XRP-7005) 1980
SUNFLOWER (Excelsior XRP-7006) 1980
DUST IN THE WIND (Excelsior XRP-7008) 1980

LOVE IS IN THE AIR (Excelsior XRP-7009) 1980
STREAKS OF LAVENDER (CD Omega W-021-2) 1993
FRANK CHACKSFIELD VOL. 1 (CD Frank Chacksfield private
  stock FCCD-1001) 1994
SOUNDS OF ROMANCE (CD Good Music Company 199927)
  1998 [2]
DINNER AT EIGHT-THIRTY (CD Vocalion 4109) 2001
THANKS FOR THE MEMORIES (CD Polygram International
  544250) 2001

RAY CHARLES SINGERS

SOMETHING WONDERFUL (Command RS 827 SD) 1961
ROME REVISITED (Command RS839 SD) 1962
PARADISE ISLANDS (Command RS 845 SD) 1963
SOMETHING SPECIAL FOR YOUNG LOVERS (Command RS
  866 SD) 1964
Al-DI-LA and Other Extra Special Songs for Young Lovers
  (RS Command 870 SD) 1964
SONGS FOR LONESOME LOVERS (Command RS 874 SD)
  1964
WHAT THE WORLD NEEDS NOW IS LOVE (Command RS
  903 SD) 1967
A SPECIAL SOMETHING . . . 12 BEAUTIFUL SONGS
  (Command RS 914 SD) 1967
AT THE MOVIES WITH THE RAY CHARLES SINGERS
  (Command RS 923 SD) 1968
MacARTHUR PARK (Command RS 936 SD) 1968
SLICES OF LIFE (Command RS 942 SD) 1969
LOVE ME WITH ALL YOUR HEART (CD Varese Sarabande
  VSD-5626) 1995

RICHARD CLAYDERMAN

(All on Compact Disc)

FROM PARIS WITH LOVE (Columbia CK-40174) 1985
PLAYS LOVE SONGS OF THE WORLD (Columbia CK-40472)
  1987
ROMANTIC AMERICA (Columbia CK-44211) 1990

REMEMBERING THE MOVIES (Quality 19126) 1992
WHEN LOVE SONGS WERE LOVE SONGS (Quality 19127) 1992
ROMANTIC BALLADS (Alex 4156) 1993
FEELINGS (Star Gala 550876) 1995
UNCHAINED MELODY (Sony Special Products 22642) 1995
ROMANCE OF RICHARD CLAYDERMAN (Sony Special
  Products 22643) 1995
THE BEST OF ABBA (Polygram 559156) 1998
THE BEST OF THE CARPENTERS (Polygram 559157) 1998
THE BEST OF ANDREW LLOYD WEBBER (Polygram 559163)
  1998
THE LOVE COLLECTION (Metro 64) 2001

CLEBANOFF STRINGS

MOODS IN MUSIC (Clebanoff and His Orchestra) (Mercury SR-
  60005)
SONGS FROM GREAT FILMS (Mercury SR-60017)
SONGS FROM GREAT SHOWS (Mercury SR-60065)
EXCITING SOUNDS (Mercury PPS-6012)
LOVE THEMES FROM GREAT FILMS (Mercury SR-60238)
TWELVE GREAT SONGS OF ALL TIME (Mercury SR-60720)
TODAY'S BEST HITS (Mercury SR-60791)
TEEN HITS (Mercury SR-60929) 1964
COUNTRY MUSIC FOR PEOPLE WHO HATE COUNTRY
  MUSIC (Mercury SR-60949) 1964
ONCE UPON A SUMMERTIME (Decca DL-74956) 1967

RAY CONNIFF (His Orchestra and Chorus)

Many of Conniff's titles have been reissued on compact disc either
through Sony/Columbia or as two-in-one discs from Collectables. What
follows is a list of original album titles and catalog numbers.

On Columbia
S'WONDERFUL (CL-925) 1957
S'MARVELOUS (CS-8037) 1958
S'AWFUL NICE (CS-8001) 1958
CONCERT IN RHYTHM (CS-8022) 1958
HOLLYWOOD IN RHYTHM (CS-8117) 1959

BROADWAY IN RHYTHM (CS-8064) 1960
CONCERT IN RHYTHM VOL. II (CS-8212) 1960
SAY IT WITH MUSIC (CS-8282) 1960
MEMORIES ARE MADE OF THIS (CS-8374) 1961
S'CONTINENTAL (CS-8576) 1962
RHAPSODY IN RHYTHM (CS-8678) 1962
THE HAPPY BEAT (CS-8749) 1963
YOU MAKE ME FEEL SO YOUNG (CS-8918) 1964
FRIENDLY PERSUASION (CS-9010) 1965
WORLD OF HITS (CS-9300) 1967
GREAT CONTEMPORARY INSTRUMENTAL HITS (C-30755)
    1971
THEME FROM S.W.A.T. AND OTHER TV THEMES 1976
SUPERSONICO (DIL 10363) 1984 (European release)
THE 30TH ANNIVERSARY ALBUM (DIL-10464) (Brazil
    release) 1986
SONGS FROM THE BIG AND SMALL SCREEN
    (CD Columbia 53197) 1993
40TH ANNIVERSARY (CD Columbia 752.274/2-460545) 1996

RAY CONNIFF SINGERS

IT'S THE TALK OF THE TOWN (CS-8143) 1959
YOUNG AT HEART (CS-8281) 1960
SOMEBODY LOVES ME (CS-1642) 1961
LOVE AFFAIR (CS-9152) 1965
HAPPINESS IS (CS-9261) 1966
SOMEWHERE MY LOVE (CS-9319) 1966
HAWAIIAN ALBUM (CS-9647) 1968
HONEY (CS-9661) 1968
I LOVE HOW YOU LOVE ME (CS-9777) 1969
JEAN (CS-9920) 1970
LOVE STORY (CS-30498) 1971 (contains Gregorian Cocktail
    version of "If You Could Read My Mind")
I'D LIKE TO TEACH THE WORLD TO SING (CS-31220) 1972
PLAYS THE CARPENTERS (CBS/Sony SOPM-129) 1974
LAUGHTER IN THE RAIN (KC-33332) 1974
LOVE WILL KEEP US TOGETHER (KC-33884) 1975
PLAYS THE BEE GEES AND OTHER GREAT HITS
    (JC-35659) 1978

DON COSTA

THEME FROM "THE UNFORGIVEN" (United Artists UAS 6119)

ECHOING VOICES AND TROMBONES (United Artists WWS 8501)

THE SOUND OF THE MILLION SELLERS (United Artists WWS 8513)

THE GOLDEN TOUCH (United Artists DCL/S 3802/6802)

HOLLYWOOD PREMIERE (Columbia CL-1880)

HITS! HITS! HITS! (Columbia CL-2041)

101 STRINGS PLAY MILLION SELLER HITS OF 1966 (Alshire S-5050) 1967

SWINGIN' THINGS (with 101 Strings) (Alshire S-5055) 1967

MODERN DELIGHTS (Verve V-8702) 1967

DON COSTA'S INSTRUMENTAL VERSIONS OF SIMON AND GARFUNKEL (Mercury SR-61177) 1970

NEVER ON SUNDAY: CLASSIC MOVIE MUSIC OF THE '50s AND '60s (CD Cema Special Products 19367) 1998

FLOYD CRAMER

LAST DATE (RCA LSP-2350) 1960

AMERICA'S BEST SELLING PIANIST (RCA LSP-2466) 1962

COUNTRY PIANO—CITY STRINGS (RCA 2800) 1964

CLASS OF '65 (RCA LSP-3405) 1965

CLASS OF '66 (RCA LSP-3650) 1966

HERE'S WHAT'S HAPPENING! (RCA LSP-3746) 1967

PLAYS THE MONKEES (RCA LSP-3811) 1967

CLASS OF '67 (RCA 3827) 1967

CLASS OF '68 (RCA LSP-4025) 1968

FLOYD CRAMER PLAYS MACARTHUR PARK (RCA LSP-4070) 1969

CLASS OF '69 (RCA 4162) 1969

CLASS OF '70 (RCA LSP-4437) 1970

ALMOST PERSUADED (RCA 2508) 1971

CLASS OF '71 (RCA LSP-4590) 1971

CLASS OF '72 (RCA LSP-4773) 1971

CLASS OF '73 (RCA 0299) 1973

PLAYS THE BIG HITS (RCA Camden ADL2-0128) [2] 1973

YOUNG AND THE RESTLESS (RCA 0469) 1974
CLASS OF '74 AND '75 (RCA APD1-1191) 1974
THE ESSENTIAL FLOYD CRAMER (CD RCA 66591) 1995

BOB CREWE GENERATION

ALL THE SONG HITS OF THE 4 SEASONS INSTRUMEN-
TALLY PERFORMED BY THE BOB CREWE ORCHES-
TRA (Philips PHS 600-150) 1964
MUSIC TO WATCH GIRLS BY (DynoVoice SLP 9003) 1967
MUSIC TO WATCH BIRDS BY (DynoVoice DY 31902) 1967

SYD DALE

LOVE ISN'T JUST FOR THE YOUNG (Go Ahead Records
GA-103) 1982
LOVE ISN'T JUST FOR THE YOUNG, VOL. 2 (Go Ahead
Records GA-104) 1982
WHERE OUR LOVE BEGAN (Go Ahead Records GA-106)
ONCE UPON A SUMMERTIME (Go Ahead Records GA-107)
WHEN I FALL IN LOVE: A MUSICAL TRIBUTE TO NAT
"KING" COLE (Go Ahead Records CALP-108)
SENTIMENTAL JOURNEY (Go Ahead Records GALP-109)
LAZY AUTUMN (Amphonic/Sound Stage AVF-70CD)
ORCHESTRAL BACKGROUNDS : A TRIBUTE TO SYD
DALE (Amphonic/Sound Stage AVF-122CD)

LENNY DEE

RELAXIN' (MCA-264) 1967
GENTLE ON MY MIND (Decca DL-74994) 1968
TURN AROUND, LOOK AT ME (Decca DL-75073) 1969
LITTLE GREEN APPLES (MCA-279) 1969
EASY COME, EASY GO (MCA-290) 1970
REMEMBER ME (MCA-26) 1971
WHERE IS THE LOVE? (Decca DL-75366) 1972
STEPPIN' OUT (MCA-455) 1974
CITY LIGHTS (MCA-476) 1975
I'LL PLAY FOR YOU (Plus 9 Other Songs) (MCA-2162) 1975
MISTY BLUE (MCA-2236) 1976

ORGAN MAGIC (MCA-2301) 1977
ORGAN CELEBRATION (MCA-2370) 1978

MARTIN DENNY

HYPNOTIQUE (LST-7102) 1959
THE ENCHANTED SEA (Liberty LST-7141) 1960
EXOTIC SOUNDS OF THE SILVER SCREEN (Liberty
    LST-7158) 1960
EXOTIC SOUNDS VISITS BROADWAY (Liberty LST-7163)
    1960
EXOTIC PERCUSSION (Liberty LST-7168) 1960
ROMANTICA (Produced by Felix Slatkin) (Liberty LST-7207)
    1961
THE VERSATILE MARTIN DENNY (Liberty LST-7307)
    1963
LATIN VILLAGE (Liberty LST-7378) 1964
A TASTE OF HITS (LST-7328) 1964
MARTIN DENNY! (Liberty LST-7438) 1966
HAWAII (Liberty LST-7488) 1968
EXOTICA CLASSICA (Liberty LST-7513) 1968
A TASTE OF INDIA (Liberty LST-7550) 1968

FRANK DE VOL

PORTRAITS (Columbia CS-8010) 1958
FABULOUS HOLLYWOOD (Columbia CS-8172) 1959
OLD SWEET SONGS (Columbia CS-8209) 1960
MORE OLD SWEET SONGS (Columbia CS-8273) 1960
RADIO'S GREAT OLD THEMES (Columbia CS-8413) 1961
MORE RADIO'S GREAT OLD THEMES (Columbia CS-8578)
    1962
OLD SWEET WALTZES (Columbia CS-8565) 1962
ITALIAN ROMANCE (ABC S-534) 1966
THE NEW OLD SWEET SONGS (ABC S-563) 1967

DUANE EDDY

TWANGY GUITAR, SILKY STRINGS (Arranger and Conductor:
    Bob Thompson) (RCA LSP-2576) 1962

LONELY GUITAR (Arranger and Conductor: Marty Paich)
(RCA LSP-2798) 1964

EXOTIC GUITARS

22 GREAT GUITAR FAVORITES (Ranwood R-7014) 1967
THE EXOTIC GUITARS (Ranwood R-8002) 1968
THOSE WERE THE DAYS (Ranwood R-8040) 1969
INDIAN LOVE CALL (Ranwood R-8051) 1969
EVERYBODY'S TALKIN' (Ranwood R-8061) 1969

PERCY FAITH

On Columbia
PLAYS CONTINENTAL MUSIC (CL-525) 1953
PLAYS ROMANTIC MUSIC (CL-526) 1953
MUSIC UNTIL MIDNIGHT (with Mitch Miller on oboe)
(CL-551) 1953
MUSIC FOR HER (CL-705) 1955
PASSPORT TO ROMANCE (CL-880) 1956
VIVA!—THE MUSIC OF MEXICO (CS-8038) 1957
THE SOUND OF MUSIC (CS-8215) 1959
BOUQUET (The Percy Faith Strings) (CS-8124) 1959
BON VOYAGE! (Continental Souvenirs) (CS-8214) 1960
CAREFREE: THE MUSIC OF PERCY FAITH (CS-8360)
1961
TARA'S THEME FROM "GONE WITH THE WIND" AND
OTHER THEMES (CS-8427) 1961
BOUQUET OF LOVE (Percy Faith Strings) (CS-8481) 1962
EXOTIC STRINGS (Percy Faith Strings) (CS-8702) 1962
HOLLYWOOD'S GREAT THEMES (CS-8583) 1962
GREAT FOLK THEMES (CS-8908) 1963
AMERICAN SERENADE (CS-8757) 1963
SHANGRI-LA! (CS-8824) 1963
THEMES FOR YOUNG LOVERS (CS-8823) 1963
MORE THEMES FOR YOUNG LOVERS (CS-8967) 1964
BROADWAY BOUQUET (CS-9156) 1965
THEMES FOR THE "IN" CROWD (CS-9241) 1966
PLAYS THE ACADEMY AWARD WINNER (CS-9450) 1967

TODAY'S THEMES FOR YOUNG LOVERS (with Chorus)
(CS-9504) 1967
FOR THOSE IN LOVE (with Chorus) (CS-9610) 1968
ANGEL OF THE MORNING (Hit Themes for Young Lovers)
(with Chorus) (CS-9706) 1968
LOVE THEME FROM "ROMEO AND JULIET" (with Chorus)
(CS-9906) 1969
WINDMILLS OF YOUR MIND (CS-9835) 1969
THE BEATLES ALBUM (Percy Faith Strings) (C-30097) 1970
HELD OVER! TODAY'S GREAT MOVIE THEMES (CS-1019)
1970
I THINK I LOVE YOU (C-30502) 1971
DAY BY DAY (KC-31627) 1972
CLAIR (KC-32164) 1973
MY LOVE (KC-32380) 1973
COUNTRY BOUQUET (KC-33142) 1974
THEMES FOR YOUNG LOVERS (CD Columbia CK-8823)
1991
INSTRUMENTAL FAVORITES (CD Time Life Music A-23065-
R986-02) 1994
THE PERCY FAITH TREASURY (CD Good Music Company
A2-25270/138727) [2] 1994
SOUTH PACIFIC/THE SOUND OF MUSIC (CD Taragon
TARCD-1075) 2000
VIVA!: THE MUSIC OF MEXICO/EXOTIC STRINGS (CD
Taragon TARCD-1076) 2000
CONTINENTAL MUSIC/ROMANTIC MUSIC (CD Taragon
TARCD-1078) 2000
TODAY'S THEMES FOR YOUNG LOVERS/FOR THOSE IN
LOVE (CD Collectables COL-CD-7429) 2002
GREAT FOLK THEMES/AMERICAN SERENADE (CD
Collectables COL-CD-7479) 2002

FANTABULOUS STRINGS

THOSE FANTABULOUS STRINGS PLAY THE SUPREMES'
HITS (Metro MS-554) 1965
THOSE FANTABULOUS STRINGS PLAY THE SONNY AND
CHER HITS (Metro MS-557) 1965

THOSE FANTABULOUS STRINGS PLAY "THUNDERBALL"
and Other Movie Hits (Metro MS-551) 1966
THE WALTZ YOU SAVED FOR ME (Metro MS-576) 1966

FANTASTIC STRINGS

The budget line of Fantastic Strings volumes contained several tracks
that were essentially Ronnie Aldrich's Decca/London recordings with
the piano tracks removed and replaced with other instruments. Regardless, these collections have lots of worthwhile moments. Many of the
same songs were released by Pickwick/San Jan Music Group under the
Moonlight Moods Orchestra.

MY FAVORITES (CD Laserlight 15062, 15063, 15054, 15065,
15066) 1988–90 [5]
MY FAVORITES: Vols. 1–5 (CD Delta 15950) [Box] 1990
GOLDEN INSTRUMENTAL HITS (CD Laserlight 15176)
1990

FANTASY STRINGS (Conducted by "Ettore Stratta"/Arranged by Hagen Galatis)

These collections, recorded in Germany, are among the last of the great
pop orchestral ensembles recording versions of "current" hits going all
the way into the eighties. Included are metarock versions of the Cars'
"Drive" and Culture Club's "Karma Chameleon."

PRELUDE TO MY LOVE (Kem Disc KD-10132) 1993
TONIGHT WE LOVE (Kem Disc KD-10142) 1993
RHYTHM OF THE NIGHT (Kem Disc KD-10152) 1993
ALMOST PARADISE (Kem Disc KD-10162) 1993
THE GREATEST LOVE OF ALL (Kem Disc KD-10172)
1993
DAY BY DAY (Kem Disc KD-10182) 1993
MEDITERRANEAN SUNSET (Kem Disc KD-10192) 1993
MAGIC MELODY (Kem Disc KD-10202) 1994
A SENTIMENTAL JOURNEY (Kem Disc KD-10212) 1994
SEASONS OF LOVE (Kem Disc KD-10222) 1994

ROBERT FARNON

PRESENTING ROBERT FARNON (London LL-812) 1953
FLIRTATION WALK (London LL-1053) 1954
TWO CIGARETTES IN THE DARK (London LL-1052) 1955
SOMETHING TO REMEMBER YOU BY (London LL-1231)
    1955
MELODY FAIR (London LL-1280) 1956
PICTURES IN THE FIRE (London LL-1667) 1957
COCKTAILS FOR TWO (Richmond B-20005) 1958
LIGHT AND EASY (Richmond B-20033) 1959
THE SENSUOUS STRINGS OF ROBERT FARNON (Philips
    200-038) 1962
IN A DREAM WORLD (Rediffusion 15-10) 1974
AT THE MOVIES (CD Horatio Nelson Records SIV-6111) 1986
    (includes some previous Muzak material)
OUT OF MY DREAMS (CD Dutton Vocalion 4102) 2000
TOGETHER/SOMETHING TO REMEMBER YOU BY (CD
    Dutton Vocalion 4108) 2001
FLIRTATION WALK/PRESENTING ROBERT FARNON (CD
    Dutton Vocalion 4118) 2002

FERRANTE AND TEICHER

On United Artists/with orchestra conducted by Nick Perito
THE WORLD'S GREATEST THEMES (UAS-6121) 1960
WEST SIDE STORY AND OTHER MOTION PICTURE AND
    BROADWAY HITS (UAS-6166) 1961
LOVE THEMES (WWS-8514) 1962
TONIGHT (UAS-6171) 1962
THE KEYS TO HER APARTMENT (UAS-6247) 1962
LOVE THEMES FROM CLEOPATRA (UAS-6290) 1963
THE PEOPLE'S CHOICE (UAS-6385) 1964
BY POPULAR DEMAND (UAS-6416) 1965
YOU *ASKED* FOR IT! (UAS-3526) 1966
"A MAN AND A WOMAN" AND OTHER MOTION PICTURE
    THEMES (UAS-6572) 1967
LIVE FOR LIFE AND OTHER GREAT THEMES (UAS-6632)
    1967

THE PAINTED DESERT (UAS-6636) 1968
A BOUQUET OF HITS (UAS-6659) 1968
LOVE IN THE GENERATION GAP (UAS-6671) 1968
MIDNIGHT COWBOY (UAS-6725) 1969
GETTING TOGETHER (UAS-5501) 1970
IT'S TOO LATE (UAS-5531) 1971
PLAY THE HIT THEMES (UAS-5588) 1972
HEAR AND NOW (UA-LA018F) 1973
DIAL "M" FOR MUSIC (UA-LA195F) 1974
BEAUTIFUL . . . BEAUTIFUL (UA-LA316-G) 1975
THE CARPENTERS' SONGBOOK (UA-LA490G) 1976
PIANO PORTRAITS (UA-LA-585-G) 1976
FEELINGS (UA-LA662G) 1977
YOU LIGHT UP MY LIFE (UA-LA908G) 1978
ALL TIME GREAT MOVIE THEMES (CD EMI E2-0777-7-
    98823-2-8) 1993
INSTRUMENTAL FAVORITES (CD Time Life Music
    S21-18343 R986-08) 1995
GREAT 1970s MOTION PICTURE THEMES (CD Capitol
    30518) 2001

FIFTY GUITARS OF TOMMY GARRETT

Producer Tommy (Snuff) Garrett marketed his talents in various guises
and produced albums for artists ranging from Julie London to Gary
Lewis and the Playboys.

50 GUITARS GO COUNTRY (Liberty LSS-14025) 1960
50 GUITARS GO SOUTH OF THE BORDER (Liberty LSS-
    14005) 1961
50 GUITARS VISIT HAWAII (Liberty LSS-14022) 1963
50 GUITARS GO ITALIANO (Liberty LSS-14028) 1964
MARIA ELENA (Liberty LSS-14030) 1964
50 GUITARS RETURN TO PARADISE (Liberty LSS-14033) 1965
50 GUITARS IN LOVE (Liberty LSS-14037) 1966
OUR LOVE AFFAIR (Liberty LSS-14041) 1967
THE 50 GUITARS OF TOMMY GARRETT (United Artists
    UAS-79) 1971
FASCINATION (CD Pair 4947) 1992

JOHN FOX

GEORGE GERSHWIN (BBC Records REB-156) [U.K. Import]
HERE, THERE, AND EVERYWHERE (BBC Records REB-168) [U.K. Import]
MANHATTAN RHAPSODY (Music of John Sbarra) (Duramore 3003) 1985
LOVE IS A MANY-SPLENDORED THING (with the Starry Night Orchestra) (CD Realm ICD-8205) 1992
TWILIGHT TIME (with the Starry Night Orchestra) (CD Good Music Company 619528) [2] 2000

JACKIE GLEASON

On Capitol

MUSIC FOR LOVERS ONLY (W 352) 1953
MUSIC TO MAKE YOU MISTY (W 455) 1954
MUSIC, MARTINIS AND MEMORIES (W 509) 1954
MUSIC TO REMEMBER HER (W 570) 1955
LONESOME ECHO (W 627) 1955
MUSIC TO CHANGE HER MIND (W 632) 1956
NIGHT WINDS (DW 717) 1956
MUSIC FOR THE LOVE HOURS (SW 816) 1957
OOOO! (SW 905) 1957
THE TORCH WITH THE BLUE FLAME (SW 961) 1958
THAT MOMENT (SW 1147) 1958
OPIATE D'AMOUR (SW 1315) 1959
APHRODISIA (SW 1250) 1960
LOVE EMBERS AND FLAME (SW 1689) 1960
THE GENTLE TOUCH (SW 1519) 1961
LOVER'S PORTFOLIO (SWBO 1619) 1961 [2]
TODAY'S ROMANTIC HITS FOR LOVERS ONLY (SW 1978) 1963
MUSIC AROUND THE WORLD FOR LOVERS ONLY (SW 2471) 1966
THE NOW SOUND . . . FOR TODAY'S LOVERS (SW 293) 1968
COME SATURDAY MORNING (ST 480) 1970
NIGHT WINDS/MUSIC TO MAKE YOU MISTY (CD Capitol C2-92088) 1991

INSTRUMENTAL FAVORITES (CD Time Life Music R986-11)
1995
THE ROMANTIC MOODS OF JACKIE GLEASON
(CD Capitol 52541) [2] 1996
TAWNY/MUSIC, MARTINIS, AND MEMORIES
(CD Collectors' Choice 168) 2000

GOLDEN DREAM ORCHESTRA [Belgian Imports]

MILLION SELLER HITS (Palette 97982)
SONGS FROM THE MOVIES (Palette 97983)
FRENCH EVERGREENS (Palette 97984)
TRY TO REMEMBER (Palette 97985)
MAGICAL GUITAR (Palette 97987)
MAGICAL TRUMPET (Palette 97988)
MAGICAL EVERGREENS (Palette 97989)

GOLDEN GATE STRINGS

THE BOB DYLAN SONGBOOK (Epic BN-26158) 1966
A STRING OF HITS (Epic BN-26160) 1966
THE MONKEES SONGBOOK (Epic BN-26248) (Produced, with
most of the arrangements by Stu Phillips) 1967

RON GOODWIN

SWINGING SWEETHEARTS (Capitol T-10177) 1958
MUSIC FOR AN ARABIAN NIGHT (Capitol ST-10251) 1959
SOMEBODY NAMED RON GOODWIN PLAYS SOMEBODY
NAMED BURT BACHARACH (George Martin, prod.)
(Capitol ST-11012) 1972
FILM FAVORITES (Parlophone PMD 1014) 1954
MUSIC TO SET YOU DREAMING (Parlophone PMD 1038) 1956
RHYTHM AND ROMANCE (EMI Studio 2 1057 LP) 1976

MORTON GOULD

MOVIE TIME (Columbia ML-4595)
COFFEE TIME (RCA LSP-1656) 1958

GOODNIGHT, SWEETHEART (RCA LSC-2628) 1964
LATIN, LUSH, AND LOVELY (RCA LSC-2752) 1964
LIVING STRINGS (RCA LSC-2317) 1960
LOVE WALKED IN (RCA LSC-2633) 1964
JUNGLE DRUMS (RCA LSC-1994) 1955
MOON, WIND, AND STARS (RCA LSC-2232) 1958
MORTON GOULD MAKES THE SCENE (RCA LSP-3771)
    1967

FRANCIS GOYA

Born Francis Weyer, this Belgian guitarist was a studio player in the seventies who focused mostly on disco and rock. By 1975, he morphed into a Latinized name and recorded many albums pairing his sentimental "Goya Style" with lush orchestras.

THE SOUND OF FRANICS GOYA (Arcade ADEHCD823) 1986
RENDEZVOUS (Mercury 836485-2) 1988
PLAYS HIS FAVORITE HITS, VOL. 1 (Cloud International
    3806022) 1992
PLAYS HIS FAVORITE HITS, VOL. 2 (Cloud International
    3806032) 1993
TOGETHER (with Richard Clayderman) (Delphine/Arcade/
    Chryslie 2102866) 2000

GEORGE GREELEY

WORLD RENOWNED POPULAR PIANO (Warner Bros.
    WS-1291) 1958
GREATEST MOTION PICTURE PIANO CONCERTOS
    (Warner Bros. W-1319) 1959
MOST BEAUTIFUL MUSIC OF HAWAII (Warner Bros.
    WS-1366) 1960
POPULAR PIANO CONCERTOS OF THE WORLD'S GREAT
    LOVE THEMES (Warner Bros. WS-1387) 1960
POPULAR PIANO CONCERTOS FROM THE GREAT
    BROADWAY MUSICALS (Warner Bros. WS-1415) 1961
POPULAR PIANO CONCERTOS OF FAMOUS FILM
    THEMES (Warner Bros. WS-1427) 1961

ARTHUR GREENSLADE

THE MOVIE AND TELEVISION MUSIC OF ROD MCKUEN
(Stanyan SR 10045) 1972
PLAYS ABBA'S GREATEST HITS: INSTRUMENTAL
VERSIONS (RCA 13036) 1975
BEAUTIFUL COUNTRY STRINGS (CNCD 5944) [Holland
Import]

RICHARD HAYMAN

GREAT MOTION PICTURE THEMES OF VICTOR YOUNG
(Mercury SR-60012)
MEMORIES OF YOU (Mercury MG-25191)
MUSIC FOR A QUIET EVENING (Mercury MG-20048)
REMINISCING (Mercury MG-20113)
SERENADE FOR LOVE (Mercury MG-20115)
TIME TO LISTEN (Mercury MG-20103)
TENDER MOMENTS (Time 2033 LP)
CINEMAGIC SOUNDS (Command 941S) 1969
THE BEST OF RICHARD HAYMAN (UA/Ascot ALS-16011)
THE BEST OF SIMON AND GARFUNKEL (Naxos CD
8.990052)
MUSIC FOR LONELY LOVERS (CD Naxos International 90022)
1990
GREAT LOVE SONGS (CD Naxos 990020) 1991

HOLLYRIDGE STRINGS

**On Capitol: Arranged and Conducted by Stu Philips unless
otherwise indicated**

THE BEATLES SONG BOOK (ST-2116) 1964
THE BEACH BOYS SONG BOOK (ST-2156) 1964
INSTRUMENTAL VERSIONS OF HITS MADE FAMOUS BY
THE FOUR SEASONS (ST-2199) 1965
THE BEATLES SONG BOOK VOL. 2 (ST-2202) 1965
INSTRUMENTAL VERSIONS OF HITS MADE FAMOUS BY
ELVIS PRESLEY (ST-2221) 1965
THE NAT KING COLE SONG BOOK (ST-2310) 1965

FEELS LIKE LOVIN' (Stu Phillips, His Orchestra and Chorus) (ST-2356) 1966

CHRISTMAS FAVORITES BY THE HOLLYRIDGE STRINGS (ST-2404) 1966

THE NEW BEATLES SONG BOOK (ST-2429) 1966

OLDIES BUT GOODIES (Perry Botkin Jr.) (ST-2564)

THE BEATLES SONG BOOK, VOL. 4 (Perry Botkin Jr. and Mort Garson) (ST-2656) 1967

THE BEACH BOYS SONG BOOK, VOL. 2 (Mort Garson) (ST-2749)

THE BEATLES SONG BOOK, VOL. 5: MAGICAL MYSTERY TOUR (Mort Garson) (ST-2876) 1968

THE HITS OF SIMON AND GARFUNKEL (Mort Garson) (ST-2998)

GEORGE, JOHN, PAUL, AND RINGO (ST-839) 1971

HITS OF THE 70's (ST-883) 1972

THE BEATLES SONG BOOK (CD EDI Cema Special Markets S23-57949) [3] 1992

THE BEATLES SONG BOOK (CD Time Life Music R-134-06/S22-18236) [2] 1995

THE BEST OF THE BEATLES SONG BOOK (CD Varese Sarabande VSD-5690) 1996

LONG AND WINDING ROAD (CD EMI TOCP-65642) [Japanese Import] 2000

LEROY HOLMES

LOVE THEMES FROM MOTION PICTURES (MGM E-3172) 1956

CANDLELIGHT AND WINE (MGM E-3288) 1956

SOPHISTICATED STRINGS (MGM SE-3833) 1960

FOR A FEW DOLLARS MORE AND OTHER MOTION PICTURE THEMES (United Artists UAS-6608) 1967

CINEMA '69 (United Artists UAS-6669) 1968

EVERYBODY'S TALKIN' (United Artists UA 6731) 1969

THEMES FROM THE NEW PROVOCATIVE FILMS (United Artists UAS-6742) 1970

A SONG OF JOY (United Artists UAS-6769) 1970

FRANK HUNTER

WHITE GODDESS (Kapp KS-3019) 1961

GREAT MELODIES FROM MOTION PICTURES (Kapp KS-3099)

MUSIC BY FRANK HUNTER (Sesac Recordings PA 203/204)
JUST A MINUTE (Sesac PA-203 LP)

HORST JANKOWSKI

BABY, BUT GRAND! (Mercury SR-21106)
THE GENIUS OF JANKOWSKI (Mercury SR-60993) 1965
MORE GENIUS OF JANKOWSKI (Mercury SR-61054) 1966
STILL MORE GENIUS OF JANKOWSKI (Mercury SR-61076) 1966
SO, WHAT'S NEW? (Mercury SR-61093) 1966
AND WE GOT LOVE (FEATURING ZABADAK) (Mercury
    SR-61160)
PIANO AFFAIRS (Mercury SR-61195)
JANKOWSKI PLAYS JANKOWSKI (Mercury SR-61219)

GORDON JENKINS

IN THE STILL OF THE NIGHT (Decca DL-78077)
STOLEN HOURS (Capitol T-884)
BLUE PRELUDE (SUNSET SUS-5149)
DREAM DUST (Capitol T-1023)
DREAMER'S HOLIDAY (Vocalion VL-3615)
HAWAIIAN WEDDING SONG and Other Sounds of Paradise
    (Columbia CS-8564)
MAGIC WORLD (Columbia CS-8682)
IN A TENDER MOOD (Columbia CS-8809)
NIGHT DREAMS (Capitol T-781)
P.S. I LOVE YOU (Decca DL-9109)
MAGIC WORLD OF GORDON JENKINS/IN A TENDER
    MOOD (CD Collectors' Choice Music 129) 2000

BERT KAEMPFERT

Many of these albums were re-released on CD from Taragon and in
Europe from Polygram.

WONDERLAND BY NIGHT (Decca DL-74101) 1960
THE WONDERLAND OF BERT KAEMPFERT
    (Decca DL-74117) 1961
AFRIKAAN BEAT (Decca DL-74273) 1962
THAT HAPPY FEELING (Decca DL-74305) 1962
LIVING IT UP! (Decca DL-74374) 1963

LIGHTS OUT, SWEET DREAMS (Decca DL-74265) 1963
BLUE MIDNIGHT (Decca DL-74569) 1965
THAT LATIN FEELING (Decca DL-74490) 1964
THE MAGIC MUSIC OF FARAWAY PLACES (Decca
    DL-74616) 1965
BYE BYE BLUES (Decca DL-74693) 1966
STRANGERS IN THE NIGHT (Decca DL-74795) 1966
HOLD ME (Decca DL-74860) 1967
THE WORLD WE KNEW (Decca DL-74925) 1967
. . . LOVE THAT (Decca DL-74986) 1968
MY WAY OF LIFE (Decca DL-75059) 1968
WARM AND WONDERFUL (Decca DL-75089) 1969
TRACES OF LOVE (Decca DL-75140) 1969
THE KAEMPFERT TOUCH (DL-75175) 1970
ORANGE COLORED SKY (Decca DL-75256) 1971
BERT KAEMPFERT NOW! (Decca DL-75305) 1971
FABULOUS FIFTIES . . . AND NEW DELIGHTS (MCA-314)
    1973
STRANGERS IN THE NIGHT (Longines Symphonette Box Set)
    (LWS-299) [5]
INSTRUMENTAL FAVORITES (CD Time Life Music R986-18)
    1996
THE VERY BEST OF BERT KAEMPFERT (CD Taragon 1014)
    1996

WAYNE KING

SONGS OF THE ISLANDS (Decca DL-74023)
DANCE TO MUSIC FROM HOLLYWOOD AND BROADWAY
    (Decca DL-74232)
GOLDEN FAVORITES (Decca DL-74309)
THE SWEETEST SOUNDS (Decca DL-74368)
MOONLIGHT AND ROSES (Decca DL 74805)
EYES OF LOVE (Decca DL 74916)
DREAM TIME (Decca DL-78663)
LINGER AWHILE (Vocalion VL 73898)
MOON RIVER AND OTHER GREAT MOVIE THEMES
    (Vocalion VL 73912)

KNIGHTSBRIDGE STRINGS

STRINGS SING (Arranged/Conducted by Reg Owen and
   Malcolm Lockyer) (Top Rank RS-603) 1959
STRINGS SWING (Top Rank RS 608) 1959
SOFT, SWAYING STRINGS (Top Rank RS 641) 1960
$^3/_4$ TIME (Monument MAS-13001) 1966
CINEMA (Monument MAS-13002) 1966
GO POP (Monument MAS-13003) 1966
REVERIE (Monument MAS 13004 LP) 1967
NASHVILLE (Monument MAS 13008 LP) 1969
GOING HOLLYWOOD (CD Sony Special Products 21560) 1995

ANDRE KOSTELANETZ

On Columbia

LURE OF THE TROPICS (CL-780) 1954
STARDUST (CL-781) 1956
CLAIR DE LUNE (CL-798) 1957
THE VERY THOUGHT OF YOU (CL-843) 1958
THE LURE OF SPAIN (CL-943) 1960
THE LURE OF FRANCE (CS-8111) 1961
LURE OF PARADISE (CS-8144) 1962
WONDERLAND OF SOUND: TODAY'S GREAT HITS
   (CS-8457) 1963
WONDERLAND OF GOLDEN HITS (CS-8839) 1964
KOSTELANETZ IN WONDERLAND—GOLDEN ENCORES
   (CS-8878) 1964
I WISH YOU LOVE (CS-8985) 1964
SHADOW OF YOUR SMILE AND OTHER GREAT THEMES
   (CS-9267) 1965
TODAY'S GOLDEN HITS (CS-9334) 1966
THE KOSTELANETZ SOUND OF TODAY (CS-9409) 1967
TODAY'S GREATEST MOVIE HITS (CS-9556) 1967
SCARBOROUGH FAIR (CS-9623) 1968
I'VE GOTTA BE ME/GALVESTON (CS-9823) 1969
GREATEST HITS OF THE SIXTIES (CS-9973) 1969
FOR THE YOUNG AT HEART (CS-9691) 1969

TRACES (CS-9823) 1969
I'll NEVER FALL IN LOVE AGAIN (CS-9998) 1970
EVERYTHING IS BEAUTIFUL (C-30037) 1970
LOVE STORY (C-30501) 1971
FOR ALL WE KNOW (C-30672) 1971
LAST TANGO IN PARIS (C-32187) 1973
PLAYS GREAT HITS OF TODAY (KC-32415) 1973
THE WAY WE WERE (C-32578) 1974
NEVER CAN SAY GOODBYE (33550) 1975
I WISH YOU LOVE (CD Good Music Company A2-26624)
[2 CD] 1996
THE ULTIMATE COLLECTION (CD Sony International
502464) [Box] 2002

FRANCIS LAI

THE BEST OF FRANCIS LAI (From the Original Motion
Picture Soundtracks of "A Man and a Woman" and "Live for
Life") (United Artists UAS 6656) 1968
LOVE STORY (MCA 27017) 1971
MORE LOVE THEMES (KAPP) (KS-3646) 1971
PLAYS FRANCIS LAI (UA UAS 5515) 1971
FRENCH THEMES (United Artists UAS 5630) 1972
FRANCIS LAI AND HIS ORCHESTRA PLAY THE COMPOSI-
TIONS OF BURT BACHARACH, GATO BARBIERI, JOHN
BARRY . . . (United Artists UA-LA095-F) 1973
LOVE IN THE RAIN (THE MAN AND HIS MUSIC)
(Audiofidelity AFE 6301 LP) 1981
BILITIS (Original Soundtrack) (CD Melodie Editions-23 80035-2)
[French Import] 1987
THE VERY BEST OF FRANCIS LAI (CD Skyline SLCD 817)
[Swedish Import] 1990
A MAN AND A WOMAN/LIVE FOR LIFE (CD DRG 12612) 1996

JAMES LAST

INSTRUMENTALS FOREVER (Polydor 184059) 1966
WENN SÜß DAS MONDLICHT (Polydor Germany 1249 363)
1969

LOVE MUST BE THE REASON (Polydor Germany 2371 281) 1972
CLASSICS FOR DREAMING (Polydor Germany 2371 320) 1972
VIOLINS IN LOVE (Polydor Germany 2371 520) 1974
HAPPY SUMMER NIGHT (Polydor Germany 2371 658) 1976

MIKE LEANDER ORCHESTRA

THE FOLK HITS (London PS-453) 1965
GREAT FILM THEMES (Ace of Clubs ACL-1207) 1966
GREAT FILM HITS, VOL. 2 (Decca EP DFE-8660) 1966
A TIME FOR YOUNG LOVE (Decca DL 75144 LP) 1970

RAYMOND LEFEVRE

THE DAY THE RAINS CAME and Other Great Hits from France (Kapp KL-1103) 1958
YOU DON'T HAVE TO SAY YOU LOVE ME (Kapp KS-3510) 1966
RAYMOND LEFEVRE AND HIS ORCHESTRA (Major Minor Records SMMLP4) 1967
LOVE ME, PLEASE LOVE ME (Four Corners FCS-4239) 1967
SOUL COAXING (Four Corners FCS-4244) 1968
LA LA LA (HE GIVES ME LOVE) (Four Corners FCS-4250) 1968
RAYMOND LEFEVRE AND HIS ORCHESTRA (Buddha 5094) 1971
OH HAPPY DAY (Buddha BDS-5109) 1972
VIENS VIENS DA TROPPO TEMPO (Riviera GP-320) [Japanese Import] [2] 1974
ROCK AND RHYTHM IN HI-FI (Barclay 80-629) 1977

MICHEL LEGRAND

I LOVE PARIS (CL-555) 1954
HOLIDAY IN ROME (Columbia CL-647) 1955
VIENNA HOLIDAY (Columbia CL-706) 1955
CASTLES IN SPAIN (Columbia CL-888) 1956
BONJOUR PARIS (Columbia CL-947) 1957

I LOVE MOVIES (Columbia CL1178) 1958
SCARLET RIBBONS (Columbia CS 8146) 1959
THE NEW "I LOVE PARIS" (Columbia CS-8440) 1960
STRINGS ON FIRE (Columbia CS-8525) 1962
THE WINDMILLS OF YOUR MIND: Original Motion Picture
Theme from "The Thomas Crown Affair" and Others (United
Artists UAS-6715) 1969
SUMMER OF '42 (Original Soundtrack) (Warner 1925) 1971
"BRIAN'S SONG" THEMES AND VARIATIONS (Bell 6071) 1972
THE BEST OF MICHEL LEGRAND (Kory KK3006) 1976
HAPPY RADIO DAYS (CD Elektra 21809) 1999

ENOCH LIGHT AND THE LIGHT BRIGADE

STRINGS IN STEREO (Waldorf) (Arranged and Conducted by
Stu Phillips)
THE MILLION DOLLAR SOUND OF THE WORLD'S MOST
PRECIOUS VIOLINS (Command RS 802SD) 1959
FAR AWAY PLACES (Command RS 822SD) 1961
GREAT THEMES FROM HIT FILMS (Command RS 835SD) 1962
1963: THE YEAR'S MOST POPULAR THEMES (Command RS
854SD) 1963
MAGNIFICENT MOVIE THEMES (Command RS 887SD) 1965
FILM ON FILM (Project 3 PR 5005 SD) 1966
FILM FAME (Project 3 PR 5013 SD) 1967
12 SMASH HITS (with the Enoch Light Singers) (Project 3 PR
5021 SD) 1968
WHOEVER YOU ARE, I LOVE YOU (with the Enoch Light
Singers) (Project 3 PR 5030 SD) 1968
HIT MOVIE THEMES (Project 3 PR 5051 SD) 1970
LET IT BE (Project 3 PR 5100) 1974
BEATLES CLASSICS BY ENOCH LIGHT (Project 3 PR 5084
SD) 1974

LIVING GUITARS

On RCA Camden: Arranged and Conducted by Al Caiola
SOMEWHERE THERE'S A SOMEONE (CAS-978) 1966
SAN FRANCISCAN NIGHTS (CAS-2192) 1968

LITTLE GREEN APPLES and Other Country Hits (CAS-2302)
1968
MUSIC FOR COUNTRY LOVERS (CAS-2320) 1969
LET IT BE and Other Hits (CAS-2425) 1969
SONGS MADE FAMOUS BY THE ROLLING STONES
(CAS-2521) 1971
A CHARLIE RICH SONGBOOK (with the Country Strings)
(RCA ACL1-0696) 1974
PLUS COUNTRY STRINGS: JOHN DENVER SONGBOOK
(RCA ACL-1-0546) 1974

LIVING MARIMBAS

On RCA Camden: Arranged and Conducted by Leo Addeo
GEORGY GIRL and Other Music to Watch Girls By (CAS-2149)
1967
PLUS STRINGS: MacARTHUR PARK and Other Favorites
(CAS 2283 LP) 1968
PLUS STRINGS: PLAY THE GLEN CAMPBELL HIT
GALVESTON and Other Hits (CAS 2329) 1969
ZORBA THE GREEK and Other Broadway and Motion Picture
Favorites (CAS 2308 LP) 1969
RAINDROPS KEEP FALLIN ON MY HEAD and Other
Bacharach/David Hits (CAS 2400 LP) 1970
LOVE IS BLUE (CAS-2087)

LIVING STRINGS

On RCA Camden: Also listed by Arranger/Conductor
MUSIC FOR ROMANCE (Hill Bowen) (CAS 637) 1960
MUSIC OF THE SEA (Johnny Douglas) (CAS-639) 1961
MUSIC OF HAWAII (Hill Bowen) (CAS-661) 1961
THE WALTZ YOU SAVED FOR ME (CAS-690)
(Johnny Douglas) (CAS-673) 1962
NIGHT THEMES (Al Nevins) (CAS-755) 1963
THE SHIMMERING SOUNDS OF THE LIVING STRINGS
(Hill Bowen) (CAS-761) 1963
CHARADE AND OTHER FILM HITS (Hill Bowen) (CAS-799)
1964

ON A SENTIMENTAL JOURNEY (Johnny Douglas) (CAS-803) 1964

MUSIC TO HELP YOU STOP SMOKING (Hill Bowen, Johnny Douglas, Bob Sharples) (CAL-821) 1964

THE MELODY LINGERS ON (Plus Harp) (Johnny Douglas) (CAS-847) 1964

THE SWEETHEART TREE and Other Film Favorites (Johnny Douglas) (CAS-926) 1965

HE TOUCHED ME and Other Beautiful Love Songs (Johnny Douglas) (CAS-951) 1966

MAKE THE WORLD GO AWAY and Other Country Favorites (Johnny Douglas) CAS-982) 1966

I'M A BELIEVER AND OTHER MONKEES HITS (Johnny Douglas) (CAS-2148) 1967

THE WORLD WE KNEW (Plus Two Pianos) (Geraldo) (CAS-2190) 1968

BY THE TIME I GET TO PHOENIX and Other Country Favorites (Henri Rene) (CAS-2285) 1968

AIRPORT LOVE THEME (Johnny Douglas) (CAS-2420) 1970

FEELINGS (Johnny Douglas) (RCA APL1 2383 LP) 1977

CLOSE ENCOUNTERS (Johnny Douglas) (ANL1-281) 1978

MUSIC FROM "CAMELOT"/MUSIC OF THE SEA (CD Collectors' Choice DMC 12434) 1999

LIVING VOICES

On RCA Camden: Also Listed by Arranger/Conductor

SONGS OF MOONLIGHT AND ROMANCE (Keith Textor) CAS-683) 1962

ON BROADWAY (Johnny Douglas) (CAS-692) 1962

RAMBLIN' ROSE AND OTHER HITS (Anita Kerr) (CAS-748) 1963

MOONGLOW and Other Great Standards (CAS-804) 1964

POSITIVELY 4TH STREET and Other Message Folk Songs (Anita Kerr) (CAS-947) 1965

WISH ME A RAINBOW (CAS 2147) 1967

THE WINDMILLS OF YOUR MIND (CAS 2319) 1969

ANGEL OF THE MORNING (CAS 2307) 1969

WHAT THE WORLD NEEDS NOW IS LOVE (CAS 2542) 1972

I WRITE THE SONGS (RCA APL1 2381) 1977
YOU LIGHT UP MY LIFE (RCA ANL1 2815) 1978

LONDON FESTIVAL ORCHESTRA

LOVE AFFAIR (GWP ST 3016) 1970
LOVE THEMES FROM THE MOVIES (GWP ST 3014) 1970
SONGS FOR LOVING PEOPLE (GWP ST 3018) 1970
SPEAK TO ME OF LOVE (GWP ST 3017) 1970
THE GENTLE TOUCH (GWP ST 3015) 1970
THE MUSIC OF BACHARACH AND THE BEATLES (GWP
ST 3013) 1970

LONDON STUDIO ORCHESTRA

**Also Listed as the STUDIO LONDON ORCHESTRA and the LONDON
STARLIGHT ORCHESTRA**

FEELINGS: Studio London Orchestra and Singers (Laser
2668022) [Holland Import] 1985
ONCE UPON A TIME IN THE WEST: 20 Famous Film Tracks
of Ennio Morricone: London Starlight Orchestra (CD Star
86007) [Swedish Import] 1986
WITH LOVE: London Studio Orchestra (CD Sound Solutions
2641322) 1992
PLAYS STING HITS: London Starlight Orchestra (CD Star
86077) 1995
16 FAMOUS FILM AND TV THEMES: London Starlight
Orchestra (CD Star 86002) 1995
GOLDEN PAN-FLUTE: London Starlight Orchestra (CD Star
86013) 1996
20 BEATLES GREATEST HITS: London Starlight Orchestra
(CD Star 86021) 1996
ANOTHER DAY IN PARADISE: Collection of Phil Collins Hits:
London Starlight Orchestra (CD Star 86052) 1996

LONGINES SYMPHONETTE SOCIETY

IN A SENTIMENTAL MOOD (Longines SYS 5073) 1970
MELODIES FROM FAR AWAY PLACES (Longines SYS 5136) [2]

CLOSE TO YOU (Longines SYS 5428 LP) 1970
ACADEMY AWARD HIT PARADE (Longines SYS 5318) 1971
10 BEST SONGS OF 73 (Longines SYS 5594) 1973
BY THE BEATLES (Longines SYS 5856 LP) 1974
ENCHANTED ISLAND (Longines SYS 5622 LP) 1973

LOS INDIOS TABAJARAS

MARIA ELENA (RCA LSP-2822) 1964
ALWAYS IN MY HEART (RCA LSP-2912) 1964
THE MANY SPLENDORED GUITARS OF LOS INDIOS
    TABAJARAS (RCA LSP-3413) 1965
IN A SENTIMENTAL MOOD (RCA LSP-4013) 1966
SONG OF THE ISLANDS (RCA LSP-4129) 1969
DREAMS OF LOVE (RCA Victor LSP-4365) 1970
THE VERY THOUGHT OF YOU (with Orchestra and Chorus)
    (RCA LSP-4496) 1971
SOFTLY, AS IN A MORNING SUNRISE (RCA FSP 310) 1972
PLAY FAVORITE MOVIE THEMES (RCA Victor APL 1-0210)
    1973
MELLOW NOSTALGIA (RCA APL1 2082) 1977
MARIA ELENA/ALWAYS IN MY HEART (CD Collectables
    2705) 1997

GEOFF LOVE (*See also* Manuel and His Music of the Mountains)

BIG LOVE MOVIE THEMES (Music for Pleasure MFP-5221)
    1971
LOVE WITH LOVE (Music for Pleasure MFP-5246) 1972
YOUR FAVOURITE TV THEMES (MFP 50091) 1973
WALTZES WITH LOVE (MFP 50192) 1975
DREAMING WITH LOVE (Music for Pleasure MFP-50244)
    1976
TAKE ME HOME, COUNTRY ROADS (MMG B 704 LP) 1976
THANKS FOR THE MEMORIES (Capitol ST-10207)
IN THE MOOD FOR LOVE (CD EMI CDB-7-92194-2) 1989
GREAT WESTERN THEMES (CD EMI CC-204.
    CDB-7-52031-2, CC211) 1997

NORMAN LUBOFF CHOIR

REVERIE (Columbia CS-8074)
BUT BEAUTIFUL (Columbia CS-8114)
SONGS OF THE SEA (Columbia CL-948) 1956
SONGS OF THE WORLD, VOL. 1 (Columbia CS-8140) 1959
MOMENTS TO REMEMBER (Columbia CS-8220) 1960
THIS IS NORMAN LUBOFF! (RCA LSP-2342) 1961
ALOHA FROM NORMAN LUBOFF (RCA LSP-2602) 1963
GREAT MOVIE THEMES (RCA LSP-2895) 1964
REMEMBER (RCA LSP-3400) 1965
ROMANTIC REFLECTIONS (RCA Camden CAS-2129) 1967
LOVE LETTERS: Featuring the Norman Luboff Choir and the
  Melachrino Strings (Longines Symphonette Society LS 200-A)
  Box [6]
MUSIC FOR DREAMERS (with Paul Weston) (CD Sony Music
  Special Products 28578) 1997
TICKET TO THE MOVIES (CD Taragon TARCD-1059) 1999

ARTHUR LYMAN

YELLOW BIRD (Hi-Fi R1004) 1961
MANY MOODS (Hi-Fi R1007) 1962
I WISH YOU LOVE (Hi-Fi R1009) 1963
CALL OF THE MIDNIGHT SUN (Life L-1024) 1964
POLYNESIA (Life L-1027) 1965
LYMAN '66 (Life SL-1031) 1966
THE SHADOW OF YOUR SMILE (Life SL 1033) 1967
THE WINNERS CIRCLE (Life SL-1039) 1968
TODAY'S GREATEST HITS (Life SL-1040) 1969

DAVID McCALLUM

MUSIC: A PART OF ME (Capitol ST-2432) 1966
MUSIC: A BIT MORE OF ME (Capitol ST-2498) 1968
MUSIC: IT'S HAPPENING NOW (Capitol ST-2651) 1969
McCALLUM (Capitol ST-2748) 1969
MUSIC IS A PART OF ME (CD EMI 533131) 2001

HENRY MANCINI

On RCA (unless otherwise indicated)
DRIFTWOOD AND DREAMS (Liberty LRP-3049) 1957
UNIQUELY MANCINI (LSP-2692) 1963
"DEAR HEART" AND OTHER SONGS ABOUT LOVE
(LSP-2990) 1965
MUSIC OF HAWAII (LSP-3713) 1966
MANCINI '67 (LSP-3694) 1967
TWO FOR THE ROAD (LSP-3802) 1967
A WARM SHADE OF IVORY (LSP-4140) 1969
SIX HOURS PAST SUNSET (LSP-4239) 1969
MANCINI COUNTRY (LSP-4307) 1970
THEME FROM "Z" AND OTHER FILM MUSIC (LSP-4350)
1970
PLAYS THE THEME FROM "LOVE STORY" (LSP-4466) 1971
BRASS ON IVORY (LSP-4629) 1972
BRASS, IVORY, AND STRINGS (RCA 0098) 1973
PLAYS THOSE EVERGREEN CLASSICS (Reader's Digest RDS
9959) 1982
SUNFLOWER: Original Soundtrack (CD Avco Embassy 11001) 1987
FILM FAVORITES (CD BMG 295.469) 1990
CINEMA ITALIANO (CD RCA 60706-2-RC) 1990

JOHNNY MANN SINGERS

GOLDEN FOLK SONG HITS, VOL. 1 (Liberty LST-7253) 1962
INVISIBLE TEARS (Liberty LST-7387) 1964
THE BALLAD SOUND OF THE JOHNNY MANN SINGERS
(Liberty LST-7391) 1964
IF I LOVED YOU (Liberty LST-7411) 1965
BEATLE BALLAD SOUND (Liberty LST-7391) 1965
I'LL REMEMBER YOU (Liberty LST-7436) 1965
DAYDREAM (Liberty LST-7447) 1966
FLOWING VOICES OF THE JOHNNY MANN SINGERS
(Sunset SUS-5115) 1966
HEART FULL OF SONG (Sunset SUS-5196) 1967
WE CAN FLY! UP-UP AND AWAY (Liberty LST-7476) 1967
A MAN AND A WOMAN (Liberty LST-7490) 1967

DON'T LOOK BACK (LST-7535) 1967
LOVE IS BLUE (Liberty LST-7553) 1968
THIS GUY'S IN LOVE WITH YOU—THE LOOK OF LOVE
    (Liberty LST-7587) 1968
GOODNIGHT MY LOVE (Liberty LST-7620) 1969

MANTOVANI

On Decca/London
SOME ENCHANTED EVENING (London LL-766) 1953
ROMANTIC MELODIES (London LL-979) 1954
WALTZ ENCORES (London PS-119) 1955
FILM ENCORES (London PS-1700) 1957
GEMS FOREVER (London PS-3032) 1958
FILM ENCORES, VOL. 2 (London PS-3117) 1959
CONTINENTAL ENCORES (London PS-147) 1959
THE AMERICAN SCENE (London PS-182) 1960
MUSIC FROM "EXODUS" AND OTHER GREAT THEMES
    (PS-3231) 1961
ITALIA MIA (London PS-3239) 1961
AMERICAN WALTZES (PS-248) 1962
MOON RIVER AND OTHER GREAT FILM THEMES
    (London PS-249) 1962
PLAY SELECTIONS FROM "STOP THE WORLD—I WANT
    TO GET OFF"/"OLIVER" (London PS-270) 1962
THE WORLD'S GREAT LOVE SONGS (London PS-280) 1962
CLASSICAL ENCORES (PS-269) 1963
MANTOVANI/MANHATTAN (PS-328) 1964
THE INCOMPARABLE MANTOVANI (London PS-392) 1964
THE MANTOVANI SOUND (London PS-419) 1965
MANTOVANI MAGIC (London PS-448) 1966
MR. MUSIC . . . MANTOVANI (London PS-474) 1966
MANTOVANI/HOLLYWOOD (London PS-516) 1967
THE MANTOVANI TOUCH (London PS-526) 1968
MANTOVANI . . . MEMORIES (London PS-542) 1968
THE MANTOVANI SCENE (London PS-548) 1969
THE WORLD OF MANTOVANI (London PS-565) 1969
MANTOVANI TODAY (London PS-572) 1970
FROM MONTY WITH LOVE (2 LPs) (London XPS-585/6) 1971

M: ANNUNZIO PAOLO MANTOVANI (Twenty-fifth
    Anniversary Album) (London XPS-610) 1972
THE GREATEST GIFT IS LOVE (London PS-913) 1975
FAVOURITE SCREEN THEMES (CD Pickwick PWK-128) 1991
INSTRUMENTAL FAVORITES (CD Time Life Music R986-05)
    1995

MANUEL AND HIS MUSIC OF THE MOUNTAINS (*See also* Geoff Love)

In 1959, Geoff Love embarked on a series of albums under this pseudonym for EMI Studio Two, combining South American themed songs
with sweet, soft, and enchanting string arrangements.

MAGIC FOUNTAINS (EMI Studio 2 TWO 219) 1968
REFLECTIONS (EMI Studio 2 TWO 266) 1969
CASCADE (EMI Studio 2 TWO 376) 1971
HORIZONS (EMI Studio 2 TWO 414) 1973
SHANGRI-LA (EMI Studio 2 TWOX 1001) 1973
THE SUN, THE SEA, AND THE SKY (EMI Studio 2 TWO 399)
    1973
MASQUERADE (EMI Studio 2 TWOX 1055) 1976
MOUNTAIN FIRE (EMI Studio 2 TWOX 1061) 1977
THE MAGIC OF MANUEL (EMI Studio 2 TWOX 1073) 1978
MANUEL MOVIE HITS (Peters Intl PLD 1020) 1979
VIVA MANUEL (EMI Studio 2 TWOX 1078) 1979
MAGIC OF MANUEL (CD EMI CDP-797527)
FOR YOUR PLEASURE (MFP 5598) 1983
MOUNTAIN FIESTA (CD EMI CC 253. CDB-7-94109-2)
REFLECTIONS/CARNIVAL (CD EMI 7243-4-95622-2-6) [2] 1998

MARIANO AND THE UNBELIEVABLES

Pop orchestral magnate Mort Garson helped assemble these talented
oddities who, photographed in eighteenth-century finery and powdered
wigs, revisited sixties pop hits with a simple yet satisfying Baroque beat.

MARIANO AND THE UNBELIEVABLES (Capitol ST-2831)
    1967
THE 25TH HOUR (Capitol ST-2875) 1968

PAUL MAURIAT

LISTEN TOO! (Philips PHS-600-197) 1966
OF VODKA AND CAVIAR (Philips PHS-600-215) 1967
FROM PARIS WITH LOVE (Mercury/Wing SRW-16403) 1968
BLOOMING HITS: PAUL MAURIAT AND HIS ORCHESTRA
    (Philips PHS-600-248) 1968
MORE MAURIAT (Philips PHS-600-226) 1968
MAURIAT MAGIC (Philips PHS-600-270) 1968
PREVAILING AIRS (Philips PHS-600-280) 1968
DOING MY THING (Philips PHS-600-292) 1969
L.O.V.E. (Philips PHS-600-320) 1969
LET THE SUNSHINE IN/MIDNIGHT COWBOY/AND
    OTHER GOODIES (Philips PHS-600-337) 1969
GONE IS LOVE (Philips PHS-600-345) 1970
EL CONDOR PASA (Philips PHS-600-352) 1971
THEME FROM A SUMMER PLACE (MGM/Verve MV-5087) 1972
LOVE THEME FROM "THE GODFATHER" (MGM SE-4838)
    1972
SUMMER MEMORIES (Philips 6332 109) [U.K. Import] 1972
PAUL MAURIAT 'SALUTES THE BEATLES (Contour) 1972
A TASTE OF FRANCE (Philips 6325 146) [Brazil Import] 1974
HAVE YOU NEVER BEEN MELLOW? (MGM SE-4999) 1975
PLAYS THE HITS OF ABBA, DEMIS ROUSSOS . . . (Power
    Exchange PXL023) [U.K. Import] 1977
LOVE IS BLUE: ANNIVERSARY COLLECTION (Featuring
    Zamfir on pan flute) (CD Verve 834259-2) 1988
LOVE IS BLUE: THE BEST OF PAUL MAURIAT
    (CD Polygram International 4101) 2000

GEORGE MELACHRINO

On RCA Living Stereo
MUSIC FOR DINING (LSP-1000) 1958
MUSIC FOR RELAXATION (LSP-1001) 1958
MUSIC FOR READING (LSP-1002) 1958
MUSIC FOR FAITH AND INNER CALM (LPM-1004) 1958
MUSIC FOR COURAGE AND INSPIRATION (LSP-1005) 1958
MUSIC TO HELP YOU SLEEP (LSP-1006) 1958
MUSIC FOR TWO PEOPLE ALONE (LSP-1027) 1959

MUSIC FOR DAYDREAMING (LSP-1028) 1959
MUSIC TO WORK OR STUDY BY (LSP-1029) 1959
MUSIC FOR THE NOSTALGIC TRAVELER (LSP-1053)
UNDER WESTERN SKIES (LSP-1676) 1958
LISBON AT TWILIGHT (LSP-1762) 1958
OUR MAN IN LONDON (LSP-2608) 1963
MUSIC FOR ROMANCE (LSP-2979) 1964
SOMETHING TO REMEMBER YOU BY (LSP-3398) 1965
THE WORLD OF MELACHRINO (Decca SPA 48) [U.K.
    Import] 1969

MIDNIGHT STRING QUARTET

Producer Snuff Garrett provided these volumes of chamber-style interpretations of pop hits and old standards.

RHAPSODIES FOR YOUNG LOVERS (Viva VS-6001) 1966
SPANISH RHAPSODIES FOR YOUNG LOVERS
    (Viva V-36004) 1967
RHAPSODIES FOR YOUNG LOVERS, VOL. TWO
    (Viva V-36008) 1967
LOVE RHAPSODIES (Viva V-36013) 1967
THE LOOK OF LOVE (Viva V-36015) 1968
GOODNIGHT MY LOVE (Viva V-36019) 1968
RHAPSODIES FOR YOUNG LOVERS, VOL. THREE
    (Viva V-36022) 1969
CHAMBER MUSIC FOR LOVERS (Viva V-36024) 1969

MIDNIGHT STRINGS ORCHESTRA

REUNITED (Excelsior XRP 7011) 1980
REMINISCING (with Syd Dale) (Excelsior XRP 7012) 1980
EVERGREEN (Excelsior XRP 7017) 1981
ON THE RADIO (Excelsior XRP 7015) 1981
RIDE LIKE THE WIND (Excelsior XRP 7016) 1981

FRANK MILLS

Mills was a member of the Canadian pop vocal group the Bells before
he began his career as an instrumental pianist. In 1972, he had a minor

hit called "Love Me, Love Me Love" but not until 1979 did he achieve his greatest fame with "Music Box Dancer," accompanied by an album with the same title that also proved popular.

MUSIC BOX DANCER (Polydor 6192) 1979
SUNDAY MORNING SUITE (Polydor 6225) 1980
PRELUDE TO ROMANCE (Capitol ST 6488) 1981
THE BEST OF FRANK MILLS: HAPPY MUSIC (CD Macola
 1172) 1994
TRANSITIONS (Capitol C2-46461) 1996
OVER 60 MINUTES WITH FRANK MILLS (EMI 46889) 1998
MUSIC BOX DANCER (CD Richmond 23) 2000

HUGO MONTENEGRO

PREMIERE PERFORMANCE (with the 20th Century Strings,
 Twentieth Century–Fox SFX-3018)
MASTERPIECES (with the 20th Century Strings) (Twentieth
 Century–Fox SFX-3019)
GREAT STANDARDS (with the 20th Century Strings)
 (20th Century Fox SFX-3030)
SOUND OF THE HUGO MONTENEGRO STRINGS
 (Movietone 71023)
MONTENEGRO IN ITALY (Time Series 2000 S/2051) 1962
GREAT SONGS FROM MOTION PICTURES (Time Series
 2000 S/2044/2045/2046) 1962
BLACK VELVET (Time Series 2000 S/2196) 1962
CANDY'S THEME and Other Sweets (RCA LSP 3332) 1965
MUSIC FROM "A FISTFUL OF DOLLARS" AND "FOR A
 FEW DOLLARDS MORE" AND "THE GOOD, THE BAD,
 AND THE UGLY" (RCA 3927) 1968
GOOD VIBRATIONS (RCA LSP-4104) 1969
THE GOOD, THE BAD, AND THE UGLY (CD RCA 07863
 66019-2) 1992

MOODS ORCHESTRAL

In 1967, Philips Records initially created the Moods Orchestral Series as audiocassettes for people to play in their cars. The eighteen-disc series, subsequently released in the LP format, included such pop orchestral arranger-conductors as Johnny Arthey, Johnny Gregory, and Ken Thorne.

On Philips

THERE'S NO BUSINESS LIKE SHOW BUSINESS
   (SBL-7793)
SMALL WORLD (SBL-7794)
FASCINATING RHYTHM (SBL-7795)
THANKS FOR THE MEMORY (SL-7796)
HIT THE ROAD TO DREAMLAND (SBL-7797)
YOU ARE MY LUCKY STAR (SLP-7798)
IT'S MAGIC (SBL-7800)
AROUND THE WORLD (SBL-7801)
BROADWAY MELODY (SBL-7802)
THE PARTY'S OVER (SBL-7803)
THANK HEAVEN FOR LITTLE GIRLS (SBL-7804)
ISN'T THIS A LOVELY DAY? (SBL-7805)
LET'S FACE THE MUSIC AND DANCE (SBL-7806)
LANGUAGE OF LOVE (SBL-7807)
HELLO, YOUNG LOVERS (SBL-7808)
FALLING IN LOVE WITH LOVE (SBL-7809)
MISTER WONDERFUL (SBL-7810)
DANCING IN THE DARK (SBL-7811)

ALAIN MORISOD

Alain Morisod, who used a special electronically modified technique to transmit his romantic piano, became another staple on the Beautiful Music stations. The 1978 melody "Lake Como" became a cult favorite among the format's listeners. He also worked with a choral group called the "Sweet People."

TWENTY MELODIES POUR REVER, VOL. 1 (CD Orchard
   801327) 2001
TWENTY MELODIES POUR REVER, VOL. 2 (CD Orchard
   801328) 2001
MELODIES POUR TOUJOURS (CD Orchard 801329)
   2001

TONY MOTTOLA

ROMAN GUITAR (Command RS-816) 1960
PLAYS COUNTRY AND WESTERN SONGS (Command
RS-823) 1961
ROMANTIC GUITAR (Command RS-847) 1962
SENTIMENTAL GUITAR (Command RS-864SD) 1964
GUITAR PARIS (Command RS-877) 1964
MEXICO/S.A.: LOVE SONGS (Command RS-889) 1966
A LATIN LOVE-IN (Project 3 PR-5010) 1967
WARM, WILD AND WONDERFUL (Project 3 PR-5025)
1968
ITALIAN FAVORITES (Project 3 PR-5032) 1968
THE TONY TOUCH (Project 3 PR-5041) 1969
WARM FEELINGS (Project 3 PR-5058 SD) 1971
TONY AND STRINGS (PR-5069) 1972
TONY MOTTOLA AND THE QUAD GUITARS (Project 3
PR-5078) 1973
I ONLY HAVE EYES FOR YOU (Project 3 PR-5094) 1974

WERNER MÜLLER

SUMPTUOUS STRINGS (London Phase 4 SP-44187)
SENTIMENTAL JOURNEY (London Phase 4 SP-44267)
MILLION STRINGS (Polydor LPHM-46012)
CASCADING STRINGS (Polydor LPHM-46028)
FIREWORKS IN STRINGS (Polydor LPHM-46062)
TWO MILLION STRINGS (with Helmut Zacharias) (Polydor
LPHM-46091)
GOLDEN AWARD SONGS (Polydor SLPHM-237518)

MUZAK

Through the years, when elevator music was the company's bread and butter, Muzak Corporation released many demonstration albums that were not available in stores and were intended strictly for prospective clients and franchisers. These albums' tracks were arranged and conducted by such names as Phil Bodner, Al Caiola, Frank Chacksfield,

Arthur Greenslade, Richard Hayman, Ted Heath, Frank Hunter, Dick Hyman, Sven Libaek, Buddy Morrow, Tony Mottola, Nick Perito, and Earl Sheldon.

REVEILLE—THE "NEW MUZAK" (H-1[1] 79) 1969
MUZAK: NEW DIMENSIONS (H-1(1) 35) 1970
MUZAK: STIMULUS PROGRESSION ONE (SZB 497) 1970
MUZAK: STIMULUS PROGRESSION TWO (SAAB 270) 1971
MUZAK: STIMULUS PROGRESSION 4: THE SOUND
    HEARD ROUND THE WORLD (SLP-8981) 1972
MUZAK: STIMULUS PROGRESSION 5 (All Arrangements by
    Nick Perito) (III, A-44) 1973
MUZAK: STIMULUS PROGRESSION 6 (40 Year Anniversary
    LP) (Misc-D-0089-A/B) 1974
MUZAK: THE ONLY ONE—STIMULUS PROGRESSION
    (111 A 0076) 1976
MUZAK MEANS CARING FOR PEOPLE (H4RS-0004) 1978
MUZAK: MORE THAN MUSIC (AA1-79) 1979
MUZAK: CELEBRATING A SOUND FUTURE—50 Years
    (TR-520689) 1984

MYSTIC MOODS ORCHESTRA

On Philips (unless otherwise indicated)
ONE STORMY NIGHT (PHS-600-205) 1966
NIGHTTIDE (PHS-600-213) 1966
MORE THAN MUSIC (PHS-600-231) 1967
MEXICO! (ALSO TITLED: MEXICAN TRIP) (PHS-600-250)
    1967
THE MYSTIC MOODS OF LOVE (PHS-200-260) 1968
EMOTIONS (PHS-200-277) 1968
EXTENSIONS (PHS-200-301) 1969
LOVE TOKEN (PHS-200-321) 1970
STORMY WEEKEND (PHS-200-342) 1970
ENGLISH MUFFINS (PHS-200-349) 1970

CD titles re-released on Cema and Capitol's "Right Stuff" Label in "Colossus" Digital Stereo
MYSTIC MOODS COUNTRY (CD Cema Special Products
    521-56928) 1993

ONE STORMY NIGHT (T2-66685) 1993
HIGHWAY ONE (T2-32048) 1995
NIGHTTIDE (T2-66687) 1995
MOODS FOR A STORMY NIGHT (T2-66686) 1995
STORMY WEEKEND (T2-66695) 1995
MORE THAN MUSIC (T2-32045) 1995
EMOTIONS (T2-32047) 1995
STORMY MEMORIES (Featuring Rene Hamaty on piano)
    (T2-66697) 1995

NASHVILLE STRINGS

THE NASHVILLE STRINGS (Columbia Musical Treasuries
    DS-583)
DANNY DAVIS AND THE NASHVILLE STRINGS PLAY
    INSTRUMENTAL VERSIONS OF THE HERMAN'S
    HERMITS SONG BOOK (MGM SE-4309) 1965
PLAY GREAT COUNTRY HITS (Arranged by Hugo
    Winterhalter) (Columbia CS-9646) 1968
PLAY GREAT COUNTRY HITS, VOL. 2 (Columbia CS-9830) 1970
BIG HARP COUNTRY CLASSICS (CD King 1502) 2001

PETER NERO

YOUNG, WARM, AND WONDERFUL (RCA LSP-2484) 1962
HAIL THE CONQUERING NERO (RCA LSP-2638) 1963
SONGS YOU WON'T FORGET (RCA LSP-2935) 1964
THE SCREEN SCENE (RCA LSP-3496) 1966
PLAYS "BORN FREE" AND OTHERS (RCA Camden
    CAS-2139) 1967
PLAYS "LOVE IS BLUE" and Ten Other Great Songs (RCA
    LSP-3936) 1968
LOVE TRIP (RCA LSP-4205) 1968
I'VE GOTTA BE ME (Columbia C-9800) 1969
FROM "HAIR" TO HOLLYWOOD (Columbia CS 9907) 1970
SUMMER OF '42 (Columbia C 31105) 1972
THE FIRST TIME EVER I SAW YOUR FACE (Columbia
    KC-31335) 1972
THE WORLD OF PETER NERO (Columbia KG-31982) [2] 1973

101 STRINGS

On Somerset/Stereo Fidelity/Alshire/Audio Spectrum

GRAND CANYON SUITE (Somerset SF-7900) 1950

CARIBBEAN CRUISE (as the Rio Carnival Orchestra) (Somerset P-5900) 1959

THE SOUL OF SPAIN (Somerset SF-6600) 1959

GYPSY CAMP FIRES (Somerset SF-8100) 1960

BACK BEAT SYMPHONY (Somerset P-11500)

HAWAIIAN PARADISE (Somerset SF-12800) 1961

I LOVE PARIS (Somerset SF-13000) 1962

PLAY THE WORLD'S GREAT STANDARDS (Stereo Fidelity SF-4300)

MILLION SELLER SONGS OF THE SIXTIES (Stereo Fidelity SF-21300) 1963

SONGS OF THE SEASONS IN JAPAN (Alshire S-5019) 1964

MOOD VIENNA (Alshire S-5023) 1965

THE QUIET HOURS (Alshire S-5026) 1965

EAST OF SUEZ (Alshire S-5027) 1965

ITALIA CON AMORE (FROM ITALY WITH LOVE) (Alshire S-5030) 1965

THE SOUL OF MEXICO (Alshire S-5032) 1966

FLY ME TO THE MOON (Alshire S-5033) 1966

A ROMANTIC MOOD FOR DINING AND DREAMING (Alshire S-5034) 1966

SOUNDS AND SONGS OF THE JET SET (Alshire S-5043) 1967

THE SOUL OF GREECE (Alshire S-5047) 1967

101 STRINGS PLAY MILLION SELLER HITS OF 1966 (with Don Costa) (Alshire S-5050) 1967

SWINGIN' THINGS (Scored by Don Costa) (Alshire S-5055) 1967

SOUNDS OF TODAY (Alshire S-5078) 1968

MILLION SELLER HITS WRITTEN BY THE BEATLES and Other "Now" Writers (Alshire S-5111) 1968

ASTRO-SOUNDS: From Beyond the Year 2000 (Alshire S-5119) 1968

AFRICAN SAFARI (Alshire S-5171) 1969

MORE HITS SONGS OF TODAY'S CHARTS (Alshire S-5175) 1969

MILLION SELLER HITS OF 1969 (Alshire S-5185) 1969
THE SOUNDS OF LOVE (A/S-199) 1969
MILLION SELLER HITS OF TODAY WRITTEN BY SIMON
    AND GARFUNKEL (Alshire S-5156) 1969
THE "EXOTIC" SOUNDS OF LOVE (A/S-201) 1970
MILLION SELLER HITS ARRANGED AND CONDUCTED
    BY LES BAXTER (Alshire S-5188) 1970
QUE MANGO! (Arranged and Conducted by Les Baxter) (Alshire
    S-5204) 1970
SPECTACULAR BRASS! FANTASTIC REEDS! (Arranged/
    conducted by Nelson Riddle) (Alshire S-5229) 1970
THEME FROM LOVE STORY (Alshire S-5232) 1971
HIT SONGS WRITTEN BY BACHARACH AND WEBB (Audio
    Spectrum 19) 1972
CAROLE KING HITS (Alshire S-5278) 1972
AMERICANA (Alshire S-5317) 1974
HITS MADE FAMOUS BY THE BEACH BOYS (Alshire S-5342)
    1976
SONGS OF THE CARPENTERS (Alshire S-5341) 1976
A TRIBUTE TO JOHN LENNON (Alshire S-5380) 1980
LOVE SONGS (CD Alshire ALCD-7) 1986
PLUS° PLUS° PLUS (CD Alshire ALCD-18) 1986
ROMANTIC SONGS OF THE SEA (CD Alshire ALCD-20)
    1986
NELSON RIDDLE with the 101 Strings (CD Alshire ALCD-27)
    1987
MAGNIFICENT DIGITAL SOUND (CD Alshire ALCD-28)
    1987
TRIBUTE TO HENRY MANCINI (CD Alshire ALCD-75) 1989
ASTRO-SOUNDS: From Beyond the Year 2000 (CD Caroline/
    Scamp SCP-9717-2) 1996
QUE MANGO!: Les Baxter with the 101 Strings (CD Caroline/
    Scamp SCP-9718-2) 1996
INSTRUMENTAL FAVORITES: THE 101 STRINGS, Featuring
    THE SOUL OF SPAIN (CD Time Life Music R986-21)
    1996
STRINGS FOR LOVERS (CD Alshire ALCD-5221) [Box]
    1996
SIMPLY BEAUTIFUL MUSIC (CD Madacy 7327) [Box] 1996

FAUSTO PAPETTI

Because of his saxophone, he might be lumped into "smooth jazz," but a tireless dedication to new and old standards with lush string backings and a relative adherence to simple melody place Papetti more securely in easy-listening territory.

I REMEMBER . . . (Audio Fidelity AFSD 6189) 1968
BONJOUR FRANCE (Durium LP. S 40.1254) [Italian Import] 1981
MY ONE AND ONLY LOVE (CD Kubaney 183) 1982
BABY BLUE MUSIC, VOL 1 (CD Kubaney 9510) 1987
US AND THEM (CD Kubaney 181) 1988
IL MONDO DI PAPETTI (CD Kubaney 182) 1988
MIDNIGHT MELODIES (CD Kubaney 184) 1988
ECOS DE HOLLYWOOD (CD Kubaney 273) 1990
MARIA ELENA (CD Kubaney 279) 1991
IN A SENTIMENTAL MOOD (CD BR. MUSIC BR 131-2)
FEELINGS (CD Huub 845001) 1991
EL CINE (CD Polygram 523136) 1994

NORRIE PARAMOR

IN LONDON, IN LOVE (Capitol ST-10025) 1956
LONDON AFTER DARK (Capitol ST-10052) 1957
THE ZODIAC SUITE (Capitol ST-10073) 1957
MOODS (Capitol ST-10130) 1958
JET FLIGHT (Capitol ST-10190) 1959
AUTUMN (with the "moody, in-and-out voice" of Patricia Clark) (Capitol ST-10212) 1960
AMOR, AMOR! (Capitol ST-10238) 1961
STRINGS! STAGED FOR SOUND (Capitol ST-1639) 1962
IN LONDON . . . IN LOVE AGAIN (with the "floating voice" of Patricia Clark) (Capitol ST-2071) 1963
WARM AND WILLING (with the "spun-gold voice" of Patricia Clark) (Capitol ST-2357) 1964
IN TOKYO, IN LOVE (Capitol ST-2526) 1964
SOUL COAXING (Studio 2 TWO 207) [U.K. Import] 1968
LOVE AT FIRST SIGHT (Polydor 184358) 1969
SILVER SERENADE (BBC REB 272) [U.K. Import] 1977

BBC RADIO TOP TUNES (CD Emporio EMPRCD-660)
IN LONDON, IN LOVE/AUTUMN (CD Collectors' Choice)

PICCADILLY STRINGS (Arranged by Ray Martin)

RAINY NIGHT IN LONDON (Capitol T-10017)
MY LONDON (Capitol T-10056)
INTERNATIONAL VIBRATIONS (Capitol T-10066)
HIGH BARBAREE: 12 FAMOUS SEA SHANTIES (Capitol
    T-10067)
GLOBAL HOP (as Ray Martin and His Piccadilly Strings)
    (Capitol T-10101) 1957

FRANCK POURCEL

POURCEL'S PORTRAITS (Capitol T-1855)
LES BAXTER'S "LA FEMME" (Franck Pourcel and His French
    Strings) (Capitol T-10015)
OUR MAN IN PARIS (Imperial LP-9304) 1965
BEAUTIFUL OBSESSION (Imperial LP-9322) 1966
SOMEWHERE MY LOVE (Imperial LP-9326) 1966
A MAN AND A WOMAN (Imperial LP-12343) 1967
LOVE IS BLUE (Imperial LP-12383) 1968
PLAYS "MIDNIGHT COWBOY" (Paramount PAS-5015) 1969
AQUARIUS (Atco SD 33-299) 1969
MEETS THE BEATLES (EMI 2C 062-11041-U) 1970
THEME FROM "LOVE STORY" (Paramount PAS 5022) 1971
L'ENFANT ROI (EMI S URL 20-866) 1972
FOR ALL WE KNOW (Paramount PAS 5035) 1972
DAY BY DAY (Paramount PAS-6036) 1972
THE WORLD IS A CIRCLE (Paramount PAS-6047) 1973
PLAYS ABBA (EMI 10 C064-016.550) 1978
HI-FI 77: 20 POP INSTRUMENTALS (EMI C-182-15570/71)
    (2) 1977
DIGITAL AROUND THE WORLD (Odeon 064-073-551T) 1981
GOLDEN SOUNDS OF FRANCK POURCEL (CD Disky
    GS-864882) 1996
THIS IS POURCEL/THE COLE PORTER STORY (CD EMI
    7243-4-98147-2-1) 1999

READER'S DIGEST RECORDS ("Pleasure Programmed")

MOOD MUSIC FOR LISTENING AND RELAXATION
   (RD 43-M) [10]
MOOD MUSIC FOR DINING (RDA 47-A) [10]
HAPPINESS IS . . . (RD4-106) [9]
BACKGROUND MOODS (RDS 6107) [10]
MAGICAL WORLD OF MELODY (RD16-E) or (RDS 6040)
   [10]
GREAT MUSIC FROM GREAT MOVIES (RDS 6315)
STARDUST MELODIES (RDS 9401-9408)
DOWN MEMORY LANE (RDA 40-A) [10]
LOVE IS BLUE: MUSIC IN A MELLOW MOOD (RD4-77-1-4)
   [4] 1969
MOOD MUSIC FROM THE MOVIES (607-ES-1-4) [4] 1971
GOLDEN FAVORITES OF THE '50s AND '60s (RDCD2581-3)
   1998

HERBERT REHBEIN

LOVE AFTER MIDNIGHT (Decca DL 74847)
LOVE MUSIC OF BERT KAEMPFERT . . . AND SO TO BED
   (Decca DL 75107)
MUSIC TO SOOTHE THAT TIGER (Decca DL 74584)
MUSIC TO SOOTHE THAT TIGER/LOVE AFTER MID-
   NIGHT/. . . AND SO TO BED (CD Taragon 1077) 2000

NELSON RIDDLE

TENDER TOUCH (Capitol T-753) 1957
SEA OF DREAMS (Capitol T-915) 1958
THE JOY OF LIVING (Capitol ST-1148) 1959
LOVE TIDE (Capitol ST-1571) 1961
LOVE IS A GAME OF POKER (Capitol ST-1817) 1962
MORE HIT TV THEMES (Capitol ST-1869) 1963
WHITE ON WHITE, SHANGRI-LA, CHARADE, AND
   OTHER HITS OF 1964 (Reprise RS-6120) 1964
THE BRIGHT AND THE BEAUTIFUL (Liberty LST-7508)
   1967
THE RIDDLE OF TODAY (Liberty LST-7532) 1968

SPECTACULAR BRASS! FANTASTIC REEDS! (with 101
    STRINGS) (Alshire S-5229) 1970
INSTRUMENTAL FAVORITES (CD Time Life Music
    S21-18406) 1995
LOLITA: Original Motion Picture Soundtrack (CD Turner/Rhino
    R2-72841) 1997
ROUTE 66 and Other Great TV Themes (CD CEMA 9452)

ROGER ROGER

From the fifties through the seventies, Roger composed and recorded movie and radio music for France's Radio-Diffusion—Television Française, Radio-Tele-Luxembourg, and Radio-Monte Carlo. He wrote incidental music with titles such as "Scenic Railway," which was inspired by a trip to Disneyland, and also contributed some Spanish-flavored numbers for Music by Muzak in the fifties.

THRILLING (MGM E-3201)
BEYOND THE SEA: THE MUSIC OF CHARLES TRENET
    (MGM E-3395)
IN PARIS IN LOVE (MGM E-3677)
FOLIES BERGERE (Decca DL 8571)
HEART OF PARIS (Decca DL-8599)
MUSIQUE POUR REVER (Vega V-30-S-725)
INVITATION TO PARIS/DANCE ALBUM
    (Everest LPBR-5093)
TOURBILLON DE PARIS (Mode MDINT-9080) 1976
GRAND PRIX (Columbia CS-8719)
MUSIQUE AUX 4 VENTS (with Marc Lanjean)
    (Pacific LDP-E-7285)

DAVID ROSE

BEAUTIFUL MUSIC TO LOVE BY (MGM E-3067) 1953
NOSTALGIA (MGM E-3134) 1954
LOVERS' SERENADE (MGM E-3289) 1955
AUTUMN LEAVES (MGM SE-3592) 1957
SECRET SONGS FOR YOUNG LOVERS (with Andre Previn)
    (MGM SE-3716) 1958
DAVID ROSE PLAYS DAVID ROSE (MGM SE-3811) 1959

SPECTACULAR STRINGS (MGM SE-3895) 1961
CIMARRON AND OTHER GREAT THEMES
    (MGM SE-3953) 1961
BONANZA (MGM SE-3960) 1961
THE VERY BEST OF DAVID ROSE (MGM SE-4155) 1962
THE VELVET BEAT (MGM SE-4307) 1965
IN A MELLOW MOOD (Masterseal ST-9000)
THEMES FROM THE GREAT SCREEN EPICS (Capitol
    ST-2627) 1967
HAPPY HEART (Capitol ST-393) 1969

JOHN SBARRA

These tracks, written by John Sbarra but arranged and conducted by
Frank Barber, Syd Dale, John Fox, and Norrie Paramor, often appeared
on both Muzak and the Beautiful Music stations.

ALL MY BEST . . . LOVE WILL ALWAYS MATTER
    (CD Fairfield JS-001) 1990
MOVE THEMES OF TOMORROW (CD Fairfield JS-003)
    1992

SENTIMENTAL STRINGS

BMG Special Products released a series of compact discs under the
"Sentimental Strings Orchestra" name, each with 10 tracks and recordings similar to those on the Reader's Digest "Romantic Strings Orchestra" collections.

CLASSICALLY ROMANTIC (44903) 1999
THE POWER OF LOVE (44904) 1999
WHAT A WONDERFUL WORLD (44905) 1999
AMERICAN SONGBOOK (44906) 1999
CONTEMPORARY CLASSICS (44907) 1999
FOREVER COUNTRY (44908) 1999
SO IN LOVE (44909) 1999
BEST OF BROADWAY (44910) 1999
SENTIMENTAL FAVORITS (44911) 1999
UNFORGETTABLE (44912) 1999

THE SHADOWS

MOONLIGHT SHADOWS (Polydor 829358-2) 1986
SIMPLY SHADOWS (Polydor 833682-2) 1987
SHADOWS ARE GO! (Caroline/Scamp SCP 9711-2) 1996
DREAM TIME (CD Karussell 550094) 2000
STRING OF HITS (CD EMI 48278) 2000
ANOTHER STRING OF HOTS HITS AND MORE (CD EMI
52005) 2000

FELIX SLATKIN

PARADISE FOUND (Liberty Premier Series LSS-14001) 1960
MANY SPLENDORED THEMES (Liberty Premier Series
LSS-14011) 1961
OUR WINTER LOVE (Liberty LST-7287) 1963
FANTASTIC STRINGS (Liberty LST-7376) 1964
LOVE STRINGS (Sunset SUS-5106) 1966
TENDER STRINGS (Sunset SUS-5170) 1967

STRINGS OF PARIS

In the mid- to late eighties, a label calling itself the Beautiful Music Collection put out a series of discs by "Robert Janssen with the Strings of Paris," conducted by "Jean Paul de la Tour." Crafted on a budget label, recorded in Eastern Europe, and packaged in Belgium, these discs contain pleasantly arranged melodies tailored for the background.

ENDLESS LOVE (BMC 87101) 1996
MIDNIGHT BLUE (BMC 87102) 1996
LOVE STORY (BMC 87103) 1996
WOMAN IN LOVE (BMC 87104) 1996
SLEEPY SHORES (BMC 87105) 1996
MOON RIVER (BMC 87106) 1996
ONLY YOU (BMC 87107) 1996
EASY TO LOVE (BMC 87109) 1996
THE MORE I SEE YOU (BMC 87110) 1997
GREAT MOVIE THEMES (BMC 87111) 1997
VIVE LE FRANCE (BMC 87113) 1997

ROMANTIC GUITAR MELODIES (BMC 87118) 1997
ROMANTIC HARMONICA MELODIES (BMC 87121) 1999
FEELINGS (BMC 87108) 2000

SUNSET STRINGS

THE SUNSET STRINGS AND VOICES (Sunset SUS-5185) 1968
FILM MUSIC ITALIAN STYLE (Sunset SUS-5188) 1968
THE IMPOSSIBLE DREAM (Sunset SUS-6208) 1968
THE ROY ORBISON SONGBOOK (Liberty LST-7395) 1965

BILLY VAUGHN

Of all the pop orchestral leaders, Billy Vaughn scored the most hits,
giving the world of rock good competition. He was a founding member
of the Hilltoppers and at Dot Records acted as the arranger behind Pat
Boone and the Fontane Sisters.

SAIL ALONG SILV'RY MOON (Dot DLP-25100) 1959
PLAYS THE MILLION SELLERS (Dot DLP-25119) 1959
BLUE HAWAII (Dot DLP-25165) 1959
THEME FROM "A SUMMER PLACE" (Dot DLP-25276) 1960
LOOK FOR A STAR (Dot DLP-25322) 1960
THEME FROM "THE SUNDOWNERS" (Dot DLP-25349)
    1961
ORANGE BLOSSOM SPECIAL AND WHEELS
    (Dot DLP-3366) 1961
BERLIN MELODY (Dot DLP-25396) 1962
CHAPEL BY THE SEA (Dot DLP-25424) 1962
A SWINGIN' SAFARI (Dot DLP-25458) 1962
1962's GREATEST HITS (Dot DLP-25497) 1963
SUKIYAKI and 11 Hawaiian Hits (Dot DLP-25523) 1963
BLUE VELVET and 1963's Great Hits (Dot DLP-25559) 1964
PEARLY SHELLS (Dot DLP-25605) 1965
MEXICAN PEARLS (Dot DLP-25628) 1965
MICHELLE (Dot DLP-25679) 1966
GREAT COUNTRY HITS (Dot DLP-25698) 1966
ALFIE (Dot DLP-25751) 1967
THAT'S LIFE AND PINEAPPLE MARKET (Dot DLP-25788)
    1967

ODE TO BILLY JOE (Dot DLP-25828) 1967
A CURRENT SET OF STANDARDS (Dot DLP-25882) 1968
THE WINDMILLS OF YOUR MIND (Dot DLP-25937) 1969
TRUE GRIT (Dot DLP-25969) 1969
WINTER WORLD OF LOVE (Dot DLP-25975) 1970
MELODY OF LOVE: BEST OF BILLY VAUGHN (CD Varese
    Sarabande 5525) 1994
INSTRUMENTAL FAVORITES (CD Time Life Music R986-15)
    1995

ANTHONY VENTURA ORCHESTRA

JE'TAIME—Traum Melodien (Dream Melodies) [German
    Imports]
Volumes 1–8 (Ariola 202 183–610, 202 184–610, 202 185–610, 202
    186–610, 202 187–610,202 188–610, 202 189–610, 202 190–
    610) 1975–1976

LAWRENCE WELK

LAWRENCE WELK AND HIS SPARKLING STRINGS (Coral
    57011) 1956
MOMENTS TO REMEMBER (Coral 57068) 1956
I'M FOREVER BLOWING BUBBLES (Dot DLP-25248) 1960
SONGS OF THE ISLANDS (Dot DLP-25251) 1960
LAST DATE (Dot DLP-25350) 1961
CALCUTTA! (Dot DLP-25359) 1961
YELLOW BIRD (Dot DLP-25389) 1961
YOUNG WORLD (Dot DLP-25428) 1962
BABY ELEPHANT WALK AND THEME FROM THE
    BROTHERS GRIMM (Dot DLP-3457) 1962
BUBBLES IN THE WINE (Dot DLP-25489) 1962
1963'S EARLY HITS (Dot DLP-25510) 1963
SCARLETT O'HARA (Dot DLP-25528) 1963
WONDERFUL! WONDERFUL! (Dot DLP-25552) 1964
EARLY HITS OF 1964 (Dot DLP-25572) 1964
MY FIRST OF 1965 (Dot DLP-25616) 1965
APPLES AND BANANAS (Dot DLP-25629) 1965
TODAY'S GREAT HITS (Dot DLP-25663) 1966

CHAMPAGNE ON BROADWAY (Dot DLP-25688) 1966
WINCHESTER CATHEDRAL (Dot DLP-25774) 1967
LAWRENCE WELK'S "HITS OF OUR TIME"
    (Dot DLP-25790) 1967
LOVE IS BLUE (Ranwood RLP-8003) 1968
MEMORIES (Ranwood R-8044) 1969
GALVESTON (Ranwood R-8049) 1969
JEAN (Ranwood R-8060) 1969
22 GREAT SONGS FOR EASY LISTENING (Ranwood
    RLP-7016) 1982
16 MOST REQUESTED SONGS (CD Columbia Legacy
    CK-45030) 1989
INSTRUMENTAL FAVORITES (CD Time Life Music R986-14)
    1995

PAUL WESTON

MUSIC FOR DREAMING (Capitol H-222) 10" 1945
MUSIC FOR MEMORIES (Capitol H-225) 10"
MUSIC FOR EASY LISTENING (Capitol H-195) 10"
MUSIC FOR ROMANCING (Capitol H-153) 10"
MUSIC FOR THE FIRESIDE (Capitol H-245) 10"
MUSIC FOR REFLECTION (Capitol H-287) 10"
MUSIC FOR DREAMING (T-1154) 12"
MUSIC BY THE FIRESIDE (T-1192) 12"
MOOD MUSIC (Columbia CL-527) 1953
DREAM TIME MUSIC (Columbia DL-528) 1953
CARIBBEAN CRUISE (Columbia CL-572) 1954
MUSIC FOR A RAINY NIGHT (Columbia CL-574) 1954
MELODIES FOR A SENTIMENTAL MOOD
    (Columbia CL-6204)
ORIGINAL MUSIC FOR EASY LISTENING (CD Corinthian
    COR102-CD) 1987
MUSIC FOR MEMORIES/MUSIC FOR DREAMING
    (CD Capitol CDP 7 92091 2) 1992
MUSIC FOR DREAMERS (with the Norman Luboff Choir)
    (CD Sony Music Special Products 28578) 1997
PAUL WESTON AND HIS ORCHESTRA WITH THE
    NORMAN LUBOFF CHOIR (Sony A28578) 1997

CARIBBEAN CRUISE/MUSIC FOR A RAINY NIGHT
(CD Collectables 6468) 2000
MOOD MUSIC/DREAM TIME MUSIC (CD Collectables 6469)
2000

ROGER WILLIAMS

On Kapp

ROGER WILLIAMS—AUTUMN LEAVES (KL-1012) 1956
DAYDREAMS (KL-1031) 1956
SONGS OF THE FABULOUS FIFTIES (KXL-5000) [2] 1957
ALMOST PARADISE (KL-1063) 1957
TILL (KL-1081) 1958
NEAR YOU (KL-1112) 1959
ALWAYS (KS-3056) 1960
TEMPTATION (KS-3217) 1961
YELLOW BIRD (KS-3244) 1961
MARIA (KS-3266) 1962
FOR YOU (KS-3336) 1963
ACADEMY AWARD WINNERS (KS-3406) 1964
PLAYS THE HITS (KS-3414) 1965
SUMMER WIND (KS-3434) 1965
I'LL REMEMBER YOU (KS-3470) 1966
BORN FREE (KS-3501) 1966
ROGER! (KS-3512) 1967
MORE THAN A MIRACLE (KS-3550) 1968
ONLY FOR LOVERS (KS-3565) 1969
HAPPY HEART (KS-3595) 1969
LOVE THEME FROM "ROMEO AND JULIET" (KS-3610)
1969
LOVE STORY (KS-3645) 1971
SUMMER OF '42 (KS-3650) 1971
LOVE THEME FROM "THE GODFATHER" (KS-3663) 1972
PLAY ME (KS-3671) 1972
IVORY IMPACT (Bainbridge BT-8002) [2] 1982
THE BEST OF THE BEAUTIFUL (CD MCA MCAD-5571)
1989
THE GREATEST POPULAR PIANIST/THE ARTIST'S
CHOICE (CD MCA MCAD2-10698) [2] 1992

INSTRUMENTAL FAVORITES (CD Time Life Music R-986-06) 1995

ROGER WILLIAMS COLLECTION (CD Varese Vintage VSD-5908) 1998

SOFTLY AS I LEAVE YOU (CD Varese Vintage VSD-5984) 1998

HUGO WINTERHALTER

THE EYES OF LOVE . . . (RCA LPM-1338) 1957

HUGO WINTERHALTER GOES . . . LATIN (RCA LSP-1677) 1957

WISH YOU WERE HERE (RCA LSP-1904) 1959

TWO SIDES OF WINTERHALTER (RCA LSP-1905) 1959

HUGO WINTERHALTER GOES . . . HAWAIIAN (RCA LSP-2417) 1962

HUGO WINTERHALTER GOES . . . CONTINENTAL (RCA LSP-2482) 1963

I ONLY HAVE EYES FOR YOU (RCA LSP-2645) 1964

THE BEST OF HUGO WINTERHALTER (RCA LSP-3379[e]) 1965

SATURDAY NITE AT THE MOVIES (Musico MDS-1001)

MOTION PICTURE HIT THEMES (Musico MDS-1040)

YOUR FAVORITE MOTION PICTURE MUSIC (Musicor M2S-3178) [2]

CLASSICAL GAS (with Eddie Heywood) (Musicor MS-32170)

LOVE STORY (Musicor MS-3196) 1972

16 BEAUTIFUL HITS (CD Deluxe DCD-7901) 1994

THE EYES OF LOVE (CD Good Music DMC2-1420) 1996 [2]

THE VERY BEST OF HUGO WINTERHALTER (CD Taragon TARCD-1080) 2000

VICTOR YOUNG (and His Singing Strings)

LOVE THEMES (Decca DL-5413)

IMAGINATION (Decca DL-5450)

CINEMA RHAPSODIES (Decca DL-8051)

HOLLYWOOD RHAPSODIES (Decca DL-8060)

NIGHT MUSIC (Decca DL-8085)

PEARLS ON VELVET (Decca DL-8285)

AFTER DINNER MUSIC (Decca DL-8350)
LOVE THEMES FROM HOLLYWOOD (Decca DL-8364)
SOFT LIGHTS AND SWEET MUSIC (Decca DL-8789)
FOREVER YOUNG (Decca DL-8798)

HELMUT ZACHARIAS (and His Magic Violins)

THEMES (Decca DL-74083)
TWO MILLION STRINGS (Decca DL-78926)
STRINGS, MOONLIGHT, AND YOU (Decca DL-85491)
MAGIC VIOLINS (Decca DL-8431)
RENDEZVOUS FOR STRINGS (Decca DL-8982)
ROMANTICALLY YOURS (Polydor SLPHM-237627)
ON LOVERS' ROAD (Polydor LPHM-46234)
BOUQUET OF STRINGS (Polydor 2485 0270) [Holland Import]
LIGHT MY FIRE (Sounds Superb SPR 90038) [British Import] 1971
MUSIC AND ROMANCE (CD Music and Romance 85714)
    [Holland Import] 1999

OTHER NOTABLE TITLES (Listed alphabetically by artist)

DICK BAKKER: SOFT MELODIES (Dureco 115-129-2)
    [Holland Import]
MYCHAEL DANNA: SKYS (CD Hearts of Space HS1 1032-2)
    1992
DEVO: E-Z LISTENING DISC (Ryko RCD 20031) 1987
CARL DOY: PIANO BY CANDLELIGHT (Time Life Music
    R139-31) [2] 1992
ROBERT DRASNIN: VOODOO! (CD Bacchus Archives BA09)
    1996 (also released as PERCUSSION EXOTIQUE! on Top
    Records/Mayfair in 1959)
ELECTRO SONIC ORCHESTRA: Presenting a New Concept
    in Sound (Coral CRL 757381) 1958
MORGAN FISHER: ECHOES OF LENNON (Global Pacific
    GPD 351) 1993
MORT GARSON (The Love Strings of . . .): LOVE SOUNDS
    (Liberty LST-7559) 1968
EARL GRANT: EBB TIDE and Other Instrumental Favorites
    (DL-74165)

CHARLES RANDOLPH GREAN SOUNDE: QUENTIN'S
THEME (Ranwood 8055) 1968
HAGOOD HARDY: THE HOMECOMING (Capitol ST-11468)
1975
DICK KESNER AND HIS MAGIC STRADIVARIUS: THE
MUSIC OF HAWAII (Coral CRL-757352)
JONATHAN KNIGHT: LONELY HARPSICHORD ON A
RAINY NIGHT (Viva V-36006) 1966
PETER KNIGHT AND HIS ORCHESTRA: INSTRUMENTAL
BEATLES THEMES FROM SGT. PEPPERS LONELY
HEARTS CLUB BAND (Mercury SR-61132) 1968
LONDONDERRY STRINGS PLAY THE LIVERPOOL
SONGBOOK (Warner WS-1580) 1967
MARBLE ARCH ORCHESTRA: TOMORROW'S
STANDARDS (Liberty LST-7567) 1968
ROBERT MAXWELL: THE VERY BEST OF . . . (MGM SE
4246)
MORNINGTOWN STRINGS: THE CARNIVAL IS OVER:
PLAY THE HITS OF THE SEEKERS (MFP-50003) 1970
MUNICH PHILHARMONIC ORCHESTRA PLAYS ABBA
CLASSIC (Atlantic 7 82362-2) 1991
ALFRED NEWMAN: THEMES (Capitol ST-1652)
JACK NITZSCHE: THE LONELY SURFER (LP Reprise
RS-6101/CD Collector's Choice CCM-195-2) 1963/2001
JACK NITZSCHE: ONE FLEW OVER THE CUCKOO'S
NEST (Original Soundtrack) (Fantasy 9500) 1976
CYRIL ORNADEL and the Starlight Symphony: HOLLYWOOD
SOUND STAGE (MGM SE-4033) 1962
RUPERT PARKER: HARPBEAT (CD Focus International 1)
1998
STU PHILIPS AND HIS ORCHESTRA: ORGAN AND
STRINGS IN STEREO (Waldorf MHK SD 1414)
BILL PURSELL: OUR WINTER LOVE (Columbia CS-8792)
1963
LES REED (with the Eddie Lester Singers): LOVE IS ALL
(London SP-44136) 1969
THE QUIETS: TAKE A FLIGHT WITH THE QUIETS
(Ovaltone OVALCD-001) [Finland Import] 2001
HENRI RENE: IN LOVE AGAIN! (RCA Camden CAL-312)

NINI ROSSO: FAR WEST: I GRANDI FILM WESTERN (Dischi Ricordi SVCD 56) 1978

MARIO SAID: EV'RYBODY'S TALKIN' (Liberty LST-7601) 1969

SANTO AND JOHNNY: THE BEATLES GREATEST HITS (Canadian American SCALP-1017) 1964

RAYMOND SCOTT: THIS TIME WITH STRINGS (Coral CRL-57174)

GEORGE SIRAVO: SEDUCTIVE STRINGS (Time Series 2000 S/2019)

SOUNDS OF THE '70s ORCHESTRA: SONGS OF THE SEVENTIES (Arranged and Conducted by William Loose) (Capitol Special Markets in Quadraphonic QL-6774) 1971

ROBERT STIGWOOD ORCHESTRA PLAYS BEE GEES' HITS (Atlantic SD-8195) 1968

BOB THOMPSON: THE SOUND OF SPEED (Dot DLP-25123) 1962

VIENNA STATE OPERA ORCHESTRA: MY FOOLISH HEART (Music from the Repertoire of Station WPAT) (Westminster WST-15014)

SOME NOTEWORTHY COMPILATIONS (Listed by release dates)

AS YOU REMEMBER THEM (Time Life Records STL1-621) [3] 1972

SILENCE AND ROMANCE (Dureco 1154132) [3] 1990

ROMANCE: Chip Davis' Day Parts (American Gramaphone AGCD 103) 1992

BEAUTIFUL DREAMER: LULLABIES THE WHOLE WORLD LOVES (London 440 117-2 LM) 1993

TIMELESS FAVORITES FROM THE FIFTIES (Realm 1CD-8372) 1994

WHISPERS OF LOVE (Surrey House Music CD-1902) 1995

BEST OF ELEVATOR MUSIC (Dominion 3509-2) 1995

INSTRUMENTAL FAVORITES: MOVIE MAGIC (Time Life Music R986-07) 1995

INSTRUMENTAL FAVORITES: POP PLEASURES (Time Life Music R986-09) 1995

INSTRUMENTAL FAVORITES: ROMANTIC MOMENTS (Time Life Music R986-16) 1996

MUSIC FOR TV DINNERS: The Moodsong® Project (Caroline/ Scamp SCP-9721-2) 1997

MUSIC FOR TV DINNERS: THE '60s: The Moodsong® Project (Caroline/Scamp SCP-9722-2) 1997

FEELINGS (Hallmark 330452) [2] 1997

LISTEN EASY: HITS FROM THE '60s (BBC WMEM-0015-2) 1998

LISTEN EASY: HITS FROM THE '70s (BBC WMEM-0016-2) 1998

INSTRUMENTAL FAVORITES: POP CLASSICS (Time Life Music R986-22) 1998

HOLIDAY FOR STRINGS (Good Music 191627-1/2) [2] 1998

HARD TO FIND ORCHESTRAL INSTRUMENTALS (Eric 11507) 1999

TEST CARD MUSIC 6 (Apollo Sound APSCD 221) 2000 (includes some previous Muzak material)

TEST CARD MUSIC 7 (Apollo Sound APSCD 223) 2001 (includes some previous Muzak material)

TEST CARD MUSIC 8 (Apollo Sound APSCD 228) 2002 (includes some previous Muzak material)

Bibliography

Periodicals and Newspapers

Ackerman, Paul. "ASCAP Board Clashes over Background Music TV Plugs." *Billboard,* December 21, 1959.

Adams, Frank. "Bomber Hits Empire State Building, Setting It Afire at the 79th Floor, 13 Dead, 26 Hurt; Wide Area Rocked." *New York Times,* July 29, 1945, pp. 1, 25.

Adams, Jane Meredith. "The Clearest Message May Be: 'Buy This Tape.'" *Boston Globe,* August 5, 1991, p. 37. [Surveys subliminal audio tapes.]

Adorian, Andrew. "Is Mood Music in the Background?" *Composer* 40 (Summer 1971), pp. 25–29.

Ahlgren, Calvin. "Ex-Sleep Musician Gets Back to Nature." *San Francisco Chronicle,* October 21, 1990, pp. 37–38.

Ahrens, Frank. "Tunes Play a Part in Many Parts of Life over the Airwaves." *Journal,* June 10, 1992, p. A6.

Allen, J. Linn. "Criticizing the Suburbs." *Baltimore Sun,* March 29, 1992.

Altman, Wilfred. "Mood Music Is Catching On . . . " *Melody Maker,* October 12, 1957. [Interview with Norrie Paramor.]

Anderson, Omer. "Church's Acoustics Heavenly Music for DGG's Prize-honored Product." *Billboard,* February 4, 1967, p. 72.

Antrim, Doron K. "Have You Tried Working to Music?" *Reader's Digest* (March 1946), pp. 127–28. [Condensed from *Forbes* 2/15/46.]

"Background Music: But It's Good For You." *Time,* August 30, 1963.

"Background Music Rule Spurs Queries." *Billboard,* November 16, 1959, p. 4.

Baldwin, Deborah. "Muzak to My Ears." *Technology Review* (November/December 1982), pp. 18–19.

Barol, Bill. "Muzak for a New Age." *Newsweek,* May 13, 1985, p. 68.

Bassman, Jim. "The Music in the Malls." *ASCAP in Action* (Fall 1989), p. 27.

"Bert Kaempfert Has Top Disk on 'Wonderland.'" *Billboard,* December 5, 1960, p. 16.

Bessman, Jim. "New Age Genre: Aging Well?" *Billboard,* June 30, 1990, p. 54.

Blum, Debra E. "A Dean Is Charged with Plagiarizing a Dissertation for His Book on Muzak." *Chronicle of Higher Education,* May 10, 1989, p. A17.

Boltz, Marilyn; Schulkind, Matthew; and Kantra, Suzanne. "Effects of Background Music on the Remembering of Filmed Events." *Memory & Cognition* 19:6 (November 1991), pp. 593–606.

Brodsky, Warren. "A Personal Perspective of the Power of Music and Mass Communication, Prior to and During the Gulf War Crisis in Israel: Implications for Music Therapy." *Music Therapy* 10:1 (1991), pp. 99–113.

Brown, Tony. "Mantovani—Spearhead of Britain's Invasion." *Melody Maker,* November 14, 1953, p. 3.

Coleman, Ray. "Acker's 30,000 Pound Stranger." *Melody Maker,* August 11, 1962, pp. 6–7.

Dawbarn, Bob. "The Version Kids Can Take Home." *Melody Maker,* October 4, 1969, p. 5.

Del Colliano, Jerry. "Reinventing Beautiful Music." *Radio Only* (April 1983), pp. 17–18.

Deutsch, Didier C. "Whatever Happened to Instrumental Film Music?" *Lone Wolf,* Indie Report 1991, pp. 26–29, 55.

Di Perna, Alan. "The 'King of Background Music' Steps Out (Major Moves from New Age Keyboardist David Lanz)." *Musician* (January 1991), pp. 76–79.

Dorfman, Andrea. "How Muzak Manipulates You." *Science Digest* (May 1984), p. 26.

Dunlap, Orrin E., Jr. "A Birdseye View: America Is Seen as a Great Music Hall by the Air-Minded Mr. Kostelanetz." *New York Times,* February 18, 1940.

Duston, Anne. "There's a Lot of Beautiful Music." *Billboard,* April 19, 1975, p. C16, C23.

"Easy Listening." *Washington Post,* August 27, 1990, p. A10. [Editorial.]

Ericson, Edward. "A Few Faks About Muzak," *Spin* (June 1989), p. 24.

Ericson, Raymond. "André Kostelanetz, 78, Conducted Symphonic and Popular Music Too," *New York Times,* January 15, 1980, p. B6.

————. "$200 a Day and They'll Pipe You Aboard." *New York Times,* March 3, 1968.

"'Erotic' Disc Seized in Italy." *Melody Maker,* September 6, 1969, p. 24.

Ferrante, Arthur, and Louis Teicher, "Two Pianos? It'll Never Sell!," *Music Journal,* September 1965, pp. 42–3.

Fields, Sidney. "Music Logic of His Own." *New York Daily News,* June 6, 1973. [Overview of Peter Nero's career.]

Fleming, John. "Common Note of Woe." *St. Petersburg Times,* June 17, 1992.

Flint, Peter B. "Lawrence Welk, the TV Maestro of Champagne Music, Dies at 89." *New York Times,* May 19, 1992, p. B8.

Foltz, Kim. "A Farewell to Mantovani." *Newsweek,* January 7, 1985, p. 44.

Fowler, Glenn. "David Rose, Composer, Dies at 80; Wrote for Television and Movies." *New York Times,* August 26, 1990, p. 44.

Franzen, Russ. "Squier's Legacy Reaches Out and Touches Everyone." *Flint Journal Lapeer Plus Edition,* March 25, 1990.

Friedrich, Otto. "Trapped in a Musical Elevator." *Time,* December 10, 1984, pp. 110–12.

Gallez, Douglas W. "Satie's *Entr'acte:* A Model of Film Music." *Cinema Journal* 16:1 (Fall 1976), pp. 36–50.

Gates, David, and Johnson, Patrice. "Muzak's Five Decades of Art-free Melody." *Newsweek,* September 10, 1984, pp. 9–10.

Genn, Lillian G. "Music by Muzak: Piping Tunes into Cafes, Factories and Homes Becomes Big Business." *New York Times,* October 12, 1941.

Giddins, Gary. "Bobby Hackett: Muzak Man." *Village Voice,* June 18, 1991, pp. S3, S17.

Green, Stanley. "Music to Hear But Not to Listen to." *Saturday Review,* September 28, 1957, pp. 55–56, 118.

Grimes, William. "Ready-to-Hear Music for Ready-to-Fix Meals." *New York Times,* July 1, 1992, pp. C1, C10.

Haden-Guest, Anthony. "The Hills Are Alive with the Sound-in-Motion of Muzak: The Search for the Ultimate Print-out." *Rolling Stone,* January 18, 1973, pp. 38–44.

Heinecke, Alan. "Coarse Groove Mood Music & Sound Effect Recordings." *Journal into Melody,* Robert Farnon Society (December 1992), pp. 41–44.

Hoffman, Marilyn. " 'Music Hath Charms'—In the Air." *Christian Science Monitor,* December 26, 1967.

Holden, Stephen. "Rock-a-Bye Baby Boomer." *New York Times,* June 3, 1990, pp. 22–24.

———. "Torch Songs with 'Twin Peaks' Overtones." *New York Times,* November 18, 1990, 1:2, p. 74.

Horowitz, Is. "If Music Be the Mood of Love (or Hate) We Got It, Says Industry." *Billboard,* May 8, 1954. p. 1.

"I Like Making Discs That Sell—Says Ray Conniff." *Melody Maker*, August 11, 1962, pp. 6–7.

"Jane Proves the Language of Love is Universal." *Melody Maker*, August 23, 1969, p. 16.

"Japan's 440 Cable Radio Stations Play It All." *San Francisco Chronicle*, November 21, 1991, p. E5.

Johnson, Robert. "Outer-Space Tunes Make Earth Debut in a Bar in Peoria." *Wall Street Journal*, September 4, 1990, pp. A1, A6.

Johnson, William. "Face the Music." *Film Quarterly* 22:4 (Summer 1969), pp. 3–19.

Johnson, Laurie. "Annunzio Paolo Mantovani Dies; Conductor of Popular Orchestras." *New York Times*, March 31, 1980.

Kahn, Henry. "French Firms Avoided 'Piped-In' Music Show." *Billboard*, July 4, 1976, p. 57.

Kerner, Leighton. "Praise for the Popularizers." *Village Voice*, February 4, 1980, p. 64.

Kilbourne. Christopher. "Lawsuit Claims 'Murder' Is Getting Away with Theft." *Bergen County Record*, March 17, 1992. [Concerning Sbarra v. Addison licensing suit.]

Klein, Joe. "Profile in What?" *New York*, March 16, 1992, p. 27.

Klemens, Ted. "Lawrence Welk Is Dead at 89." *New York Daily News*, May 19, 1992.

Knauf, Ken. "Background Music Booms—But Softly." *Billboard*, January 13, 1958, p. 1.

Kohanov, Linda. "Taking Top 40 by Strategy." *Pulse!* (November 1990), pp. 96–139.

Koledin, Irving. "Gilels, Mantovani, Briggs & Fonteyn." *Saturday Review*, October 22, 1955, pp. 31–32.

"Kostelanetz Constructs Bridges for Audiences." *Down Beat*, January 12, 1955, p. 10.

Lanza, Joseph. "Music—More Than a Mask for the Cacophony Clusters." *Park World* (November 1991), pp. 72–74.

———. "The Sound of Cottage Cheese." *Performing Arts Journal* (September 1991), pp. 42–53.

Levy, Alan. "The Muzak Men." *Horizon* (Summer 1965), pp. 39–45.

Lufkin, Liz. "The Real Thing on Muzak." *San Francisco Chronicle*, September 14, 1990, pp. B3, B5.

MacLeod, Bruce. "Facing the Muzak." *Popular Music & Society* 7:1 (1979), pp. 18–31. [One of the best and fairest Muzak assessments, which refuses to succumb to anti–elevator music prejudice.]

Mancini, Anthony. "The Personal Piano of Peter Nero." *New York Post,* July 27, 1968.

"Massed Strings." *Time,* October 15, 1956, p. 60.

McBride, Caryn A. "Muzak Fine-tunes Its Sounds to Maintain Productivity, Boost Morale." *Westchester County Business Journal,* June 29, 1992, p. 15.

McDermott, Jeanne. "If It's to Be Heard But Not Listened to, It Must Be Muzak." *Smithsonian* 20 (January 1990), pp. 70–82.

McKee, Sally. "Peorian's Music Moves Soviets." *Journal Star,* Peoria, Ill., May 6, 1991, back page.

Minard, Lawrence. "Move Over, Muzak." *Forbes,* August 27, 1984, p. 142.

"Money Music." *New Yorker,* November 29, 1958, pp. 42–43.

"Mood Merchant." *Time,* August 17, 1962, p. 62. [Brief overview of Arthur Lyman, including performance at Chicago's Edgewater Beach Hotel.]

Morris, Edmund. "Oases of Silence in a Desert of Din." *New York Times* (Travel & Leisure Resorts), May 25, 1975, pp. 1 and 14.

"Music from Soup to Nuts." *Billboard,* January 13, 1958.

"Muzak, at 40, Develops Plan to Play a New Tune." *New York Times,* August 19, 1974.

"Mysterious Melody Malady." *Science Digest* (April 1981), p. 102.

Nash, Nathaniel C. "Muzak's Global Music." *New York Times,* March 16, 1975.

"Nelson Riddle Is Dead at 64; Orchestrated Sinatra Songs." *New York Times,* November 8, 1985.

Oestreich, James R. "Is It Mahler? Or Is It Happy Talk?" *New York Times,* January 6, 1991, 2, pp. 1, 30.

Parker, Jim. "Muzak's Not Just for Elevators." *Contra Costa Times,* July 14, 1987, p. 3C.

Pascual, Psyche. "Muzak Attack." *Los Angeles Times,* November 17, 1991, p. A3.

Perkins, Francis D. "Mantovani and His Music Are Heard at Carnegie Hall." *New York Times,* October 6, 1955.

Ramirez, Anthony. "Muzak's New Owners Seek Broader, High-Tech Market." *New York Times,* October 13, 1992.

Randle, Bill. "Bill Randle 'Discovered' Mantovani." *Billboard,* February 11, 1967, p. M30.

Rich, Alan. "Lincoln Center Strikes Again!!!" *New York,* October 30, 1972, p. 66.

Rios, Carol E. "George Squier." *Signal*, April 16, 1986.

Rockwell, John. "Rock vs. Disco: Who Really Won the War?" *New York Times*, September 16, 1990, pp. 1, 50.

Rosenfeld, Anne H. "Music, the Beautiful Disturber." *Psychology Today* (December 1985), pp. 48–56.

Ross, Sean. "AC Stands Firm Atop Format Rankings." *Billboard*, June 9, 1990, pp. 12, 15, 20, 21.

———. "Fallen on Hard Times, Easy Moves Toward Soft AC." *Billboard*, May 26, 1990, pp. 1, 89, 97.

Schonberg, Harold C. "Scalpel, Sponge, a Bach Partita . . . " *New York Times*, July 22, 1984.

Schumach, Murray. "It All Started on a Train in Saskatchewan." *High Fidelity* (February 1958), p. 77. [André Kostelanetz profile.]

———. "The Music Between." *High Fidelity* (February 1957) [Includes profile of Mantovani.]

Scott, David Clark. "Siren Song of Background Music to Buy By." *Christian Science Monitor* (Business), September 5, 1986, p. 22.

Sharpe, Ivan. "Muzak's Music—Heard But Not Listened To." *San Francisco Chronicle*, December 18, 1967.

Sherman, Robert. "Carnegie Crowds Hear Mantovani." *New York Times*, November 28, 1966.

Signal Corps Bulletin, July–August 1934, Washington, D.C.: War Dept., Office of the Chief Signal Officer, pp. 1–2.

Silver, John. "The Fascinating World of Mood Music." *Journal into Melody*, Robert Farnon Society (April 1992).

Smucker, Tom. "Percy Faith's Challenge to Mewzick." *Village Voice*, April 7, 1975.

"The Sound of Selling" (background music; study by Gerald J. Corn). *Psychology Today* 19 (December 1985), p. 56.

Steinfield, Aaron. "A Decade of Experience Cracking Plush Locations." *Billboard*, March 25, 1955.

Stokes, Carol E. "George Owen Squier: 'Soldier-Scientist'." *Army Communicator* (Spring 1989)

Sutherland, Alastair. "Sorry, No Kazoo Players Required." *Canadian Composer* (Summer 1990), p. 4. [Some standards Muzak and AEI have for their instrumental channels.]

Tatham, D. G. "The Squire of Bournemouth—Monty at Home." *Billboard*, February 11, 1967.

Taubman, Howard. "Curtain of Sound." *New York Times*, January 13, 1960.

Taylor, Angela. "She Spends Her Day Piping in Music, Then Listens to More of Same at Home." *New York Times,* March 12, 1973.

Thomas, Robert McG., Jr. "Percy Faith Dead at 67; Conductor and Arranger." *New York Times,* February 10, 1976.

Tiegel, Eliot. "The Anita Kerr Style: Soft Sound with Sock." *Billboard,* December 17, 1966, p. 22.

————. "Movie Music Maestro." *Pulse!* (February 1991), pp. 71–72. [Profile of Henry Mancini.]

Tooley, Jo Ann. "Making Muzak." *U.S. News & World Report,* October 30, 1989, p. 82. [Top twelve songs on Muzak's Environmental channel and the original artists are listed.]

Turkington, Gregg. "101 Strings." *Goldmine,* November 30, 1990, pp. 56, 154.

Weidenbaum, Marc. "Big Orchestral Soundtracks Are Back—Hold Your Applause." *Pulse!* (August 1991), p. 136.

Wein, Bibi. "Body and Soul Music." *American Health* (April 1987).

Wickman, Jim. "Background Music: Challenge and Opportunity." *Billboard,* March 26, 1955.

Wilson, John S. "Mantovani Ignores Music Critics and Strings Along with Success." *New York Times,* October 4, 1963.

————. "Peter Nero." *International Musician* (November 1972), pp. 4–5.

Wolf, William. "The Turntable Never Stops on a Mantovani Record." *New York Sunday News,* November 7, 1971, p. 10.

Wood, Terry. "New Age Has Affected Baby Boomers." *Billboard,* October 28, 1989, p. 11.

Woodley, Richard. "Music by Muzak." *Audience,* September 10, 1971.

Woodward, Josef. Review of *Twin Peaks* Soundtrack and *Industrial Symphony No. 1 (Dream of the Broken Heart). Musician* (February 1991), p. 91.

Yaron, Adele. " . . . and the Listening Is Easy." *The Wire* 106/7 (January 1993), pp. 34–36.

Zemen, Ned. "Gently Roll over Mantovani: On FM, It's Lite over Easy." *Newsweek,* December 14, 1992. [A semi-lament that "dentist office" strings are being replaced by the grunts of Michael Bolton as "Beautiful Music" FM converts to Adult Contemporary.]

Zrzavy, Helfried C. "Issues of Incoherence and Cohesion in New Age Music." *Journal of Popular Culture* 24:2 (Fall 1990), pp. 33–53. [How New Age's first efforts were directed toward providing musical background for album cover art.]

Books, Monographs, and Dissertations

Attali, Jacques. *Noise: The Political Economy of Music.* (Translated by Brian Massumi.) Minneapolis: University of Minnesota Press, 1985.

Barnes, Stephen H. *Muzak: The Hidden Messages in Music.* Studies in the History and Interpretation of Music, vol. 9. Lewiston, N.C.: Edwin Mellen Press, 1988.

Baudrillard, Jean. *Simulations.* (Translated by Paul Foss, Paul Patton, and Philip Beitchman.) New York: Semiotext(e), 1983.

Bellamy, Edward. *Looking Backward (2000–1887).* New York: New American Library, 1960.

Cardinell, Richmond L. *Music in Industry.* Three-part Monograph. New York: ASCAP, 1944.

Cheney, Margaret. *Tesla: Man out of Time.* New York: Laurel, 1981.

Clarke, Donald, ed. *The Penguin Encyclopedia of Popular Music.* London: Penguin Books, 1990.

Darby, William, and DuBois, Jack. *American Film Music: Major Composers, Techniques, Trends: 1915–1990.* Jefferson, N.C., and London: McFarland, 1990.

David, Hans T., and Mendel, Arthur, eds. *The Bach Reader: A Life of Johann Sebastian Bach in Letters and Documents.* New York: W. W. Norton, 1966.

Debord, Guy. *Society of the Spectacle.* Detroit: Black & Red, 1983.

Diserens, Charles Murdock. *The Influence of Music on Behavior.* Princeton, N.J.: Princeton University Press, 1926.

Doelle, Leslie L. *Environmental Acoustics.* New York: McGraw-Hill, 1972.

Dunlap, Orrin E., Jr. *Radio's 100 Men of Science.* Freeport, N.Y.: Books for Libraries Press, 1944. ["George Owen Squier: Champion of Wired Wireless."]

Ellis, J. Dee. *Pioneer Families and History of Lapeer County, Michigan,* Lapeer, Mi.: Ellis Publishing Co., 1978.

Eremo, Judie, ed. *New Age Musicians.* Milwaukee: Hal Leonard, 1989.

Ewen, David. *All the Years of American Popular Music.* Englewood Cliffs, N.J.: Prentice-Hall, 1977.

Federal Communications Commission Reports, Docket No. 15084, 1964, pp. 1515–40. [Summary of 1964 FCC decision regarding FM/AM simulcasting.]

Gillmor, Alan M. *Erik Satie.* Boston: Twayne, 1988.

Gorbman, Claudia. *Unheard Melodies: Narrative Film Music.* Bloomington: Indiana University Press, 1987.

Hay, James. *Popular Film Culture in Fascist Italy.* Bloomington and Indianapolis: Indiana University Press, 1987.

Henry, William A., III. *The Great One: The Life and Legend of Jackie Gleason.* New York: Doubleday, 1992.

Hitchcock, H. Wiley, ed. *The Phonograph and Our Musical Life: Proceedings of a Centennial Conference, 7–10 December, 1977.* I.S.A.M. Monographs, No. 14, Institute for Studies in American Music, Brooklyn College of the City University of New York.

Husch, Jerri A. *Music of the Workplace: A Study of Muzak Culture.* Ph.D. Dissertation: University of Massachusetts, 1984.

Huxley, Aldous. *Brave New World.* New York: Harper & Row, 1969.

Kahn, Steve. *The Mall.* New York: Pocket Books, 1983.

Kowalke, Kim H., ed. *A New Orpheus: Essays on Kurt Weill.* New Haven, Conn.: Yale University Press,

Lewis, Tom. *Empire of the Air: The Men Who Made Radio.* New York: Edward Burlingame, 1991.

Limbacher, James L., ed. *Film Music: From Violins to Video.* Metuchen, N.J.: Scarecrow Press, 1974.

London, Kurt. *Film Music.* New York: Arno Press & New York Times, 1936, 1970.

Mancini, Henry (with Gene Lees). *Did They Mention the Music?* New York: Contemporary Books, 1989.

Mast, Gerald, and Cohen, Marshall, eds. *Film Theory and Criticism.* New York: Oxford University Press, 1974.

McLuhan, Marshall. *The Gutenberg Galaxy.* New York: Signet, 1969.

More, Sir Thomas. *The Utopia of Sir Thomas More.* New York: Classics Club/Walter J. Black, 1947.

Mumford, Lewis. *The Future of Technics and Civilization.* London: Freedom Press, 1986.

Muzak-Free London: A Guide to Eating, Drinking and Shopping in Peace. London: Kogan Page, 1991.

Myers, Rollo H. *Erik Satie.* New York: Dover, 1948, 1968.

Packard, Vance. *The Hidden Persuaders.* New York: Pocket Books, 1957.

Peck, Bradford. *The World a Department Store: A Study of Life Under a Cooperative System.* Boston: Arno & New York Times, 1900, 1971.

Public Utilities Commission v. Pollek, U.S. Supreme Court Reports (October 1951), vols. 342-343, pp. 1069–1080.

Russell, Ken. *Altered States: The Autobiography of Ken Russell.* London: Bantam, 1989.

Sadie, Stanley, ed. *The New Grove Dictionary of Music and Musicians, Vol. 1.* New York: Macmillan, 1980.

Schafer, R. Murray. *The Tuning of the World.* New York: Alfred A. Knopf, 1977.

Shemel, Sidney, and M. William Krasilovsky. *More About This Business of Music.* 3d ed. New York: Billboard, 1982.

Siegmeister, Elie, ed. *The Music Lover's Handbook.* New York: William Morrow, 1943.

Simon, George T. (& Friends). *The Best of the Music Makers.* Garden City, N.Y.: Doubleday, 1979.

Spiller, Roger J., ed. *Dictionary of American Military Biography, Vol. III.*

Stewart, R. J. *Music, Power, Harmony: A Workbook of Music and Inner Forces.* London: Blanford, 1990. [A lofty cosmic perspective with worthwhile look into the influence of computers and electronics on modern music.]

Tame, David. *The Secret Power of Music.* Rochester, Vt.: Destiny Books, 1984.

Tamm, Eric. *Brian Eno: His Music and the Vertical Color of Sound.* Boston and London: Faber & Faber, 1989.

Thomas, Tony, ed. *Film Score: The Art & Craft of Movie Music.* Burbank, Calif.: Riverwood Press, 1991.

Tisdall, Caroline, and Bozzolla, Angelo. *Futurism.* New York: Thames & Hudson, 1977, 1989.

Volta, Ornella. *Satie: Seen Through His Letters.* (Translated by Michael Bullock.) London: Marion Boyars, 1989.

Wakeman, John, ed. *World Film Directors: Volume One (1890–1945).* New York: H. W. Wilson, 1987.

Warhaft, Sidney, ed. *Francis Bacon: A Selection of His Works.* Indianapolis: Bobbs-Merrill, 1965, 1982.

Weatherby, W.J. *Jackie Gleason: An Intimate Biography of the Great One.* New York: Pharos Books, 1992.

Welk, Lawrence (with Bernice McGeehan). *Wunnerful, Wunnerful!: The Autobiography of Lawrence Welk.* Englewood Cliffs, N.J.: Prentice-Hall, 1971.

Zamyatin, Yevgeny, *We,* translated by Mirra Ginsburg, New York: Avon Books, 1972, 1987.

Muzak Studies and Monographs

"Effects of Muzak Programming on Supermarket Customers." *Muzak Research Review,* 1989.

Harvey, Arthur W., D.M.A. "Utilizing Music as a Tool for Healing." Muzak Research Study, 1991.

History of Muzak: 1922–1973. (From the Muzak Archives.)

"How Muzak Affects Profits: Three Case Histories Showing Beneficial Effects of Muzak on Employee Performance." Muzak, 1974.

"The Impact of Music by Muzak on Financial Customers, Employees and Managers." *Muzak Research Review,* 1992.

"The Impact of Music by Muzak on Shoppers." *Muzak Research Review,* 1989.

Keenan, James J. "Study of Clerical Task Performance Under Different Conditions of Programmed Music." Fairfield University.

"Maps to Music." Muzak Study #547, *Research Department of Muzak Corporation,* 1948.

"Muzak Improves Productivity." Muzak, 1972.

"The Right Music Style Can Successfully Promote the Image You Desire for Your Business." *Muzak Research Review,* 1990.

Roballey, Thomas C., Colleen McGreevy, Richard R. Rongo, et al. "The Effect of Music on Eating Behavior." *Bulletin of the Psychonomic Society,* 23(3), 221–222, Muzak Research Study, 1989.

"Special Report: Business Music: A Performance Tool for the Office/ Workplace." *Research Department, Muzak Limited Partnership,* 1991.

Wokoun, William. "Vigilance with Background Music." U.S. Army Human Engineering Laboratories.

Wokoun, William. "Work Performance with Music: Instrumentation and Frequency Response." U.S. Army Human Engineering Laboratories.

Index

●